SOCIAL INTELLIGENCE
Measuring the Development of Sociomoral Reflection

SOCIAL INTELLIGENCE

Measuring the Development of Sociomoral Reflection

JOHN C. GIBBS
Department of Psychology
The Ohio State University

KEITH F. WIDAMAN
Department of Psychology
University of California at Riverside

———— *In collaboration with ANNE COLBY* ————

———— *With a foreword by* ————

LAWRENCE KOHLBERG

Prentice-Hall, Inc., Englewood Cliffs, N.J. 07632

Library of Congress Cataloging in Publication Data

Gibbs, John C.
   Social intelligence.

   Bibliography: p.
   Includes index.
   1. Social ethics. 2. Reasoning (Psychology)
--Testing. I. Widaman, Keith F. II. Colby,
Anne. III. Title.
HM216.G453   303.3'72   82-3824
ISBN 0-13-815910-6   AACR2

Editorial/production supervision
   and Interior design by Virginia Livsey
Cover design by 20/20 Services, Inc.; Mark Berghash
Manufacturing buyer: Edmund W. Leone

ISBN 0-13-815910-6

Printed in the United States of America

10 9 8 7 6 5 4 3 2 1

Prentice-Hall International, Inc., London
Prentice-Hall of Australia Pty. Limited, Sydney
Prentice-Hall of Canada, Ltd., Toronto
Prentice-Hall of India Private Limited, New Delhi
Prentice-Hall of Japan, Inc., Tokyo
Prentice-Hall of Southeast Asia Pte. Ltd., Singapore
Whitehall Books Limited, Wellington, New Zealand

Dedicated to

Larry Kohlberg

CONTENTS

CONTENTS

FOREWORD

Lawrence Kohlberg

John Gibbs, the first author of this volume, was a valued member of a Harvard team which developed a method of assessing stages of spontaneous moral reasoning (Standard Issue Scoring) and validated this method against 20-year American longitudinal data and 10-year longitudinal data from Turkey and Israel (Colby, Kohlberg, Gibbs, & Lieberman, in press). Building from this Standard Issue Scoring method, John saw the possibility of developing an alternative open-ended instrument which would be easier to administer and score than the Harvard method, and yet would retain the qualitative nature of responses lost in Jim Rest's (1979) multiple-choice recognition test (the Defining Issues test). In part, John was inspired by the format of the Loevinger & Wessler (1970) group-administerable Sentence Completion Test. Like the Loevinger test, Gibbs and Widaman's Sociomoral Reflection Measure (SRM) has a defined stem (in this case, moral norms) to which the subject responds. The value content is precoded, and the rater need only attend to the stage structure of the response. This simplification of test administration and scoring seems to retain much of that captured by the more complex Standard Issue Scoring method. This volume reports a correlation of .85 with the Standard method in an age-heterogeneous sample, and a correlation of .50 with age controlled. Given the test-retest reliability of both instruments (higher for the Standard Issue method), these correlations represent considerable concurrent validity of the SRM. To the extent that the correlation between the two measures is moderately good, the SRM can claim the basic validity (e.g., invariant sequentiality, structured wholeness) of the Standard Issue method of assessment. Eventually, factor-analytic and longitudinal studies by the authors should establish the construct validity of the measure in its own right.

While in general agreement with the rationale and usefulness of the SRM, I differ with John Gibbs on one major point, the existence and inclusion of a post-conventional fifth stage of moral judgment. Adapting from distinctions made by Gibbs (1977, 1979a), Kohlberg, Hewer, and Levine (Note 1) distinguish between "hard" Piagetian structural stages and "soft" qualitative stages, such as the Perry (1968), Loevinger (Loevinger & Wessler, 1970) and Fowler (1981) stages. Both "hard" and "soft" stages represent qualitative changes in development and define developmental sequences. In addition, "hard" stages represent: (1) new thought operations; (2) internalized schemata of action; (3) logically or philosophically formalizable systems in equilibrium; and (4) culturally universal patterns. Soft stages are new levels of reflection on the self and the world, rather than new operations of thought and judgment. I believe that Stage 5 meets all the criteria of "hard stages"; Gibbs does not. Further research is clearly needed on this point. I personally would recommend, in using the SRM, that one treat Gibbs's "theory-defining level" (specifically, Theoretical Principles) responses as indicating a fifth stage.

In summary, this book and the measure it provides represent a useful introduction to moral stages and their measurement--even for those who will wish to go on to master Standard Issue Scoring for more intensive research purposes (requiring exactness in assigning stage scores to individual subjects in longitudinal and clinical work). For those who want a measure of group means, educational effects, and correlations with other variables, the greater efficiency of the SRM may make it the method of choice. It is a pleasure to recommend this volume to anyone interested in research method in moral development.

June, 1981
Cambridge, Massachusetts

PREFACE

This book is dedicated to Lawrence Kohlberg, one of the most influential developmental psychologists of our era. Although Kohlberg has made important contributions in areas such as sex-role development and early childhood education, his major work has been in moral development. Indeed, were it not for Kohlberg's work over the past several decades, it is doubtful that moral reasoning would have attained its distinct and major status in developmental psychology.

When, in the late 1950s and early 1960s, Lawrence Kohlberg undertook to study moral reasoning and conduct, his choice of topic made him something of an "odd duck" within American psychology . . . . Social scientists were not nostalgic for that period when morality seemed to be mainly a bludgeon for controlling sex and, possibly, swearing. No up-to-date social scientist, acquainted with psychoanalysis, behaviorism, and cultural anthropology, used such words at all. To appreciate what Kohlberg has done to deepen the intellectual interest in what is, after all, a very substantial aspect of human psychology, one must have some sense of the tide he swam against. Moral reasoning, as a process, was something of which behavioral scientists were at least professionally unaware. Certain aspects of the process entered into behavior research under such concepts as "attitude," "norm," "custom," and "value." But in a very muddled way that usually failed to take account of even the most elementary distinction of moral philosophy . . . . The study of attitudes, customs, norms, and values had the effect, in the past, of "trivializing" the subject of morality. In general, attitudes were just "pro" or "con" some object of social concern (a politician, a policy, an ideology); one toted up the pros and cons, rather like a preelection poll, and that was thought to be the end of it. Customs and norms were described as relatively concrete guides to behavior, and a culture was likely to seem a kind of bundle of these, like so many unrelated sticks tied together with a string. People were not often asked to think about cases in which norms were in conflict--as norms, in fact, often are--or to try to reason their way to a resolution of such conflict. When people are asked to deal with ethical dilemmas, as in Kohlberg's research, a complex and hard-to-understand process emerges. (Brown & Herrnstein, 1975, pp. 307-308)

Kohlberg found, then, that moral thinking is a complex process not reducible to the expression of moral attitudes, norms, or values. He has claimed that morality is not totally relative, that individual, social-class, and cultural differences in moral reasoning permit--upon sufficient probing--the discernment of common structures. Further, these structures are claimed to evolve in a standard sequence of developmental stages, with individual and cultural variation accounting mainly for differences in rate of development through the sequence. Kohlberg's theory of moral stages has attracted attention from extraordinarily diverse areas in the contemporary intellectual community. Kohlberg's Center for Moral Development and Education at Harvard has been visited not only by psychologists and educators, but also by philosophers, theologians, counselors, and others interested in ethics from numerous countries. Kohlberg's theory is controversial: in the social science literature, Kohlberg's claims have attracted at least as many adversaries as proponents (e.g., Kurtines & Greif, 1974, vs. Broughton, 1978).

Kohlberg's reaction to this theoretical controversy has generally consisted of pointing out that his claims are, after all, essentially empirical. While I (Gibbs) was a research associate and part of the Kohlberg group at the Center from 1975 to 1979, I frequently heard Kohlberg explain that his stages were more a matter of discovery than of invention, that moral reasoning structures could be discerned by anyone willing to take the time to investigate. Nonetheless, those of us at the Center who were helping to construct a systematic assessment manual based on Kohlberg's 20-year longitudinal moral judgment study were also mindful of the truth of another Kohlberg comment: namely, that social cognition does not emerge from subjects with moral stage tags already attached. Constructing a manual, in other words, was hard work.

That work has, however, provided the basis for an empirical answer to Kohlberg's critics. Blind scoring of that portion of the longitudinal data not used in the initial manual construction has yielded a clear picture of a stage-sequential development in moral reasoning (Kohlberg, 1981). Further, the manual itself (Colby, Kohlberg, Candee, Gibbs, Hewer, Kaufman, Power, & Speicher-Dubin, in press) has been found to provide a reliable and valid instrument for the stage assessment of moral judgment (Colby, Kohlberg, Gibbs, & Lieberman, in press).

As Kohlberg explains in the Foreword, this book provides a simplified and group-administerable equivalent to the Harvard assessment instrument. The prominent developmental psychologist James Rest was a research associate at the Harvard Center during the late 1960s. Over the course of his involvement as part of the Kohlberg group, Rest (1979) gained the impression that Kohlberg's primary aim in guiding manual construction "was not to put together a handy instrument, but to devise a theoretical system to represent the logic of moral thinking, analogous to Chomsky's work on syntactical structures" (p. xviii). I believe Rest's inference was--and continues to be--essentially correct. The Standard Issue Manual is a brilliant systematization of the content and structure of moral thought--but its intricacies limit the readiness and ease with which it can be used as a research tool. A "handy instrument" it isn't.

Rest recollects that, during his years at the Center, "alternative schemes for assessing moral judgment became a compelling interest" (p. xviii) for him. This "compelling interest" led Rest to develop his Defining Issues Test (DIT), which assesses moral judgment (specifically, moral evaluation) through a multiple-choice format. During my work at the Center in the late 1970s, I came to be captured by the same "compelling interest" in the possibility of "alternative schemes" referred to by Rest. Yet my departure has not been as radical as Rest's. Rest (1975) has rejected interpretations of the DIT as simply a more "handy" way of indexing moral reasoning (the correlations are low anyway), and has instead championed the referent for the DIT--moral <u>evaluation</u>--as a form of moral judgment worthy of study in its own right.

Our Sociomoral Reflection Measure (SRM), in contrast, remains within the realm of the justification or reasoning sense of moral judgment. The SRM unabashedly rides piggyback on the parent Standard Issue manual. Like its parent, the SRM is a production-task measure of moral reasoning whereby subjects must express their thinking with respect to moral dilemmas and associated normative values. Whereas sociomoral norms constitute only one classificatory feature of the Harvard manual, however, norms become the crucial feature defining the questionnaire and scoring format used in the SRM. Systematic use of the norms has enabled us to amplify the strength of the dilemma questions and to simplify the procedures for stage assessment of the responses (see Chapter 2). These innovations have in turn made possible the convenience of group administration (rather than individual interviewing) for data collection and of self-training (rather than workshop participation) for learning reliable stage assessment.

The extensive assistance of the second author, Keith Widaman, in the construction and validation of the SRM was, of course, crucial. As I was making a career move from Harvard to Ohio State in 1979, Keith (then a graduate student at Ohio State) introduced himself and expressed his wish to work with me in the moral development area. I was soon delighted to discover how well my project was supported not ony by Keith's quantitative expertise, but as well by his ability to make keen inferences as to the qualitative meanings of sociomoral responses. Keith's highly successful completion of Kohlberg's June 1979 Moral Judgment Scoring Workshop provided the foundation for Keith's substantive participation in the new reference manual construction, in preliminary work on scorability and other assessment rules or procedures, and in the training of our vanguard group of SRM raters: Helen Ahlborn, Kevin Arnold, and Miriam Galevi (these raters are also thanked for their subsequent contributions to the project). Keith's participation was also major in the data collection phase, and in the psychometric analyses of the new instrument's properties. His contributions to the SRM project continued during 1980 and early 1981 despite his busy first year as assistant professor at the University of California, Riverside.

Many persons (and in some cases, the institutions they represent) made crucial contributions to the success of our instrumentation project. Especially crucial on a practical level was the funding for the project provided by the Small Grant Program of the National Institute of Mental Health. Larry Kohlberg consistently encouraged this work from its very start in January of 1979 and provided an invaluable early critique of the manuscript draft. Anne Colby (Radcliffe), who is the foremost authority on Kohlberg's theory and stage constructs (apart from Kohlberg himself), served as a consultant on the project. The importance of her contributions to the sharpening of the reference criteria is reflected in her status as collaborator. Marvin Berkowitz (now at Marquette University) conducted for us the first psychometric study of the SRM, specifically, of its concurrent validity with the Harvard instrument. We owe considerable thanks to Ted Fenton (Carnegie-Mellon University) for his early belief in the SRM and his inclusion of it as one of the evaluative measures used in connection with his Civic Education Project. Various personnel associated with the Ohio Youth Commission, the Columbus Public Schools, and the Ohio State University also provided crucial assistance in other aspects of the data collection. We thank Janina Jolley, Scott Mullarky, Catherine O'Connor, Mark Tappan, and Bedonna Weiss for their diligent work as self-trainees. Most recently, we thank Phil Clark (Ohio State), Bill Damon (Clark University), and Fred Damarin (Ohio State) for their constructive comments regarding portions of the manuscript and Mark Tappan (again) and Kevin Arnold for extensive proofreading assistance. Our gratitude also goes to our families for their unfailing sympathy and support throughout this project.

The "reference manual" in this book is comprised of Chapters 5 through 12. These chapters provide the criteria to which the scorer refers in making developmental assessments of the responses provided by subjects on the SRM questionnaire. Other portions of the book should make possible the informed and effective use of the reference manual. Chapter 1 introduces the developmental approach to the assessment of intelligence by contrasting it with the individual differences approach, and then makes a corresponding--and more specifically pertinent--contrast within the framework of <u>social</u> intelligence. In Chapter 2, we elaborate on the developmental approach to the measurement of social intelligence, specifically with reference to the measurement of moral judgment (or what we call sociomoral reflection). Chapter 2 concludes by overviewing our psychometric evaluations of the SRM. Chapter 3 discusses at length the sociomoral stages themselves and their relation to situational action as well as to the concept of maturity. The discussion in this chapter represents a consolidation of the revised view of the stages previously articulated by Gibbs (1977, 1979a). Chapter 4 provides guidance for self-training and for scoring by reference to Chapters 5-12. Appendices B and C provide the materials for the self-training program outlined in Chapter 4; Appendix A contains the SRM questionnaire itself (Forms A and B), plus the standard rating form. With its arious parts, this book should be sufficient to make possible research use of the Sociomoral Reflection Measure.

September, 1981
Columbus, Ohio

SOCIAL INTELLIGENCE

Measuring the Development of Sociomoral Reflection

TWO APPROACHES

TO

INTELLIGENCE

The precise focus of this book is on the measurement of reflective sociomoral thought. Since sociomoral reflection is a specified form of social intelligence, however, our work more fundamentally relates to intelligence. Elkind (1969) has compared and contrasted the "psychometric" with the "Piagetian" approach to the conceptualization and measurement of intelligence. It is important for an understanding of our assessment work to articulate this distinction. The terms we will use for the two approaches, however, are "individual difference" (or differential) and "developmental": psychometric techniques are not the exclusive possession of the former approach, nor is Piaget the only theorist important in the latter. Thanks to works by Elkind and others (Cowan, 1978; DeVries, 1974; Furth, 1973; Stephens, McLaughlin, Miller, & Glass, 1972; Tuddenham, 1971), psychologists have come to grasp the fundamentally distinct conceptualization of intelligence provided by the developmental approach; yet the point has been made primarily with respect to nonsocial intelligence. A parallel point remains to be grasped with respect to social intelligence. In this chapter we will articulate our developmental approach to reflective sociomoral thought against the backdrop of a discussion of the individual-differences approach.

"I.Q." is a quintessential symbol of the individual differences approach. Tests such as the Stanford-Binet provide an "Intelligence Quotient" (I.Q.), which represents the intellectual brightness, power, or agility of an individual relative to that of his or her same-aged peers. Assessment of such individual differences is based on the relative numbers of items correctly answered on a test typically containing a large number of questions tapping simple as well as complex cognitive abilities. These items derive from diverse sources, and the criterion for their inclusion is essentially empirical: those questions which are correctly answered by a gradually increasing percentage of persons in successively older age brackets are retained as test items —and those which show no such age trends are eliminated. As Tuddenham (1971) observed, "Current tests consist of items chosen more for their statistical properties than for their content" (p. 65). Large cross-sectional samples are then typically used to establish the "normal" or average percentage of items passed at specified ages. An individual's I.Q. is defined and evaluated as bright or dull relative to these age norms. Since one's degree of intellectual brightness is considered by many differential theorists to be a stable and possibly inherited trait, one's relative position as one gets older is expected to remain fairly constant. Hence, although intelligence tests do entail use of age-related (and therefore to some extent developmentally related) differences, the aim in doing so is to establish age-constant individual differences.

A psychometrically acceptable intelligence test--or any psychometrically serious test--must meet certain standards, chiefly those pertaining to reliability and validity. The test must be demonstrated to be a valid measure of that which it purports to measure, e.g., by correlating highly with an already accepted measure of the variable or by appropriately discriminating among persons who can already be described on other grounds as possessing high or low levels of that variable. The test must also show some stability or reliability, e.g., by correlating highly with the results of a second testing administration or by showing good consistency across its component parts. Reliability is thought to be promoted by standard procedures of test administration, perhaps even by using tape-recorded instructions to guard against subtle variations.

The developmental approach is not concerned with intellectual brightness so much as with intellectual maturity. An individual who can infer or work out the correct answers to a relatively large quantity of miscellaneous problems may be bright but is not necessarily intellectually mature. Criteria for maturity must be derived from studies of normal human cognitive development, with an eye to identifying the basic and maximally generalizable patterns of the individual's mental evolution--in other words, to identifying the character of intelligence at different ages. Although complexity is not necessarily to be equated with maturity, there is a theoretical assumption that development from birth to maturity fundamentally entails progressive differentiations and integrations in, for example, thought processes. This assumption is common to Piaget's cognitive-structural perspective as well as Werner's organismic perspective, and for that matter can be found in the nineteenth-century writings of J. M. Baldwin. For all these theorists, the experiential differentiations and integrations of intelligence represent active and responsive modes of adaptation which extend beyond relatively "closed" processes of instinctual and other regulations (see especially Piaget, 1969/1971).

Further, there is an assumption that these differentiations and integrations lead to a sequence of hierarchically arranged cognitive structures, or "stages," that has maturity as a normal end-state. Indeed, the structuralist view--which we adopt in our work--is that one cannot even properly speak of the development of a psychological variable unless a progressive organizational complexity (usually entailing a hierarchical sequence) can be discerned. (This does not mean that developmental psychologists necessarily should confine their interests to "development" defined in this narrow sense. We accept Wohlwill's 1973 position that any robust age-related change in a psychological function over time is fair game for the developmental psychologist--although we do feel that those functions of greatest significance for the developmentalist are those which undergo an evolving complexity.) In this strict sense of development, an age-related increase in the percentage of correct problem solutions (as reflected in mental age) is viewed as epiphenomenal to developmental processes--not as development itself.

The development of progressively mature mental structures cannot be discerned at the surface level of problem-solving solutions; it must instead be studied at the level of the processes which underlie and generate those solutions. For example, psycholinguists find transformational patterns not at the surface level of literal syntactical combinations but rather in terms of the deep or generic functional level of language constructions and operations. To investigate the cognitive dynamics which underlie a task performance, the developmental researcher may probe by introducing task variations and extensions at opportune points during the subject's task activity. When one is working with verbally fluent subjects, it is helpful to elicit justifications or explanations of their various task decisions. These justifications often provide significant indications of how the subject is approaching and thinking about the problem. In this phase of the developmental approach, the completely "standard" procedures associated with the differential approach would actually block rather than facilitate research progress. As Tuddenham (1971) noted, rigidly standardized procedures "would never have provided the insights which have led Piaget, Inhelder, and their co-workers to their theoretical formulations" (p. 74). Although the task format must be standard enough to allow for comparisons across subjects (particularly comparably aged subjects), the experimenter must be procedurally flexible and alert to unexpected features of the subject's reasoning that may yield new structural discoveries. As Cowan (1978) argues, "standardized" does not necessarily mean "scientific." It is an instructive point that some of the most replicable findings in developmental psychology have come not from perfectly standardized investigations but instead from Piaget's nonstandard but penetratingly flexible and inquisitive méthode clinique.

Individualized inquiry need not characterize the full saga of developmental research, however. In the context of moral development, Kohlberg (1979) has suggested that the trajectory of developmental research entails three phases. In the first phase, the emphasis is on exploration. One works with cross-sectional, longitudinal, and cross-cultural samples to identify the "broad outlines" (p. x) of sequential, structural development, typically using the méthode clinique for this purpose. Eventually, however, one becomes reasonably confident that the "transcontextual validity" (Weisz, 1978) of the basic sequence has been sufficiently explored, and one perceives diminishing returns from further exploratory investigations. At this point, a second, primarily methodological phase becomes appropriate, and emphasis shifts from exploration to assessment. Thanks to one's phase-one work, one can bring to the assessment phase a considerable knowledgeability of the relevant structural sequences and of the most efficacious techniques for eliciting them. With the phase-one experience as a foundation, then, effective assessment methodology can be developed. Standard procedures can now be introduced with reasonable confidence that their use will not preclude the discovery of important new structures. Indeed, in the second phase it is entirely appropriate, scientific, and beneficial to develop systematically structured and standard tests and to apply the traditional psychometric criteria of validity and reliability to those tests.

Kohlberg then sees a third phase, not yet fully attained in moral development, whereby the assessment advances achieved in the second phase enable one to return to the basic theoretical questions not fully answered in the first phase (e.g., questions as to the developmental relationship of sociomoral intelligence to other relevant variables or as to the degree of unitariness to the stages) with one's new, scientifically powerful assessment tools at one's disposal. It is to the advent of this third phase that we trust the assessment tool presented in this book will contribute.

The distinctions noted between the differential and the developmental approaches can be elaborated specifically with reference to social intelligence (cf. Greenspan, 1979). As Walker and Foley (1973) note, most investigators of social intelligence have from the start "approached their problems with an individual difference orientation" and with a "definite interest in psychometrics" (p. 840). The psychology of social intelligence has a research history, beginning with Thorndike's (1920) conceptualization of the construct as "the ability to understand and manage men and women, boys and girls--to act wisely in human relations" (p. 228). Although Thorndike viewed social intelligence as an ability distinct from those of "abstract" and "mechanical" intelligence, that view has become controversial. Guilford (1967) shares the Thorndike view, reserving for social intelligence distinct factor combinations in his complex multifactorial theory of human intelligence. Wechsler (1958), on the other hand, although using the term "social intelligence," views it as merely the application of general intelligence to social contexts. This controversy continues to be reflected in recent literature (e.g., Keating, 1978; Osipow & Walsh, 1973). Most researchers on both sides, however, have conceptualized social intelligence in individual-difference rather than in developmental terms.

Among the most widely used tests of social intelligence are those innovated by Guilford and associates. Guilford's social intelligence tests include tasks eliciting performances such as: choosing the most appropriate interpersonal episode; identifying the drawing which does not belong in a set of drawings of socioemotional facial expressions, gestures, and postures; and identifying the type of interpersonal situation in which a given verbal statement will have appropriate meaning. On the basis of the age-normative data compiled for these tests (O'Sullivan & Guilford, 1975), one can assess an individual's degree of interpersonal brightness, in much the same spirit as one determines an individual's I.Q.

Although most investigators have been concerned with social intelligence as a fairly stable trait or facility, some have been interested in social intelligence as an evolving, progressively mature capacity. These researchers have typically used more open-ended techniques, consistent with the first-phase concern in the developmental approach with flexible inquiry into more spontaneous modes of behavior that may reveal features of organization or structure. Piaget's chief method in his early work (1932/1965) on the topic was to use children's comparative evaluations of moral concepts such as naughtiness or fairness as a vehicle for probing their reasoning. After a subject made a comparative evaluation with respect to a given pair of stories differing in certain morally relevant respects, the subject would then be asked to explain or justify that evaluation. Feffer and colleagues (e.g., Feffer & Suchotliff, 1966) studied social cognitive capacities at diferent ages by assessing whether subjects retain thematic coherence as they retell TAT-inspired stories from the viewpoint of each of the story protagonists. Similarly, Flavell, Botkin, Fry, Wright, and Jarvis (1968) used adaptability in story re-telling performance as a method for studying the development of role-taking and communication skills. Kohlberg (1969), followed by Selman (1980) and Damon (1979), retained and intensified the Piagetian focus on justification by presenting moral or social problems and then probing the ways in which subjects justify their decisions and evaluations with respect to their proposed solutions to the problems.

All of the above researchers have used cross-sectional (and in Kohlberg's case, longitudinal and cross-cultural) samples for studying social intelligence. This commonality is not accidental, of course, since by definition the developmentalist is concerned with the ways in which a psychological function evolves from birth to maturity. Many developmentalists, most prominently Piaget and Kohlberg, have inferred and attempted to establish the existence of qualitative, sequential stages that successively emerge and consolidate over the course of this evolution. Hence, whereas the individual-difference researcher may seek to assess ability-related traits of social brightness, the developmentalist may seek to study stage-related manifestations of progressive social maturity.

One unfortunate trend discernible in the differential literature has been its increasing rejection of moral valuing as an aspect of social intellectual ability. Whereas the developmentalists are open to exploring moral maturity no less than social maturity, the individual-difference researchers--while generally accepting the concept of ability in terms of strictly social intelligence--shift to the concept of attitude when focusing on the moral features of social intelligence. Indeed, the chief point of Pittel and Mendelsohn's 1966 critique of assessment work on moral values was that such work could only become "scientific" once personal and societal-value biases were eliminated from what was properly the study of "subjective attitudes of evaluation" ("whether these attitudes would be approved or disapproved by society is a subsequent question which need not be considered in the construction of measures of evaluative attitudes"; p. 34). In the wake of the Pittel and Mendolsohn, critique, Hogan (1970) innovated an explicitly nondevelopmental study of individual dispositional differences in adult moral judgment, based on the assumption that "the determinants of moral values are similar to the factors which support social attitudes" (p. 206). Identifying an attitudinal polarity between "personal conscience" and "social responsibility," Hogan established a discriminative instrument termed the Survey of Ethical Attitudes, which was designed "to scale quantitatively the disposition to adopt one or the other of the two viewpoints" (p. 19). The test items (empirically derived from a large preliminary item pool) consist of brief sociopolitical statements evaluated by subjects on an agree/disagree scale. For example, agreement with the item "Rebellion may be a sign of maturity" contributes to a personal-conscience weighting, whereas agreement with "Civil rights are always bad" would strengthen a social responsibility weighting.

The defensibility of this divorce of moral "attitudes" or values from social intelligence must be questioned. Thorndike's original definition of social intelligence was hardly free of moral value connotations, although the particular connotations were ambiguous: was the final value of "understanding others" and acting "wisely in human relations" that of empathic sensitivity, diplomacy, and magnanimity? Or was it manipulative self-interest? We suspect that the attempt to eliminate moral values from social intelligence mainly succeeds in impoverishing the concept, in robbing the concept of refined moral connotations (e.g., social wisdom) while leaving other connotations intact. Indeed, in Weinstein's (1969) "interpersonal competence" model of social intelligence, "the ability to accomplish interpersonal tasks . . . boils down to the ability to manipulate the responses of others . . . . Competence is relative to the actor's purpose" (p. 755). Social intellectual ability, then, inevitably entails a moral value orientation--one way or another.

One constructive value of the Pittel and Mendelsohn review, however, was in their essential point that moral judgment should mean something more basic than the demonstration of favorable evaluations and knowledgeability regarding the moralistic norms provincial to a particular society. Sociomoral brightness, whatever its precise nature, should not be considered reducible to the degree of one's content learning of "morals" (cf. Hartshorne & May's

1927 "moral knowledge" tests). Like the individual-difference theorists, the developmentalists seek to distinguish from content learning something more "basic." The developmentalists, however, distinguish from content not abilities or evaluative attitudes but structural capacities. In the developmentalists' terms, specific informational knowledge is at the level of surface content rather than at the level of basic reasoning, where transcontextually valid, evolving structures may be found. Damon (1977) expresses this point with respect to the social sphere of intellectual development:

> Learning the characteristics of persons and institutions contributes only marginally to the possession of understanding the social world. More central and difficult is understanding the nature of the relations between persons (or between persons and their institutions) and the transactions that serve to regulate, maintain, and transform these relations. A child experiences and makes sense out of society only by gaining knowledge of such social relations as authority, attachment, and friendship, and of such social transactions as punishment, sharing, kindness, and hostility. . . .It is the child's knowledge of relations and transactions between persons that determines the characteristics of the child's social functioning. Knowledge of social relations and transactions cannot be derived from knowledge about the objective traits of others; in fact, it can be more easily claimed that a child learns to objectify traits of others through the establishment of a succession of relations with them. (pp. 2, 6-7)

Unlike the individual-difference investigators, developmentalists have generally accepted the moral value aspect of social intelligence. Social intelligence, at least at the reasoning level, inextricably entails prescriptive and ideal features which must be encompassed in any broad study of the "relations" and "transactions" of social intellectual development. Indeed, we conceptualize our own work on social intelligence, which extends most directly from the developmental research of Piaget, Kohlberg, and Selman, as concerned with reflective sociomoral thought; that is, with subjects' reflective justifications of prescriptions that one should help a friend, save a life, obey the law, and so on.

The developmental approach to social intelligence, then, is fundamentally distinct from the differential approach. Instead of assessing social intelligence as a trait-like ability or attitude, the developmental aim is to explore social intelligence as an evolving capacity or worldview. Instead of seeking to establish differences among people in terms of mental power or brightness, or dispositional attitude or style, the developmental approach searches for the commonalities among people (especially those comparable in age and age-related variables) in order to determine basic patterns or structures of social intelligence. Yet this book, which adopts the developmental approach, is most immediately about assessment rather than exploration. We present a standardized test, the Sociomoral Reflection Measure, which has been validated using traditional psychometric criteria and which is designed for uniform administration in groups. By reading through the ensuing chapters and working through the assessment training materials provided in the appendices, you the reader should be able to develop effective skills in the use of the SRM as an assessment tool.

The SRM does not, however, provide a "moral quotient" of the degree of sociomoral "brightness." The SRM rests squarely upon decades of research exploring the evolution of sociomoral cognitive maturity and represents a contribution to what Kohlberg (as noted earlier) has called the "second phase" of research in moral development: a phase in which the methodology of the earlier exploratory work is refined and standardized. Of course, exploratory developmental work using the méthode clinique continues, most notably Damon's (1977) work investigating sociomoral thought in young childhood. Indeed, it remains to be seen whether a fully standardized procedure will ever prove fully applicable with young children, although Enright, Franklin, and Manheim's (1980) instrumentation work represents a promising start. Currently, much of the Piaget-based developmental work on sociomoral thought (including not only ours but also that of Kohlberg himself) has been devoted to methodological refinement, to the end of making possible Kohlberg's prospective "third phase" or what Kuhn (1962) might refer to as "normal science": the phase of scientific activity in which a new paradigm has developed in its procedures and instrumentation to the point where precisely communicative and replicative scientific progress can take place.

2

THE DEVELOPMENTAL APPROACH

TO

SOCIAL INTELLIGENCE

In this chapter, we will focus on the methodological aspect of the developmental approach to social intelligence. Certainly the central figure over the past two decades in this area has been Lawrence Kohlberg. In recent years, Kohlberg (and his associates at Harvard) have constructed a standard interview instrument for assessing an individual's developmental level with respect to Kohlberg's stages of moral judgment, or what we call reflective sociomoral thought. Kohlberg's goal has been ambitious: to achieve a psychometrically standardized assessment measure which nonetheless retains a Piagetian focus on justificatory or explanatory reasoning, i.e., which is nonetheless sensitive to the reflective sociomoral meanings of the individual (Colby, Kohlberg, Gibbs, & Lieberman, in press).

Kohlberg's standard interview format has made possible the valid and reliable assessment of a subject's stage of sociomoral reasoning. The new instrument (the Standard Issue Scoring Manual, to be discussed) represents a clear advance in Kohlbergian stage assessment methodology. However, the data must still be collected through individual interviews, and raters must still engage in a complex conceptual classification of the interview responses before being able to initiate assessment. For many research purposes, these limitations may not be necessary. Our Sociomoral Reflection Measure (SRM) is a group-administerable pencil-and-paper questionnaire which utilizes certain strengths of the Kohlberg interview questions to maximum advantage. The SRM retains the Piagetian focus on subject-produced reasoning, relying on a strengthened question format to insure that--despite the lack of individual probing--subjects' responses are nonetheless "deep" enough to be structurally significant. The SRM also frames the contexts for the subjects' responses so precisely that raters need do no preliminary content classification of the responses: time and energy are saved as raters concentrate on structural stage assessment. The SRM has been subjected to a thorough psychometric evaluation, the favorable results from which will be summarized in the latter part of this chapter.

BACKGROUND

One of Kohlberg's fundamental methodological innovations is the moral dilemma. As Kohlberg points out, the true moral dilemma is one which counterposes two or more sociomoral norms of comparable prima facie value and rightness. Indeed, these basic normative values (Kohlberg calls such normative value sets "issues") have a truistic quality. For example, most of us feel that we should of course help a friend or save a human life, just as we feel that we should refrain from theft and obey the law. We may even be tempted, if we are asked out of the blue about these values, to say that they are self-evident. We become much more reflective, however, once we experience a value conflict. What if the only way we can save a friend's life is by stealing and breaking the law? Then our minds are "set. . . working" (Brown & Herrnstein, 1975, p. 310) as we struggle to achieve and defend an answer to this dilemma. Kohlberg's counterposing of some normative values (e.g., life affiliation) against others (e.g., law, property) has proven to be an excellent tool for revealing and studying the cognitive structures by which we coordinate and evaluate values--even though we are not ordinarily conscious of those structures.

The latest version of the Kohlberg et al. Moral Judgment Interview (MJI) assessment system, Standard Issue Scoring (previously referred to as Standard Form Scoring), achieves a rather ingenious blend of standard controls with allowance for individual spontaneity. Parallel forms of the MJI use dilemmas that, although different in concrete content, are carefully matched on the "issues" (or sets of normative values) that can be elicited per dilemma. Whereas a previous assessment system had allowed the number of issues tapped per dilemma to vary with the proclivities of particular subjects and interviewers, Standard Issue Scoring fixes the number of issues to be scored per subject at two per dilemma (and three dilemmas per protocol). Further, the Standard Issue system virtually insures that every protocol will yield a score on both issues of each dilemma by including multiple probe questions for each issue in the question format. Yet a particular subject's dominant thinking on a dilemma--represented by the issue associated with the individual's dilemma choice--is assigned greater psychometric weight in recognition of the greater evaluative importance of that issue for the subject.

Besides the standardization of issues per dilemma, another methodological advance embodied in Standard Issue Scoring is the specification of an appropriate unit of analysis, one that is "narrow enough to be homogeneous (and thereby capture what seems to be a single, discrete moral concept or idea), yet broad enough to represent the idea's full conceptual significance for the subject" (Colby, 1978, p. 93). The mass of responses as encompassed within each dilemma issue had proven to be too large a unit, since one finds not a single justification of the issue but numerous, often heterogeneous justifications of the different normative values (or norms) encompassed within an issue. On the other hand, Kohlberg had known since 1958 that a single sentence was often too small a unit, since a subject may take several sentences to express a moral idea. The optimal specification proved to be somewhere between the issue-clustered mass of sentences and the single sentence. This optimal unit of analysis is called the criterion judgment, which is defined formally as a mode of justification (or element) applied to a particular norm within an issue. Although subjects often use several sentences to express a criterion judgment, criterion judgments in the Standard Issue Manual are typically sentence-length since nonessential aspects of expression have been deleted. In other words, the criterion judgment represents a skeletal, generic, or core expression of a sociomoral justification. It is important to note that the value to which the criterion judgment is applied (specifically the norm, more generally the issue) is identified as content rather than structure: the norm and issue identify the context for the justificatory element, but it is exclusively the justification which is scored. Previous assessment systems had not made this distinction, much to the detriment of research in moral development.

These terms and procedures can be illustrated with Kohlberg's near-famous Heinz dilemma, in which a man named Heinz must decide whether to break the law and steal an exorbitantly priced drug in order to save his dying wife's life. The Heinz dilemma is considered to be fundamentally a conflict between the norm of life and the norm of law, and hence the two standard issues for the dilemma are so named. Within the life issue, however, one also finds the norm of affiliation (between husband and wife), and within the law issue one also finds the norm of property (not stealing from the druggist). On the MJI, the Heinz dilemma is followed by seven core questions:

1. Should Heinz steal the drug?
1a. Why or why not?
2. If Heinz doesn't love his wife, should he steal the drug for her?
2a. Why or why not?
3. Suppose the person dying is not his wife but a stranger. Should Heinz steal the drug for the stranger?
3a. Why or why not?
4. (If you favor stealing the drug for a stranger:) Suppose it's a pet animal he loves. Should Heinz steal to save the pet animal?
4a. Why or why not?
5. Is it important for people to do everything they can to save another's life?
5a. Why or why not?
6. It is against the law for Heinz to steal. Does that make it morally wrong?
6a. Why or why not?
7. Should people try to do everything they can to obey the law?
7a. Why or why not?
7b. How does this apply to what Heinz should do?

Raters scoring protocol responses from these questions must engage in two phases of work: classification and assessment. In terms of classification, the first step is to code by issue. Operationally, the responses to the dilemma questions are issue-defined mainly on the basis of whether the given response supports action alternative X or Y of the dilemma. The issue associated with the subject's opinion choice as to what should be done in the dilemma is termed the "chosen" issue, and the alternative issue the "nonchosen issue." (Chosen-issue scores are given 1.5 times the weight of the nonchosen issue score in the overall protocol rating.) Thus, a "yes" to the first question asked, whether Heinz should steal the drug, would indicate that life is the chosen issue and law the nonchosen issue. One would then code the succeeding responses according to whether they serve to justify the chosen or the nonchosen issue. Since the scorable unit of analysis is typically much smaller than that represented by the material on the issue (chosen or nonchosen), however, it is necessary further to classify the response within, say, the chosen issue by norm and element. For example, a response that Heinz should steal the drug "because a good husband should care about his wife" would be coded as applying a "duty" element (since "a good husband should . . ." implies a role obligation) to an affiliation norm (relations between husband and wife) on the chosen issue (life). To give another example, a subject who responds to question 2 by stating that, even if Heinz doesn't love her, he should still steal it because "he has a basic responsibility to save a human life" would provide a case of the same "duty" element (albeit at a different stage) applied to the life norm of the life issue. To establish the interview judgements to be assessed, one must pool the similarly coded features of the data: a given discrete idea may recur sporadically throughout the issue responses, and a valid assessment of the stage level of the idea require consideration en masse of its various content expressions.

Once the responses for the given issue have been coded and grouped by norm and element, the classification phase in the Kohlberg system is completed, and stage assessment can begin. The essence of stage assessment is to find the stage level which offers the closest match between a given interview justification (i.e., a given element as applied to a given norm within the issue) and an available criterion judgment in the manual on that issue. Once the assessment for the chosen issue is completed, one proceeds to code the norms and elements evident in the nonchosen issue material in similar fashion, and then to find the best stage matches for those isolable justifications. The overall procedure is then repeated for the remaining two dilemmas in the protocol. The total protocol score is then reported both globally as a function of the most dominant stage or stages represented among the six issue ratings, and more quantitatively on the basis of all of the issue-score stage weightings.

The SRM, although based on the MJI, has been designed to facilitate: (1) scoring (and learning to score) by eliminating the classification phase of the work; and (2) data collection by eliminating the need for individualized follow-up questions. The techniques used in the SRM to accomplish these objectives derive from certain implicit features in the MJI questions, and can be introduced through the discussion of those features. It should be understood that Kohlberg's standard probe questions are those interview questions which have been found, over the past two decades, to be the most efficacious in eliciting structurally significant justification responses. These questions promote the yield of structural scorability in several basic ways.

One basic feature of some of the questions contributes to both classification and assessment endeavors. Notice that, after the first several items, the questions (presented earlier) start to broaden the frame of reference for the subject's discourse beyond the single sentence or specific action choice to the level of general prescriptive practices or normative values. Question 5 asks the subject to evaluate the importance of saving another's life and then asks the subject to justify that evaluation. Questions 6 and 7 ask abstract value questions pertaining to the law norm. These questions augment the structural yield of the data because they challenge the subject to reflect upon and justify values such as life and law in direct and general terms. Yet we know that these questions are far less efficacious when posed out of the blue, divorced from the context of the dilemma and preceding questions. The dilemma and the immediate action-choice questions which follow evidently serve as concrete "props" for the abstract reflective reasoning, since the subject can still reflect on the value as it was embodied in the dilemma. Probably also facilitative is the fact that the opening general question, question 5, asks subjects to evaluate the normative value of life by having subjects judge whether it is important to save another's life (which most subjects judge affirmatively). The evaluation may serve to warm up the subject to the general norm, since in order to judge a value we must at least attend to it and in some minimal sense reflect on it. Overall, the concrete dilemma context with its action questions, followed by questions asking for evaluation, brings subjects to the realm of reflective sociomoral thought.

Another equally important methodological contribution made by these general norm questions is the reduction they afford in the classification work which must be done by the rater. Unlike other questions which require scorers to identify issues, norms, and elements among the responses, questions 5 and 7 are automatically tagged on both issue and norm (question 5 elicits life and question 7 elicits law). With the need for content classification mostly eliminated by such "norm framing," scorers can proceed to focus on stage assessment of the data, or at least on how these question responses contribute to it.

A tactical feature which also helps account for the efficacy of the questions is implicit in the earlier questions on the dilemma. Notice that questions 2, 3, and 4 extend or vary the core Heinz dilemma in various ways (what if Heinz doesn't love his wife? What if it is a stranger? A pet?) and then ask the subject to reconsider his or her choice in light of these new circumstances. These circumstantial modifactions promote scorability by making the dilemma more of a _dilemma_, especially for those subjects whose reflective wheels need scarcely to turn to justify stealing to save one's beloved spouse. Further, the changes promote the likelihood that the major norms implied by the dilemma will be addressed by the subject's justification. Probably a related function is also served by question 6, which highlights an alternative norm in the core dilemma that may have been neglected by the subject (e.g., "It's against the law for Heinz to steal . . ."). Again, it is when the subject experiences the task as a _problem_ and must therefore do some fresh thinking that we gain the best position for validly assessing a subject's developmental level of thought. The technique of task variation is the best Piagetian tradition, as demonstrated by even a cursory inspection of Piaget's experimental applications of the _méthode clinique._

The SRM amplifies the assessment and classification efficacy of the MJI by incorporating these implicit features of general norm questioning and dilemma varying and converting them into deliberately and systematically applied techniques. Notice that on the MJI, the dilemma-variation feature has been used in probe questions for some of the norms (affiliation, life) but not others. Similarly, the general norm questions are asked for life and law, but not for affiliation or property. Why should this be? If these features have proven to be efficacious, then why not use them for _every_ norm? Indeed, it is possible to combine the two features for every question. One can vary (or at least highlight) each major normative circumstance of the dilemma and then, for each such variation, ask for the subject's evaluation and justification of the norm involved. Further, the inclusion of a general-norm level for every question means that every question, not just some, can be norm-tagged. The specific manner in which the SRM incorporates the best features of the MJI into every question can be discerned by perusal of Form A or B of the SRM (Appendix A). For example, the Form A life norm question first elicits an evaluation of the importance of saving a stranger's life, which then defines the "life" frame of reference for the ensuing sociomoral justification.

As will be reported later in this chapter, this greater efficacy through probe-question systematization has made possible several benefits. For one thing, it means that the SRM can be group-administered without fear that the lack of opportunity for individual follow-up will cause an insuffficient yield in the data. It also makes possible benefits pertaining to scoring work. To learn to do reliable Standard Issue Scoring of the MJI, one must participate in an intensive, tuition-fee workshop lasting one or two weeks at Harvard (extensive practice even after the workshop is also essential). Scoring the protocol transcripts in one's research is a lengthy process, with

some transcripts taking as long as several hours to rate. Scoring and learning
to score the MJI is so arduous and time-consuming partly because one must
engage in extensive classificatory judgments before even beginning stage
assessment work. Since the SRM cuts down drastically on classificatory requirements, scoring and learning to score are thereby facilitated. Indeed, our
research results demonstrate that, after working through the training
exercises provided in the appendices, you will in all probability be in a
position to do sociomoral assessment at criterion levels of reliability--
without the necessity for a special intensive workshop.

We view the SRM, then, as extending the trend toward standardization represented by the advent of MJI Standard Issue Scoring. Although the SRM makes
possible some important gains for future scientific research, however, there
are also some losses and limits. After all, the MJI, since it is an open-
ended vehicle for individual interviewing of persons at different ages, has
been an excellent tool for descriptively rich structural investigation. By
the same token, since the SRM frames the reference and probes for the subject's thoughts more strictly, the possibility of discovering new structures
using the SRM is considerably curtailed (although not eliminated). Also,
relative to the SRM, the MJI allows a closer tracking of the problem-solving
dynamics of the subject's thought, granting greater weight to those justifications entailed in the subject's chosen approach to solving the problem.

We do not feel that these losses are major ones. After twenty years of
open-ended structural investigation in numerous countries, the point of diminishing returns seems to have been reached with respect to the discovery of
new structures. As described in the previous chapter, we believe that the
path has been adequately cleared in sociomoral development for the introduction and use of more standard instruments. Regarding the MJI's greater problem focus, the greater retention of the particular problem's dynamics also
means that the structural raters must read through a greater amount of dross
in the interview material (since preoccupation with particular details about
the Heinz situation tends to obscure the general values that need to be the
referent for structurally significant reflection). The need for differential
weighting of the subject's responses (see discussion of "chosen" vs. "nonchosen" issue) can be reduced by slanting the dilemma variations so as to
dispose a subject to evaluate and justify a normative value which might
otherwise be slighted. For example, asking: "What if the druggist just wants
Heinz to pay what the drug cost to make, and Heinz can't even pay that?" leads
many subjects to grant more serious attention to the general-norm question,
"How important is it for people not to take things that belong to other
people?" (SRM question 5a).

One virtue of the SRM can also be viewed as a limitation. As noted, the SRM
like the MJI retains the Piagetian focus not simply on the subject's selection of prestructured choices and evaluative options, but more importantly on
the subject's production of reflective justifications of those choices and
evaluations. Through the study of spontaneous justificatory production, we
can gain central access to an individual subject's thinking about the task
problems. To achieve this advantage, however, the researcher must develop
skill in stage assessment of the subject's justificatory reflections. Although a workshop is unnecessary, self-training of SRM assessment skill takes
at least one month and usually longer. Also, the insistence on production
raises the question of the extent to which the presence or absence of verbal
and writing skills in a particular subject may have the effect of inflating

or depressing the assessment of the subject's actual sociomoral competence.

Are these limitations outweighed by the virtue of using an instrument which taps the relatively "deep" process of subject-produced reflective justification? We think so, for most purposes, and the SRM minimizes the methodological and logistical complexities required for the assessment of such data. Numerous researchers in the past ten years (Bloom, 1977; Enright, et. al., 1980; Hogan, 1970; Maitland & Goldman, 1974; Page & Bode, 1980; Rest, Cooper, Coder, Masanz, & Anderson, 1974), however, have constructed sociomoral tests which do not entail a production component—and which therefore do not require extensive assessment work and training. The most prominent of these tests is the Defining Issues Test (DIT; Rest, 1979). The DIT has achieved preeminence partly because Rest has conducted quite thorough and favorable psychometric evaluations of the test but probably also because the DIT evolved directly from Rest's collaborative work with Kohlberg. Like the MJI (and the SRM), Rest's DIT uses dilemmas and requires subjects to make evaluations of importance. Whereas Kohlbergian dilemma questions ask for the evaluation of certain normative values as a prelude to asking for the justification of those values, however, the Rest dilemma questions ask only for evaluations—but the evaluations are of the importance of certain substantive considerations which are in fact stage-significant (cf. Kohlberg's criterion judgments). In other words, whereas Kohlbergian norm questions provide only the norm and reserve the justificatory consideration for the subject to produce, the Rest items produce the full justificatory consideration for the subject and then tap only the subject's evaluation (in terms of both ratings and rankings) of these considerations. Such data show how a subject basically construes a moral dilemma by indicating those issues which the subject perceives as most important for the situation, i.e., as definitive of the dilemma (hence the "Defining Issues" Test). Differential patterns among subjects' comparative rankings of the considerations then permit distinctions along a developmental scale. For example, a subject whose top rankings consistently go to high-stage considerations would be placed more highly on the scale than would a subject whose top rankings go to lower-level considerations.

It is important to understand what the DIT does—and does not—validly assess. The DIT does provide a developmental assessment of people's sociomoral and sociopolitical evaluative judgment. A measure of this construct can be quite valuable. For example, demagoguery is especially dangerous where citizens perceive social problems mainly in terms of low-level issues, whereas a high-level appeal may not be futile if tests show that voting citizens do understand and appreciate social problems in terms of relatively sophisticated issues. Although the DIT is a valid test of sociomoral evaluative thought, however, it is not a valid test of sociomoral justificatory thought. As Rest (1975) himself asserts, "The DIT was not designed simply to be an easier way of assessing moral judgment than Kohlberg's test" (p. 748). Hence, it is not surprising that the DIT has poor concurrent validity with the MJI (Davison & Robbins, 1978; Froming & McColgan, 1979). The various reported concurrent validity levels, as Rest et al. (1974) note, are "not high enough to regard the two measures as equivalent tests" (p. 497). Yet the attempt to use the DIT in precisely this fashion abounds in the literature. Again, the DIT is a valid test of moral evaluation, but it is certainly not a test of moral reasoning in any structural sense. (This is not to say that an objective assessment of sociomoral reasoning is in principle impossible. Indeed, we are currently working on such a test.)

Psychometric Evaluation

In general, then, the SRM may considerably facilitate the research of those investigators interested in reflective or justificatory sociomoral thought. For the past several years, we have studied the psychometric properties of the SRM in terms of several kinds of reliability and validity. In connection with these studies, more than 600 subjects have so far been tested, persons of both sexes, of several races and SES levels, and ranging in age from 8 to 66. The results of these studies, which are generally quite favorable, are reported in detail elsewhere (Gibbs, Widaman, & Colby, Note 2, in press; Gibbs, Widaman, Colby, & Fenton, Note 3). The rest of this chapter will report the essential results in relatively general and nontechnical fashion.

Psychometric research on the SRM has made use of two primary indices representing the overall stage ratings of the protocols. The simpler index is modal stage, or the stage (1, 2, 3, or 4) most frequently represented among the protocol responses. Psychometrically far more differentiated is the Sociomoral Reflection Maturity Score (SRMS), which entails a 400-point scale extending from Stage 1 (lowest possible rating = 100) to Stage 4 (highest possible rating = 400; justifications at the "theory-defining level" may also be noted, however; see Chapter 3). A secondary index which represents the SRMS in more qualitative summary form is global stage, which indicates either a pure stage (not necessarily identical to modal stage) or a major-minor stage combination. The global stage index summarizes the SRMS data along a 10-point scale; SRMS ratings 100 through 125 = Stage 1; 126-149 = Transition 1(2); 150-174 = Transition 2(1); 175-225 = Stage 2, etc.). In defining scoring discrepancies along the global scale, a "within 1/3 stage" discrepancy is any disparity (between raters, between times of administration, between forms of the test) which represents at most two adjacent global ranges on the scale (including those which fall within a single global range--such cases, however, are also separately evaluated as "exact global agreement"). Examples are: 321 and 326, 3 and 3(4), respectively; and, 326 and 374, 3(4) and 4(3), respectively. Although the global stage index is helpful where percent agreements must be calculated, it is not considered a primary index since it represents merely a less differentiated, monotonic transformation of the SRMS.

The full procedure by which modal stage and SRMS are calculated from the component ratings of the SRM is described in Chapter 4. Essentially, the SRM indices are based on stage or stage-transitional assessments of the subject's evaluative justifications of eight normative values: life, affiliation, law, legal justice, conscience, family affiliation, contract, and property. Briefly, modal stage is the stage most heavily represented among the stage ratings. The SRMS is the arithmetic average of the norm ratings multiplied by 100.

The psychometric evaluation of the SRM has entailed investigations of its reliability as well as its validity. Reliability pertains to the question of whether a test has stable or consistent properties, whereas validity pertains to the question of whether the test actually measures that which it is assumed to measure. We assessed four kinds of reliability using age-homogeneous samples: test-retest, parallel-form (separate sessions of administration), internal consistency, and interrater. Test-retest and parallel-form reliability pertain to the question of stability over time; internal consistency and interrater reliability pertain to other senses of stability. The SRM's parallel-form reliability was comparable to its test-retest reliability: exact modal agreement percentages were acceptable (mean of 71; modal agreement within one stage was 100 percent), and SRMS correlations were in the 70's and 80's (.90 and .87, respectively, for the entire age-heterogeneous samples). Absolute SRMS differences averaged slightly under 20 points, and mean signed differences were negligible. Percent global agreement was high for agreement within one-third stage (in the 90's for both parallel-form and test-retest reliability), although mean percent exact global agreement was markedly lower for parallel form (48 vs. 60). In general, the SRM appears to generate consistent results across successive testing administrations, even where different (although parallel) dilemmas are used across time of testing.

Parallel-form reliability is generally considered to provide a strong assessment of stability, since the different content across forms reduces the possibility that a high correlation across testing times is attributable to subjects' memory and imitation of their previous responses. The question of whether the test index is stable across different content can also be assessed by measuring internal consistency. Our primary internal consistency indicator was the alpha coefficient, which reflects the average extent to which the component scores (our eight norm ratings) covary with one another. The alpha for the total reliability sample (time 1 tests) was .85 (.74 with age partialled out). Also, the mean percent of overall stage ratings attributable to modal stage was 58. Hence, individual norm ratings on the SRM appear to be fairly homogeneous and consistent with one another. (Nonetheless, one should not attempt to do research with the SRM using only one particular norm rather than the overall protocol scores.)

Interrater reliability received particular attention in our evaluation program, since a primary objective was to determine whether reliable SRM assessment could be learned simply through self-training. We distinguished three types of raters: highly trained, trained, and self-trained. We (Gibbs and Widaman) constituted the first category: we were "highly trained" because we had intensive experience in corroborating our assessment inferences through the process of construction of the manual. This optimal background was reflected in the reliability results: the SRMS correlation of our independent protocol ratings was .98, our exact global agreement was 93 percent, and our exact modal agreement was 85.7 percent (agreement within one modal stage was 100 percent).

The trained raters were three students: a female developmental psychology graduate student, a male developmental psychology graduate student, and a female undergraduate senior. The graduate students were moderately familiar—and the undergraduate only slightly familiar—with Kohlberg's work on moral development. These raters worked through the training materials (see Appendices) and were tutored by us over the course of six weekly sessions (taken together, these sessions probably provided the equivalent of Kohlbergian workshop training). The trained raters achieved good interrater reliability, although not at the outstanding level of the highly trained raters. SRMS correlations were generally in the 80's, and percent global agreement with one-third stage in the 90's (the highest exact agreement, 75, was achieved by the undergraduate). Exact modal agreement averaged in the 70's (modal agreement within one stage was again 100 percent).

After the training materials were annotated on the basis of the initial training work, five prospective raters trained themselves by working through the training exercises over a period of approximately two months (October and November 1980). The self-trained raters included males and females, as well as graduate students and undergraduates, all of whom were moderately familiar with Kohlberg's work. Generally, the interrater performance of the self-trained raters was comparable to that of the trained raters. However, one self-trained rater, an undergraduate female, consistently performed below minimum acceptable standards. On the other hand, the other undergraduate self-trained rater (a male), performed as well as or better than the most reliable of the trained raters (the female undergraduate). We tentatively conclude that success in SRM self-training can be anticipated more confidently for graduate students, but that achievement of excellent interrater reliability by undergraduates is not impossible.

As noted, the psychometric evaluation of the SRM has also entailed investigations of its validity. Two kinds of validity have been evaluated: criterion-related (specifically, concurrent) and construct. One of our earliest studies was of the concurrent validity of the SRM with the MJI. Since the SRM is a direct derivative of the MJI, a subject's standing on the two measures should be comparable and correlative. The data, based on parallel-form administration of the two tests, support this expectation. Modal stage agreement between the SRM and MJI was 75.4 percent, and 100 percent of the modal discrepancies were within one modal stage. The correlation between the two tests was .85 (.50 with age partialled out, but still highly significant). Although exact global agreement between the two tests was only 38.6 percent, agreement within one-third stage was 78.9 percent (Berkowitz, Note 4).

Construct validation of the SRM has been a continuing endeavor, since "judgments of construct validity are based upon an accumulation of research results" (APA, 1974, p. 30). Construct validation, in fact, is an ongoing process intimately involved with theory development:

> In obtaining the information needed to establish construct validity, the investigator begins by formulating hypotheses. . . .Taken together, such hypotheses form at least a tentative theory about the nature of the construct the test is believed to be measuring. . . .If the investigator's theory about what the test measures is essentially correct, most of his predictions should be confirmed. If they are not, he may revise his definition of the construct, or he may revise the test to make it a better measure of the construct he had in mind. Through the process of successive verification, modification, or elimination of hypotheses, the investigator increases his understanding of the qualities measured by the test. Through the process of confirmation or disconfirmation, test revision, and new research on the revised instrument, he improves the usefulness of the test as a measure of a construct. (p. 30)

Since its concurrent validity with the MJI is strong, the SRM thereby gains some degree of construct validity deriving from the 20-year construct validation process which has established the MJI (see Colby, 1978; Kohlberg, 1981). Perhaps the greatest piggyback benefit from the parent instrument is the evolved effectivenes of the MJI Standard Issue Scoring System in measuring the consecutive, nonregressive characteristic of longitudinal stage data collected over two decades (Colby, Kohlberg, Gibbs, & Lieberman, in press). "Invariant sequence," as this property is termed, is the star stage-construct hypothesis in structural-developmental theory, and its confirmation simultaneously bolsters the test and the theory.

Nonetheless, concurrent validity per se is not sufficient for establishing the construct validity of a new test, no matter how well established the criterion test may be. We have directly assessed the construct validity of the SRM chiefly in two ways: first, by investigating whether it correlates positively with certain relevant summary variables (age, SES, education); and, second, by investigating whether it can detect sociomoral gains attributable to relevant treatment experiences (also, a short-term longitudinal study of the SRM is underway; Kernan & Gibbs, Note 5). Highly significant correlations (in the 70's) between the SRM and age and grade, and a more modest but still significant correlation of .23 between the SRM and SES, were found using the time 1 data from the reliability sample. It is also noteworthy that we have found no sex differences at any age level in any of the samples. It is possible, however, that there are systematic content frequency differences in the usage of the various aspects of a given stage; research on this question is planned, Gibbs & Burkhart, Note 6). SRM age norms by grade for the construction and reliability samples are provided in Tables 1 and 2.

Table 1

Mean Protocol Rating and SES
By Grade and Sample

Protocol Rating						
Grade	n	Age	SRMS	Adjusted[a] SRMS	Global	SES
Construction Sample						
4th	26	9.8	173.5	200.7	2(1),2[b]	32.3
5th	30	10.2	202.4	211.4	2	44.4
7th	23	12.4	234.6	242.9	2(3)	44.8
9th	18	14.3	291.8	276.1	3	60.7
10/11th	23	15.2	287.3	292.7	3	46.8
College	51	18.6	342.8	323.5	3(4),3[b]	63.1
Adult	30	37.8	367.4	366.8	4(3)	50.7
Combined	201	17.6	280.3	280.3	3	50.3
Reliability Sample						
7th	35	12.1	260.4	264.3	3(2)	52.9
10th	34	15.5	290.5	289.0	3	61.7
College	38	18.8	343.2	341.0	3(4)	62.9
Combined	107	15.5	299.4	299.4	3	59.2

[a]SRMS was adjusted to control for variance attributable to SES.
[b]The two global ratings are based on SRMS and adjusted SRMS, respectively.

Table 2

Modal Stage Frequencies
By Grade and Sample

	Modal Stage			
Grade	1	2	3	4
Construction Sample				
4th	5	21	0	0
5th	0	29	1	0
7th	0	16	7	0
9th	0	3	12	3
10th/11th	0	3	17	3
College	0	1	22	28
Adult	0	0	2	28
Reliability Sample				
7th	1	14	19	1
10th	0	6	25	3
College	0	0	14	24

Another evaluation of construct validity was the SRM's assessment performance with respect to theoretically relevant experimental enhancement
studies. We conducted two intervention projects (Gibbs et al., Note 3; Arnold,
Ahlborn, & Gibbs, Note 7), and on both of them the SRM proved to be an effective discriminator of experimental change. One discriminative assessment
opportunity was afforded by the inclusion of the SRM in a battery of tests
used to evaluate the Civic Education Project at Carnegie-Mellon University.
The Civic Education Project was designed to promote social, intellectual, and
ethical development in high school students. Students are exposed to justice-
and democracy-oriented instructional innovations in social studies and Eng-
lish, discuss conflicting views generated by sociomoral dilemmas, and participate in rule-setting school fairness committees. The treatment was introduced
and maintained by teachers who had been trained at a Carnegie-Mellon University workshop led by Dr. Edwin Fenton. Five participating high schools in the
United States and West Germany yielded six experimental groups, plus one
control group comparable in curriculum (social studies) but without the Civic
Education Project innovations. In terms of the SRMS index, the experimental
groups did show significant gains in sociomoral reasoning relative to control
group. There were no significant differences in terms of using modal stage,
however.

Our other intervention project was conducted with adjudicated male and female juvenile delinquents incarcerated at medium-security institutions under
control of the Ohio Youth Commission. Our theoretical expectation was that a
delinquent sample would manifest a depressed developmental level of sociomoral
reflection, in light of the dearth of role-taking opportunities afforded by
the family and ecological backgrounds of most delinquents (Welsh, 1976). This

expectation was confirmed. Even after the scores were adjusted for age and SES, the delinquents scored significantly lower on SRMS than did the Civic Education Project and reliability samples, 261.8, Transition 3(2), vs. 299.4, Stage 3. The difference can also be expressed in terms of modal stage. In the nondelinquent samples, 14 percent of the subjects evidenced a modal Stage of 4, 71 percent were at modal Stage 3, and 15 percent were at modal Stage 2. In the delinquent sample, no subjects were at modal Stage 4, 59.5 percent were at modal Stage 3, and 40.5 percent were at modal Stage 2.

We construed this developmental depression as a case of delay or arrest and conducted an intervention project using dilemma discussions as the vehicle for remedially facilitating the sociomoral development of the pretest modal Stage 2 delinquents. Subjects were randomly assigned to experimental or control groups, and the experimental subjects participated in a two-month series of weekly sociomoral dilemma discussions. The discussion leaders attempted to promote role-taking opportunities by asking subjects to justify their differing views to one another. The results in terms of modal stage were particularly dramatic. Whereas 87.5 percent of the experimental subjects who had evidenced Stage 2 as their modal stage in the pretest shifted in modal stage usage to Stage 3 on the posttest, only 14.3 percent of the control subjects in this category did so. Similar results were obtained using SRMS, although the level of significance was lower ($p < .05$ rather than $p < .001$). Subjects who had evidenced modal Stage 3 on the pretest for the most part remained at the stage on the posttest, with no significant differences using either modal stage or SRMS.

In general, then, the SRM would appear to be a stable, appropriate, and sensitive test of an individual's developmental level of reflective sociomoral thought. The test has good internal consistency and yields reliable scores even with self-trained raters. It correlates highly with chronological age and effectively discriminates the results of sociomoral enrichment experiences. The SRM can be group-administered, yet its open-ended component affords researchers the opportunity to use production data in their studies. For these reasons, the SRM may contribute valuably to developmental research on social intelligence.

3

THE

STAGES

We have depicted two approaches to the concept of intelligence and have elaborated on the developmental approach to the evolution from childhood to maturity of reflective sociomoral thought. Not yet discussed, however, is the point that this evolution is assumed to take place through a sequence of stages. In the domain of social intelligence, our assessment instrument measures the maturity of reflective sociomoral thought in terms of a progressive sequence of four standard stages (the relation of these four stages to Kohlberg's six stages will be discussed later in this chapter).

Reflective sociomoral thinking concerns the justification of one's sociomoral decisions and evaluations. We speak of reflective thinking because we assume that the justifying of a decision or evaluation entails reflection upon it (at least in some minimal sense). We speak of reflective sociomoral thinking because social intelligence in its broadest sense inextricably entails prescriptive decisions and evaluations referring to socially good and right action (helping a friend, saving a life, not stealing from others). On the other hand, "sociomoral" is helpful because the unadorned "moral" is for many people rife with misleading solipsistic connotations. In the tradition of Piaget, Kohlberg, and Selman, "morality" is understood as deeply and inextricably rooted in social interaction. Morality in this tradition refers to that which is good and right not simply for oneself but more profoundly for the quality of interactions between oneself and others, society, and humanity. One's sociomoral justification, then, is structured by one's understanding of "the nature of the relations between persons (or between persons and their institutions) and the transactions that serve to regulate, maintain, and transform these relations" (Damon, 1977, p. 2).

Although some social developmentalists (most notably Damon) have studied stages in early childhood--and others (especially Kohlberg) have posited uniquely adult stages--our focus is on childhood and adolescence. Our data show that, by late adolescence, the broad features of normative sociomoral reflection as it is found in adulthood have been formed. Of course, social intelligence in the adult years may evidence some "quantitative" advances (e.g., in the relative proportions of the higher stages or in the scope and transforming power of high-stage usages), as well as the qualitative advance of philosophical sophistication; and, on the other hand, there may be structural deficiencies in some special adult populations. These areas are worth studying. We have not, however, found any uniquely adult sociomoral stages in the Piagetian sense that can serve as the referents for developmental research.

The main aim of this chapter is to describe the basic developmental stages of social intelligence as they have been fleshed out in our research. Although interesting in their own right, the descriptions will also be functionally valuable for the stage assessment work entailed in the succeeding chapters. Beyond this descriptive discussion, we will consider a crucial issue surrounding the stages, namely, the question of their possible relations to moral actions and moral maturity.

A given sociomoral stage refers primarily to the character of one's prescriptive understanding of relations and transactions between people. Furthermore, a given approach to coordinating actions and perspectives (e.g. dispositions, needs, attitudes, claims) across persons intrinsically relates to a certain prescriptive understanding of people's motivations for their actions and perspectives. We can illustrate these dynamics—which characterize the structure of the stages—through an adaptation of Selman's (1980) extensive work on the development of social perspective-taking (our distinction between coordination and motivation relates to Selman's distinction between "relations" and "persons").

At Stage 1, human relations are construed unilaterally: sequences of observable, absolute one-way actions of one person "upon" another person are appreciated and appealed to in sociomoral justification. Accordingly, the Stage 1 understanding of human social motivation is simplistic: a person's perspective is simply read off from a one-way action or anticipation, without the deeper understanding that would come from a perspectival coordination.

The understanding of social interaction at Stage 2 entails the insight that human relations can be "two-way" in the sense that person A can not only anticipate person B's reaction to A's perspective but can also take that anticipated reaction into account in fashioning A's perspective in the first place. Moreover, it is understood by A that B's perspective can be similarly fashioned in part by considerations of A's own potential reactions. In general, it is implicitly understood that A or B in a dyadic situation may momentarily suspend his or her own perspective in order to inform that perspective with considerations deriving from the other person's perspective. This "exchanging" type of perspective-taking is intrinsically associated with an instrumental view of human sociomoral motivation: people should act morally if and when such actions make sense considering their enlightened self-interest; for example, you should help a friend because otherwise, stepping into the friend's shoes for a moment, you can anticipate that the friend won't want to help you the next time you need a favor.

In the context of sociomoral justification, we can intuitively recognize that Stages 1 and 2 are socially immature: they both lack a certain quality of reflective ideality (although in a narrow sense we can say that Stage 2 is more "rational" than Stage 1). As long as one relates another's perspective to one's own in a temporally linear fashion—and sees others as doing the same— one has not attained reflective maturity even on the simplest, dyadic level. Reflective sociomoral ideality first emerges at Stage 3 as one simultaneously interpenetrates one's own perspective with another's. In other words, mature sociomoral thinking requires that the thinker transcend the spatiotemporal contiguities and contingencies of one-way and two-way relations and view an ongoing relationship from what Selman calls a "third-person" perspective. From the third-person (overall and ideal) perspective, one constructs and experiences genuine mutualities, e.g., a caring for the "we-ness" of a relationship, which become in themselves sufficient justifications for one's sociomoral evaluations. Further, this third-person perspective eventuates into an understanding of social motivation as not necessarily limited to instrumental pragmatics. It is implicitly understood that persons may act at least in part out of an underlying, stable caring for other persons and relationships as values in their own right--although it is also understood that, in practice, people often do things because of their momentary "interests" in the narrow sense. (Indeed, in economic transactions, such as bartering or marketplace bargaining, the interchange of individual pragmatic interest may be appropriate and is not necessarily "morally immature.")

Stage 3 may itself represent sufficient reflective maturity in the context of a face-to-face rural village or tribal community, where social systems are scarcely more complex than are those of one's interpersonal relationships. In pluralistic, urban societies, however, ethical problems arise which must be resolved by expanding one's frame of reference beyond dyadic relations to encompass networks of positional relationships, i.e., social systems (cf. Edwards, 1975). As one enters adulthood in a complex society, one increasingly must deal with a social diversity which gains viability and coherence only through the common acceptance of basic rights, responsibilities, and other standards or procedural practices by the citizens of that society. Stage 4, then, marks an expanded application of third-person ideality beyond dyadic relations to the differentiated, hierarchical networks of complex social systems. This systemic level of conceptualizing human relations intrinsically entails the understanding that adult persons may be structured in their social actions by certain consistent standards which--although flexible in certain cases--do not totally accommodate to the interpersonal sentiments deriving from particular face-to-face relationships.

The preceding global depiction of the stages prepares the way for a fine-grained analysis which will be helpful in your development of sociomoral stage assessment skill. Your work with the stages should also be informed by an understanding of the unit of analysis to be used in stage assessment. Our unit of analysis is essentially the same as that used by Kohlberg et al. in Standard Issue Scoring: namely, the discrete, unitary justification of a single sociomoral value and decision. Kohlberg's unit is called the "criterion judgment," and it is technically described as the application of a stage-significant element to a norm on an issue (see Chapter 2). Our counterpart to the criterion judgment is the criterion justification (CJ), technically defined as a specific application of a stage-significant "aspect" manifestation to the evaluation of a norm. There are two operational differences between the criterion judgment and the criterion justification. First, whereas the MJI Standard Issue scorer first classifies an individual subject's various responses according to issue (chosen vs. nonchosen) and norm (variable within issue), the SRM scorer does not. We do not use the issue system at all, and the norms are framed and thereby fixed by question (as described in Chapter 2). The 16 questions on the SRM yield justificatory responses addressed to the following eight norms, labeled as follows: (1) affiliation (marriage and friendship), (2) life, (3) law (and property), (4) legal justice, (5) conscience, (6) family affiliation, (7) contract, and (8) property. A second difference is that, whereas in Standard Issue Scoring coding by element is necessary (although it is often done only informally), SRM coding by aspect is not necessary (although familiarity with the aspects can facilitate scoring), since each norm on the SRM frames such a small quantity of responses.

Since Kohlberg used the term "aspect" in a previous scoring system, an explanatory note may be helpful. In Kohlberg's old terminology and in our current system, an aspect is a feature of reflective and justificatory sociomoral thought which is functionally integral to a broader structure of thought, i.e., a stage. Kohlberg's old aspects (their contemporary Standard Issue equivalents are called "modes"), however, were defined abstractly enough to serve as vertical dimensions along which corresponding features of the stages could be arrayed. We found this approach to be too abstract to be helpful in stage assessment, so we have fashioned a more inductively based aspect system whereby entirely discrete sets of aspects are used to describe each of the respective stages.

Each of the stages can be described in terms of approximately six aspects (Stage 1 has only five, Stage 4 has seven). Virtually all of the aspects, for all the stages, are represented by criterion justifications (CJs) on each of the eight norms of the SRM. Thus there are approximately 200 official "locations" for reference criteria in the system. Indeed, the logically possible number of reference criteria is even greater: stage-transition levels are also represented in the reference chapters, and each stage aspect typically differentiates into several discrete criterion justifications. Since the key to grasping the empirical unit of analysis of the stages is the aspect, the aspects of the stages are described in detail below.

THE STAGES

Stage 1: Unilateral and Simplistic

Justifications at this level are characteristically rather stark and unqualified. There is no coordination of alternative perspectives; opposite opinions, where presented, are simply juxtaposed with no apparent attention to the contradiction. Reflection is usually couched in the simple tenses (past, present, future), although hypothetical anticipations ("would," "could," "might") are not entirely absent. Justifications which are incomplete (from higher-level perspectives) are presented by the Stage 1 thinker as if they were quite sufficient and even self-evident (e.g., obeying the law is important because otherwise "stealing is bad" or "your parents don't like it"). Piaget's (1932/1965) description of this level as "heteronomous" rather aptly captures its external and authority-oriented character. The aspects (abbreviated labels in parentheses) of Stage 1 are illustrated below.

Aspect 1: Edicts of Unilateral Authority (Unilateral Authority). This aspect consists of a simple appeal to an authority figure (parent, spouse, God) or other embodiment of authority (the law, the Bible). The appeal is usually unelaborated, as if the very invocation of the authority's name were a sufficient justification in itself. The authority seems to be taken as a given prior presence (e.g., Law and Property: "the law is there for you to follow") and may be granted considerable power (e.g., property norm: letting one's children keep their money is not important because "maybe the child didn't obey").

Aspect 2: Immediate or Physical Status (Status). Stage 1 normative evaluations may also be justified by appeal to the most salient role or status of the person or persons involved. For example, on the affiliation norm, helping one's wife may be evaluated as important because "it's his wife" or because she "might be an important person." Elaborations of this justification are usually physicalistic (e.g., on Family Affiliation: helping one's parents is important because "they're your parents, they're grown up"; or on Life: a person "may be important, may own a lot of furniture"). A particularly interesting manifestation of the status aspect occurs on Conscience, where a jail sentence is advocated because the conscientious lawbreaker's conscience after all "was only his mind"--that is, was an entity which, having no physical status, should have counted for very little.

Aspect 3: Maxim-Like Rules, Prescriptions, or Proscriptions (Rules). This aspect of Stage 1 reflection consists of flat assertions which have a maxim-like ring and which are often couched in absolute terms (e.g., Life: saving a stranger's life is <u>not</u> important because "you should never go near strangers"). The assertions are usually proscriptive, but may be prescriptive (e.g., Contract: "you should always keep your promises"). The adverbs "always" and "never," especially as in "you should always/never . . .," facilitate the correct classification of justification data as Stage 1, but maxim-like assertions may sometimes be Stage 1 without showing this form. Applied to roles, the Rules aspect contributes a quite rigid and narrow or constraint-oriented conception: on Legal Justice, sending lawbreakers to jail is important because "a judge has to send people to jail."

Aspect 4: Unqualified Positive or Negative Labels or Affective States (Labels). This facet of Stage 1 thinking consists of the justificatory use of fairly gross or undifferentiated labels (e.g., good/bad, nice/mean, or right/wrong) or affective terms (happy/sad). The labels represent statuses which will come to exist as consequences of one's action; the eventuation of these labels may be either favorable (e.g., Affiliation: helping one's spouse is important in order "to be nice") or unfavorable (e.g., Contract: keeping a promise is important because otherwise the other person, "will cry" or "won't be your friend"). In some instances, the Labels aspect is quite close to the Rules aspect, differentiated only by use of a noun (rather than verb) form (e.g., Contract: "You shouldn't be a tattletale"). A particularly interesting manifestation of the Labels aspect is found on Life, where stereotyped role labels define allowable exceptions to an opinion against saving a stranger's life: saving the stranger's life is not important "unless you are a firefighter, police officer, or hospital person."

Aspect 5: Punitive Consequences. This aspect consists of the evaluation of the importance of normative values by the criterion of whether or not one is punished for violating them. Usually the anticipation of punitive consequences is expressed in the simple future tense, suggesting that the punishment is felt to be inevitable or unavoidable. Also, the punitive event is usually represented physically (spanked, beat up, killed), or at least figuratively (get found out, punished, sent to jail). The physical content is so strongly suggestive of Stage 1 that it is so classified even where a conditional tense is used (e.g., "might get spanked").

Stage 2: Exchanging and Instrumental

The heteronomy of Stage 1 is succeeded at Stage 2 by an "autonomous" morality (to use another of Piaget's terms). In other words, sociomoral justifications now reflect an understanding of morality as deriving not from edicts, rules, or consequences external to oneself, but instead as deriving directly from the perspectives which arise through one's interactions with others. Accordingly, Stage 2 represents a more rational morality than does Stage 1. On the other hand, the "rationality" of Stage 2 thinking is peculiarly narrow; for example, the ethical dynamics of social relationships are treated as a matter of quasi-economic exchanges (e.g., Affiliation: helping one's spouse is important "if she has done you favors" or "because she may return the favor"). The six aspects of Stage 2 are as follows.

Aspect 1: Quid Pro Quo Deals or Exchanges (Exchanges). This aspect of Stage 2 reflection is comprised of justifications by appeal to "tit-for-tat" exchanges or deals with others. A given sociomoral norm may be prescribed if it is seen as a quid pro quo reciprocation for a past favor (e.g., Family Affiliation: helping one's parents is important because "they have done a lot of things for you") or past offenses (e.g., Law and Property: "the druggist was trying to steal from him, so why wouldn't he steal back?"). The Exchange aspect may also be evidenced in the justificatory appeal to anticipated reciprocations from others (e.g., Life: the saved stranger may "return the favor") or to straightforward deals with others (e.g., Affiliation: helping one's wife is important because "he married her; he shouldn't have gotten married if he didn't want to help").

Aspect 2: Strict Equalities or Inequalities (Equalities). Especially in reaction to the authoritarian relations so acceptable to Stage 1 thinking, Stage 2 is emphatically egalitarian. For example, on Family Affiliation, keeping promises to one's children may be evaluated as not important because "children are equal to their parents" and "if parents don't keep promises, why should the children?" This egalitarian aspect also applies to instances of pragmatic role-taking (e.g., Life: save the stranger because "everyone just has one life") or when possible inequalities are anticipated and protested (e.g., Affiliation: saving one's spouse is not important because "he would [be the one who would] have to go to jail, not she").

Aspect 3: Concrete Rights or Freedoms (from Constraints) (Freedoms). This aspect generally covers appeals to unfettered or unconstrained freedoms as concrete rights. For example, on Life (Form B), living even when you don't want to may be deemed unimportant because "if she doesn't want to live, she doesn't have to." Autonomy or freedom from interference is also emphasized on Life (Form A): saving the stranger's life is not important because "you shouldn't butt in; it's the stranger's problem." Similarly, lenience may be recommended for Heinz or Mr. Jefferson (Legal Justice, Conscience) in protest against a coercive understanding of the conscientious motivation ("his conscience was forcing him to do it"). Expression of the Freedoms aspect in terms of a rudimentary idea of entitlement or merit is found on Legal Justice ("The druggist has a right to complain") and on Property ("She worked for it, she can do what she wants with it").

Aspect 4: Contingent Preferences or Dispositions (Preferences). This aspect generally covers justifications where the prescription of a norm is made contingent upon the given actor's wishes, desires, or inclinations. For example, on Affiliation (Form A), helping one's spouse is important "if one wants to" or "because he may like his wife." Occasionally, there is a generalized appeal to preferences (e.g., Law and Property: Obeying the law is important because "no one wants to go to jail"). The preferential appeal may also be prescriptive (e.g., Life Form B: living even when you don't want to is important because "you should want to live"). Anticipations of dispositional consequences (e.g., Contract: keeping promises to a friend is important because otherwise "you won't like yourself"), on the other hand, are classified under Advantages (see below).

Aspect 5: Pragmatic Needs (Needs). This aspect consists of justificatory appeals to assumed or probable pragmatic needs or practical necessities. For example, the Life value may be justified as important because "the stranger needs someone to help" (Form A) or because "her husband still needs her" (Form B). Sending lawbreakers like Heinz to jail may be justified as not important because "he was too poor to pay." On the Affiliation norm, helping another is appreciated as important because of the scarcity value to the helper: helping one's spouse is important because "your parents may be all you have." The Needs justification is sometimes couched in an incipient role-taking appeal (e.g., Affiliation: helping one's spouse is important because "if you needed to, you'd steal too").

Aspect 6: Calculative Advantages or Disadvantages (Advantages). This aspect of Stage 2 thinking consists of appeals to anticipated benefits or liabilities ensuing from the enactment of specified normative values. For example, on Law and Property, obeying the law may be evaluated as important because "you shouldn't take the risk," "you don't know what you're getting into," or "stealing gets you nowhere." The appeal to possible advantages may take the form of appreciating the capacity for new opportunities (e.g., on Life Form B, living even when you don't want to is important because "you only live once; there are still many things you can do"). The Advantages aspect may also be manifested in terms of an individualistic idea of general deterrence (.e.g., Legal Justice: sending lawbreakers to jail is important because otherwise "everyone will figure they can get off easy"). The Advantages aspect occasionally is quite difficult to distinguish from the Exchanges aspect previously discussed; the operational rule is that appeals to anticipated benefits or liabilities are classified as Advantages unless an explicit element of exchange is specified. For example, on Affiliation, helping one's spouse is important because then "she might do you a favor someday" is still considered Advantages, but "she might return the favor" is classified Exchanges.

Stage 3: Mutual and Prosocial

As described earlier in the chapter, third-stage thinking transcends the pragmatics of instrumental preferences and exchanges to encompass the more intrinsic mutualities and expectations of prosocial feeling, caring, and conduct. Stage 3 is manifested in terms of six aspects as follows.

Aspect 1: Relationship-Based Values or Mutualities (Relationships). This aspect consists of appeals to the mutualistic and emotionally interpenetrative sentiments which emerge once there is an overall understanding of interpersonal relationships. For example, on Contract, keeping promises is justified for the sake of "a good relationship," because a friend "becomes a part of you," or so that the other person won't "lose faith in you." Similarly, on Life (Form B), living even when you don't want to is important because "life is a gift which should be appreciated." Instead of the simpler reciprocations of Stage 2 (or even the hypothetical reciprocations of Transition 2/3), Stage 3 bases moral reciprocity upon a genuine mutuality of expectations and feelings. For example, on Affiliation, helping a friend may be justified as important because "you would hope the friend would help you." On Property, letting one's children keep their money may be justified with the question, "How would the parents feel if the children took the parents' money?"

Aspect 2: Empathic Role-Taking or Intrinsic Concern (Empathic Role-Taking). This aspect is generally comprised of strongly empathic considerations pertaining to another's welfare. For example, on Affiliation, helping one's spouse may be evaluated as important in order "to spare the children from suffering," or because otherwise "she may feel crushed or unloved," or "he would feel tortured watching her suffer." On Property, letting one's children keep earned money is important because the child "worked so hard" for the money. On Law and Property, obeying the law is important because "people can feel attached to their property." There may be an appeal for compassion, expressed in terms of role-taking appeals to be "forgiving" or "understanding" of others.

Aspect 3: Normative Expectations. This aspect consists of appeals to normally expected role conduct and sentiment or to the consequences if normative expectations are typically violated. Illustrative justificatory phrases are "that's what friends are for," "that's what is expected of judges," or "children are supposed to honor their parents." On Law and Property, there is the concern that if laws are broken there will be "chaos," "confusion," or "havoc." Normative expectations play a very important role in the Stage 3 worldview.

Aspect 4: Underlying Prosocial or Antisocial Intentions or Personality (Prosocial Intentions). This aspect generally covers justificatory appeals to the prosocial intentions or features of the normal social personality. Prosocial prescriptions of sympathy or sacrifice, or judgments of antisocial intentions ("inhumane," "selfish," "greedy"), are used not as unqualified labels (Stage 1), but rather as characterizations reflecting underlying motivational features of personality. For example, on Affiliation, helping one's spouse is seen as important, not in order "to be good" or because "that's kind" (Stage 1), but rather in order "to show his love" or "to act out of love." The latter phrasing reveals an understanding of love as an underlying sentiment which needs to be expressed in, or which is a wellspring for, prosocial conduct. Justificatory concerns with being a "better person" (Law and Property) or with "leaving a good impression" on others (Contract) are also grouped under the Prosocial Intentions aspect. Even though Prosocial Intention justifications reflecting an other-orientation are close in content to Empathic Role-Taking (e.g., Legal Justice: sending lawbreakers like Heinz or Mr. Jefferson to jail is not important because "he did it for her sake"), they are still classified under Prosocial Intentions unless the empathic element is explicit.

Aspect 5: Generalized Caring or Valuing (Generalized Caring). This aspect covers justificatory appeals which generalize prosocial or normative prescriptions beyond the context of particular relationships or roles. For example, on Affiliation, the importance of a husband's helping his wife even if he doesn't love her may be justified by the consideration that "she is still a human being," or that "saving a life is more important than obeying the law." Similarly, on Life (Form A), the importance of saving the stranger's life may be justified by a prescription that "you shouldn't just care about your friends" or "should care for everyone." This aspect also covers certain expressions of generalized valuing (e.g., "life is precious").

Aspect 6: Intrapersonal Approval or Disapproval (Intrapersonal Approval). In terms of this aspect, the importance of given normative values is supported by references to conscience, self-esteem, or self-disapproval for misconduct. For example, obeying the law may be evaluated as important for the sake of one's "peace of mind," or because otherwise, "she would feel guilty," or "How can we live with ourselves?" The importance of keeping promises may be supported by the consideration that "it makes you feel good inside." An interesting manifestation of Intrapersonal Approval occurs on Legal Justice, where lenience might be important because "he has probably punished himself enough already."

Transition 3/4 Type R

The transitional phases generally do not lend themselves to distinct analysis since their content categories are blends of certain of the aspects of the adjacent stage levels. There is one type of transitional phase, however, an orientation between Stage 3 and Stage 4 which we call "Type R" for "relativism of personal values," which does merit discussion. This orientation starts with Stage 3--its justifications refer to intentions or feelings--but extends beyond Stage 3 by relativizing those intentions or feelings as subjective values which, if sincerely held by a person, cannot be questioned or invalidated by other persons. Thus on Affiliation (Form A), helping one's spouse is important "if he feels that saving her is more important than obeying the law" or "depending on whether he really loves his wife." There is generally a strong emphasis on "following your own judgment" (e.g., Life), which suggests some movement toward the achievement of conscientious standards (Stage 4). Although transitional phases are almost by definition unstable, we suspect that 3/4 Type R can remain functionally stable in a person's sociomoral reflection for an indefinitely extended period of time--especially because of the cultural support it receives from the popular ideological themes of Western societies.

Stage 4: Systemic and Standard

By the fourth stage level, one sees an expansion (Selman, 1976, p. 307) in the referent for the overall perspective achieved at Stage 3 to encompass functional systems or networks more complex than the essentially dyadic relationships of Stage 3. The seven aspects of Stage 4 are described below.

Aspect 1: Societal Requirements or Functional Priorities (Societal Requirements). This aspect covers those justifications where the specified normative value is supported as a requirement or priority for society or for social institutions. As an example, Law is justified because it "makes possible order in society," and Contract is justified because "society is based on trust." In terms of institutions such as marriage or family, there may be the consideration (see Affiliation) that the husband (or someone) "must be the one in charge" if the institution is to function in an orderly fashion. That these norms are valued at the level of institutional practices is made clear by the act- vs. rule-utilitarian distinction, which is sometimes made explicit. For example, on Legal Justice, the importance of sending lawbreakers to jail is justified by the consideration that "the law must be enforced even if a particular law is incorrect or unfair." Even Life may be treated as a quasi-institutional value: saving a human life or remaining alive no matter what may be construed as "God's law" or a "higher law" and, as such, is granted functional priority over "written law" or "human law." Note, however, that a representation of life as a basic value which is "more important than society" is classified under Basic Rights or Values (see below). Also, a justification which specifies a priority of rights, i.e., life as a human right or claim which takes precedence over law or the right or claim to property, is considered to be at the level of theory-defining discourse (see "The Theory-Defining Level," this chapter).

Aspect 2: Basic or Society-Based Rights or Values (Basic Rights/Values). This aspect generally relates to justifications of norms as embodying universally applicable rights or values which are or should be recognized as such by members of society. There is usually an assertive or categorical quality to these justifications. Examples are "Honesty is a standard everyone can accept," "Everyone has a right to have promises kept," and "One has a right to a fair return on one's investment." This aspect also refers to society or societal institutions themselves as a basic value. For example, laws are justified not only "to protect people's rights" but also to serve "the common good." On Life, living even when you don't want to (Form B) is evaluated as important because "only through everyone contributing will there be progress" in society or because even as a cripple "one can still be useful or productive" for society. Leniency for acts of conscience is important if they were "in society's best interest," and helping one's parents is important because "the family must come before individual desires." The categorical quality to the basic valuing of norms is sometimes expressed without a societal context. Saving lives or keeping promises is important because life or promises are "sacred," and, indeed, life may be "more important than society."

Aspect 3: Societal Positions or Contractual Responsibility (Responsibility). In terms of this aspect, the enactment of given normative values is viewed as essentially a responsibility, obligation, or commitment which the actor has incurred or should accept. For example, sending lawbreakers to jail may be evaluated as important because "the judge has sworn to uphold the law." Prescriptions of obligation are sometimes themselves justified as contractually fair, since certain counterbalancing liberties or privileges are allowed as correlates with the responsibilities. Thus, on Law and Property, the point may be made that "there are obligations as well as privileges" that go with living in society and that a decision to break a law can only be (possibly) justified if "one is prepared to accept responsibility" for the consequences of one's actions. The Responsibility aspect can also apply to members of a relationship, as in the justification of the Contract value as a "pact" or "matter of honor" between the promiser and promisee.

Aspect 4: Responsible Character or Integrity (Character). This aspect of Stage 4 reflection refers to normative justifications which appeal to considerations of responsible character or integrity. For example, on Contract, keeping promises may be evaluated as important because doing so "is a sign of character or integrity, or shows self-respect," or because it "shows respect for others." This concern with character may also be expressed in terms of its development (although some versions are Transition 3/4). On Family Affiliation, keeping promises to one's children may be evaluated as important because parents should "provide a model of integrity, honor, or character." On Property, letting one's children keep their money is important because "children should be given a sense of responsibility."

Aspect 5: Procedural Precedents or Consistent and Objective Practices (Consistent Practices). This aspect consists of justifications which view given normative values in terms of procedures which must be practiced consistently because the alternative—arbitrary and subjective actions—is unacceptable. Thus, on Affiliation, stealing to help one's spouse is evaluated as not important because then "who can say when stealing is O.K. and when it isn't?" Similarly, on Life (Form A), saving a stranger's life may be evaluated as important because "who is to say that one life is 'worth more' than another?" Varied manifestations of this aspect occur on Legal Justice, where the importance of sending lawbreakers to jail may be justified as necessary in order "to avoid setting a dangerous precedent," because "exceptions will lead to subjective actions" and because "the judge must not be influenced by subjective feelings." It is this understanding of consistency as an ingredient in objectivity--and as the principle which can turn a poor judgment into an un-favorable precedent--which motivates the Conscience norm concern that "conscience" may be "too vague to use in court" as a reason for leniency. The Consistent Practices aspect is sometimes quite close in content to justificatory responses classified under Societal Requirements, since an understanding of the necessity of consistent practices for society may be implicitly or even explicitly expressed. For example, on Conscience, Leniency may be seen as not important because "there must be a common standard or rule for judging acts of conscience." Responses entailing concerns with uniform procedure are classified under Consistent Practices, then, even where the necessity for those practices is also suggested.

Aspect 6: Procedural Equity or Social Justice (Procedural Equity). This aspect complements the Responsibility and Consistent Practices aspects discussed above. Whereas the Responsibility aspect stresses what the individual owes the society or societal institutions, Procedural Equity emphasizes what society or authority owes the individual. Examples are the Law-and-Property suggestion that "society is responsible for criminals or crime" and Legal Justice suggestions that "flexibility should be a part of the law," and that "the individual should be the basis of the society." Similarly, on Family Affiliation, there is the prescription that parents "should not abuse their authority" or "must earn or deserve respect." (Again, a concern with not "losing respect" is classified with Character). Therefore, whereas the emphasis in Consistent Practices is on the need for standard procedures for the sake of fairness in the sense of equality or objectivity, the emphasis in Procedural Equity is on adjustments in the case-by-case application of those standards for the sake of fairness in the sense of equity. For example, on Law and Property, the consideration is raised that laws "cannot take into account every particular case or circumstance," and on Legal Justice there is the prescription that the judge should "interpret the law" or "realize that each case is unique."

Aspect 7: Standards of Conscience. In terms of this aspect, the enactment of a given normative value is justified by appeal to standards of individual or personal conscience. The appeal may be to "self-respect," one's "sense of self-worth," "personal satisfaction," "dignity," "honor," "consistency," or "integrity" (an appeal specifically against "compromising one's integrity" is classfied under Character). The Standards of Conscience aspect is expressed on Life (Form A) in terms of suggestions that "Heinz was responding to a higher law or was going by a personal law" (direct justifications of normative values such as life as representing a "higher law" are classified under Societal Requirements).

The Theory-Defining Level: Social, Ethical, and Political Philosophy

Beyond the four stages discussed above, some adult respondents evidence a level of justificatory discourse which Kohlberg (1973b) describes as "defining a moral theory and justifying basic moral terms or principles" (p. 192). This theory-defining level of discourse entails the explicit formulation of intellectual or philosophical positions with respect to issues such as the relation between individualistic vis a vis societal rights. The question of whether this theory-defining level entails higher Piagetian stages (e.g., Kohlberg's "Stage 5," 1973a, 1973b) will be considered in the context of the relationship between sociomoral reflection and sociomoral action (discussed later in this chapter). In this manual, we do provide for recognition of theory-defining patterns of thoughts (see below) but do not assign to them the technical status of Piagetian stages.

There are two types of theory-defining discourse which may be occasionally noted in the data. The first type espouses a relativism of individual vs. societal rights or ethical systems and is labeled "TR" for "theoretical relativism." It is similar to the Transition 3/4 Type R orientation described earlier, except that TR specifically expresses relativism as a philosophical position concerning the claims of individuals vis a vis those of societies: the two sets of ethics are viewed as radically incommensurable with one another, and hence any priority of one set of claims over the other reflects a purely arbitrary or subjective inclination. Transition 3/4 Type R applies relativism not to the class of "the individual" vs. "society" (sociopolitical discourse), but rather to the values of various individual persons. TR has been referred to as "4 1/2" by Kohlberg (1973a, p. 191).

The second type, called TP for "theoretical principles," represents a more affirmative philosophical orientation than does TR. Human rights such as life are analyzed as logically prior to other rights or claims, and rights such as liberty are explicitly discussed in social contract terms. TP is functionally and perhaps even analytically superior to the TR orientation; we do not, however, assign TP a higher "stage" status (Kohlberg's "Stage 5" designation notwithstanding; see discussion below). Stages 1 through 4 were definable in terms of five or more differentiated aspects, each of which was manifested in diverse normative contexts; it is perhaps theoretically significant that TR and TP do not lend themselves to aspect-differentiated treatment and are found on only a few norms.

REFLECTION AND ACTION

Is the assessment of a person's developmental stage of reflective sociomoral thought helpful in predicting how that person will act in a given sociomoral situation? Although Kohlberg (1976) rejects this question in the strong sense, i.e., as a test of criterion-related validity, he does assert that "moral stage is a good predictor of action in various experimental and naturalistic settings" (p. 32). The question is a fair and important one. What if one's reflective behavior were found to bear absolutely no relation to one's situational behavior? Study of the stages would still have some scholarly value, but their ecological significance would be severely diminished. For most of us, the excitement of studying sociomoral stages is greatly enhanced by the possibility of their impact upon human social-situational behavior.

Logically prior to the prediction question is the question of whether reflective moral structures and situational moral action are related in any sense. The answer to this question would seem to be affirmative, since it is hard to see how a given action could be classified moral or nonmoral unless one knows something of how the actor defines the situation and what the actor's motivation is in performing the act. In other words, morality does not inhere exclusively in the objective properties of a situational act, but instead necessarily encompasses a reference to the meaning of that situation for the actor (the epistemological and research implications of this point are explored by Gibbs, 1979b, 1980). An ostensibly compassionate sacrificial act, for example, does not have a moral import if it turns out that the act was done accidentally or under hypnosis; and it does not have the same moral import if it was done for secretly self-aggrandizing purposes.

The larger point is that moral reasoning and moral action are related because together they constitute a continuum of moral behavior. Although moral reasoning usually allows for relaxed abstraction and moral action usually requires an on-the-spot concrete reaction, there is no radical divorce between the two. There are action implications to even the most hypothetical moral reflection, and there is some cognitive mediation in even the most practical and "immediate" moral act. As Damon (1977) explains,

> One must consider both judgment and action together as inseparable components of <u>knowledge</u> and . . . recognize that knowledge may be expressed in different contexts. One possible context is the hypothetical-verbal context of an interview composed of story dilemmas; we may say that the kind of knowledge tapped by such an interview is theoretical, reflective knowledge. Another context, of course, is the immediate context of real-life social situations; we may call this a real-life, "practical" knowledge (that is, knowledge in <u>practice</u>). (p. 19)

It does not necessarily follow from the functional relationships between reflective and practical moral behavior, however, that a particular developmental stage level of reflective moral thought will be helpful in the unique prediction of a particular course of situational moral action. After all, two different sociomoral stages, although they may yield quite different definitions of a practical situation--and quite different reasons for a particular situational action--may nonetheless support the same act. Conversely, the same sociomoral stage may be equally conducive to entirely opposite courses of action in a situation, depending on how the situation is construed. Thus, it is logically possible that reflective moral stage and situational moral action could be functionally related, yet bear no predictive relation from stage to action.

Empirically, however, we know that the relationship is not totally indeterminate. Consider as an example the depressed sociomoral levels of delinquents relative to nondelinquents, found by us (see Chapter 2) and by others (see review by Blasi, 1980, pp. 11-17). This fairly robust finding suggests specifically that the developmentally prolonged use of sociomoral Stage 2 into the adolescent years--or, in other words, the failure to achieve Stage 3 in adolescence--promotes the likelihood of straying into self-interested situational actions legally classified as delinquent. Other examples of the prediction of differential sociomoral action as a function of different sociomoral stage are provided by Blasi (1980) and by Brown and Herrnstein (1975).

Empirical evidence for predictability reflects the fact that, through comparative analyses of the stages' implications for various types of situational definitions and actions, differential compatibilities of stage with action can sometimes be identified. Brown (Brown & Herrnstein, 1975) suggests that the degree to which a given stage of sociomoral thought is conducive to action X rather than action Y in a situation can be assessed on the basis of whether the implication from the stage to action X is relatively uncomplicated and straightforward, i.e., whether there is no need to introduce gratuitous, farfetched, and dubious assumptions in order to apply the stage structure to situational act X. Specifiable applications which entail relatively little translative "strain" (p. 32)--both within that stage and in comparison with other stages--represent prime areas for the study of discriminative reflection-action hypotheses. The work of constructing an "articulated and theoretically clear rationale for eliciting certain specific stage-action relations (Blasi, 1980, p. 37), although difficult, is essential for valid research on the reflection-action question.

A fully satisfactory treatment of the reflective stage-situational action question will probably require some integration of the developmental with the individual-difference (see Chapter 1) approaches. This point is brought home by the consideration that, even in the case of an action that can be discriminatively predicted by a certain stage, that action may not be engaged in by a person at that stage because of the intervention of any number of person-related variables. As Blasi (1980) notes,

> It is plausible that prediction can only be improved by including in the equation personality characteristics that are unrelated or only partially related to more cognitive structures . . . . The processes that fill the space between a concrete moral judgment and its corresponding action should be determined. One could ask, for instance, in what way a general structure of moral reasoning is applied to a concrete situation to invest it with moral meaning. Do people differ in their readiness to interpret the world in moral terms? What types of motivational forces lead individuals from judgment to action? What kinds of defensive or coping strategies are used to avoid an unpleasant decision that follows from one's moral judgment, or what kinds of strategies are used to keep the consistency between judgment and action, in spite of external or internal interfering factors? (p. 40; cf. Brown & Herrnstein, 1975, pp. 334-338; and Greenspan, 1979, pp. 510-511)

Of course, certain situational factors, e.g. hectic circumstances, or diffusion of responsibility in a group, may interact with person variables (e.g., "ego strength") to complicate further the prediction from stage to action.

STAGES AND MATURITY

One area of stage-action research which has attracted particular attention has concerned the study of situational action relevant to Kohlberg's highest stages, 5 and 6. For example, in a celebrated study, Haan, Smith, and Block (1968) found that a significantly higher percentage of students at Kohlberg's highest stages participated in acts of civil disobedience (specifically, the 1964 sit-in that started the Berkeley Free Speech Movement) than did students at Kohlberg's Stages 3 and 4. Interestingly, however, students at the lowest stages, especially Stage 2, also participated to a greater extent than did the intermediate-stage students. These results were accounted for broadly in terms of the basic developmental levels--preconventional, conventional, and postconventional--used by Kohlberg to group, respectively, his (1963) Stages 1 ("Punishment and Obedience") and 2 ("Naive Instrumental Hedonism"); Stages 3 ("Maintaining Good Relations, Approval of Others") and 4 ("Social Order and Authority"); and Stages 5 ("Contract and Democratically Accepted Law") and 6 ("Individual Principles of Conscience"). Kohlberg (1976) suggests that

> one way of understanding the three levels is to think of them as three different types of relationships between the self and society's rules and expectations. From this point of view, Level I is a preconventional person, for whom rules and social expectations are something external to the self; Level II is a conventional person, in whom the self is identified with or has internalized the rules and expectations of others, especially those of authorities; and Level III is a postconventional person, who has differentiated his self from the rules and expectations of others and defines his values in terms of self-chosen principles. (p. 33)

In terms of the levels, the Haan et al. results are explained on the grounds that students with "conventional" stage orientations, involving identification with authority, were thereby less disposed to civil disobedience than were the "postconventional" students, for whom "self-chosen principles" may have conflicted with the dictates of authority. (Civil disobedience was also relatively attractive to the "preconventional" stage students, however: they may have perceived the situation as one in which they needed to assert their own instrumental interests against the demands of powerful external authorities.)

Unfortunately, the certainty of the Haan et al. results (and other results obtained prior to the mid 1970s) has been seriously compromised by the major substantive revisions in the stage definitions undertaken by Kohlberg and associates in recent years. Since these revisions have especially affected the criteria for defining the highest stages, early studies of the reflection-action relation at the "post-conventional" level have been particularly affected. Indeed, we will argue that these changes have been so major as to call into question the continued appropriateness of the preconventional/conventional/postconventional trichotomy.

Following Piaget's (1932/1965) early work on the subject, Kohlberg sought to identify qualitative age trends in justificatory moral reasoning that would prove to be general and uniform across social class, culture, sex, race, and social epoch. To determine whether his cross-sectionally-derived six-stage sequence was in fact general and uniform, Kohlberg embarked on extensive studies of the stage typology both cross-culturally and longitudinally. The longitudinal research also enabled Kohlberg to assess the typology in relation to certain additional Piagetian stage expectations, such as consecutive sequence (no stage skipping in development) and nonregression (no stage reversals). It was the nonregression criterion, based on the Piagetian expectation of a naturally upward tendency in stage change (see Gibbs, 1977), which was to pose a crucial and very consequential problem for the theory.

The most substantial revisions in the stage definitions have been prompted by a stage-regression problem discovered in the late 1960s. Kohlberg and his colleagues discovered that many of the longitudinal subjects who had shown Stage 5 or Stage 6 thinking as 16-year-old high school students apparently regressed to Stage 2 during the college years (only to return to Stage 5, however, after college). Following an initial interpretation of the sequence anomalies as genuine functional regressions (Kohlberg & Kramer, 1969), Kohlberg subsequently (1973b) eliminated the apparent regression by making certain structural revisions in his stage definitions.

Kohlberg's revisions rested on a reinterpretation of the apparent regression as in fact a transition ("4 1/2") from the coventional to the postconventional levels of moral judgment. The key to Kohlberg's reinterpretation was the argument that, although the moral thinking of the "regressed" college student resembled in content the naive hedonism and egoism of the young Stage 2 subjects, the college-student thought was actually far more abstract and philosophical than was that of the young subjects. To make this distinction, Kohlberg introduced the concept of "level of discourse," i.e., the order of abstraction or reflection evident in subjects' modes of judgment. Whereas naive Stage 2 thinking aimed at "justifying moral judgment to an individual selfish actor," the college-student discourse was aimed at "defining a moral theory and justifying basic moral terms or principles from a standpoint outside that of a member of a constituted society" (p. 192). The "theory" emphatically "defined" by the "4 1/2" thinkers was a rather sophisticated meta-ethical relativism (Turiel, 1974). The immediate effect of the discourse analysis, then, was to eliminate the notion that subjects at Stages 5 and 6 in high school had really regressed to Stage 2 in college. Yet regression was still indicated to a certain extent, since it was still a regression to drop from the highest stages to the transitional phase 4 1/2. In using the level-of-discourse analysis to eliminate this remaining regression, Kohlberg was to introduce truly substantial revisions in his stage definitions.

These revisions resulted from an analysis of the ostensibly postconventional moral judgments of the high school subjects in comparison with the postcollege versions of postconventional justification that several of those same subjects had subsequently generated. Kohlberg (1973a) concluded that, whereas the level of discourse of the adult data was genuinely theory-defining, the discourse of the high-school thought was actually that of a "generalized member of society."

> Specifically, whereas the principled adults proposed a priori theories in their discourse (natural rights, a universal value hierarchy, social contract), the idealizations of the adolescent discourse (appeals to moral law, love for all humanity, etc.) evidenced no such systematizations. Kohlberg therefore refined his post-conventional stages into more philosophical constructs, and expanded his conventional-level stage definitions to include the formerly "principled" idealizations as new "B" substages. Correspondingly, the previous definitions of stage 3 and stage 4 became merely "A" substage versions of the stages. Alongside concerns with others' approval and role-stereotypical good conduct (3A) were placed concerns for mutual good faith or understanding and for universalized caring (3B); alongside concerns with fixed responsibilities or authority and the givens of the law (4A) were placed concerns with ideal responsibility to contribute to a better society and with moral law (4B) . . . .

> The challenge to a structural-developmental model from the stage-regression discovery had been a serious one, and Kohlberg was bold enough to meet the challenge with pervasive revisions in his stage definitions and stage theory. In the upheaval of revision a new transitional phase (4 1/2) was born, Stages 3 and 4 gained A and B substages, and Stages 5 and 6 became philosophically purified . . . . In Kohlberg's neo-Kohlbergian theory, the stages of moral judgment development march right through the life span, with moral judgment maturity reserved for those adults showing the sophistication of ethical theory. (Gibbs, 1979a, pp. 93, 94-95)

It should now be clear why the Kohlberg stage revisions in the 1970s have been so consequential for early studies such as that by Haan et al. Given the rarification of Stages 5 and 6 (indeed, Stage 6 is so rare that Kohlberg, 1981, no longer even considers it to be an empirical construct), most of what Haan and associates classified as at these stages would probably now be assessed as "B" versions of Stages 3 or 4. This would probably be true irrespective of whether Kohlberg's MJI or our SRM were used in the assessment, since our Stages 1 through 4 correspond to Kohlberg's Stages 1 through 4 as defined in the current Standard Issue Scoring system (see Chapter 2).

Although we believe that Kohlberg's stage revisions constitute an advance in the structural characterization of the stages, we also believe that these innovations have introduced a certain tension vis a vis the basic tri-level typology, which after all has not been revised. For example, now that much of the prescriptive ideality formerly associated with "postconventional" reasoning has been integrated with Stages 3 and 4, is it still appropriate to characterize these stages as "conventional"? Although the older "A" versions of the stages may still reflect a conventions-bound acceptance of authorities and law, it is hard to see how such a "conventional" orientation is reflected in the "B" versions. On the Heinz dilemma, a 3B justification for stealing the drug even for a stranger is that Heinz should care about the life of any human being; and a 4B justification may be that, after all, any society which allows concern for property to usurp a human life is unjust in the first place. Does not the inclusion of such justifications shatter the general ascription of the term "conventional" to Stages 3 and 4? Perhaps we should call such (formerly postconventional) justifications "transconventional" since they seem to transcend and even transform the given conventions of interpersonal relationships and society to achieve a broader perspectrive.

Again, perhaps some integration of the developmental with the individual-difference approaches will be helpful, this time with respect to our theory of the stage orientations. Consider the point that, on the dilemmas (and presumably in situational behavior), the "A" approach is to work within the given context of the problem, whereas the "B" approach is to get at the root of the problem. For example, on the Heinz dilemma, an A-oriented justification at Stage 4 would "center" on a contextual given (such as Heinz's responsibility to the law), whereas a B-oriented justification would consider this given in relation to deeper considerations in such a way as to extend or transform the immediate context of the problem (for example, by appealing to the injustice of such a society in the first place). The B tendency to home in on the generative essence of a moral problem would seem to relate to the analytic (as opposed to global or synthetic) orientation which characterizes the well-known cognitive style of field independence (vs. field dependence; Witkin, 1978). Also, the B tendency to initiate a transformation of (rather than simply to accommodate to) a problematic situation would seem to presuppose a belief that the locus of control for events can be "internal" or personally caused (Rotter, 1966). Hence, the B/A orientation difference may reflect individual differences in certain personality or cognitive style variables (field independence/field dependence, internal/external locus of control). Indeed, considering the extraordinary depth and breadth that these factors have been demonstrated to have in personality research, would it not be odd if they were without any significant influence upon an individual's modes of sociomoral justification? The issue would appear to be at least partly an empirical one: Is there a significant association between field dependence/field independence or external/internal locus of control and the sociomoral A/B stage orientations? Although there are some studies showing correlations between cognitive style and sociomoral development across stages (e.g., Bachrach, Huesman, & Peterson, 1977; Connolly & McCarrey, 1978; Maqsud, 1980), the work within stages is only beginning (Fuller, Gibbs, Clark, & Goodrick, Note 8).

One point worth noting is that internal locus of control and field independence would seem to be particularly conducive to active, independent, and critical thinking. In this connection, these cognitive sets become more than simply alternative styles, since "thinking for oneself" is a rightly valued ability. This is especially true in the sociomoral domain, where a discerning intellect is a crucial ingredient to social concern in a world rife with embedded or implicit "givens" of injustice and intolerance. Our view is optimistic: morally transformational orientations may represent the application of abilities and attitudes that are commonly in evidence--rather than of high-order "postconventional" stages that are reached only by an elite few.

The tension between the stages and the levels in Kohlberg's work must be resolved, then, and we believe it is the levels that must be revised in order to accommodate to our improved structural understanding of the stages. After all, the overarching "level" trichotomy has always been a second-order construct system, imposed upon the more inductively derived stages. The three levels were initially suggested by Dewey and Tufts in 1908. These philosophers distinguished "three levels of conduct" which they referred to, respectively, as levels of "instincts and fundamental needs" (cf. Kohlberg's preconventional level), "custom" ("the man acts of the group, and does not conceive his own good, as distinct from that of the group," p. 38; cf. Kohlberg's conventional level), and "conscience" (whereby the person "chooses" moral values and principles "freely and intelligently," p. 39; cf. Kohlberg's postconventional level). Although Dewey and Tufts did articulate their concept of "levels" in anthropological (and hence somewhat empirical) terms, they did not attempt to relate their scheme to possible corresponding age trends in individual psychological development. Hence, if there is a conflict between the stages--as they have been fleshed out through extensive developmental study--and the levels, it should be the "levels" construct which does most of the accommodation.

We propose that there are two, not three, basic levels of normative sociomoral development: immature (composed of Stages 1 and 2) and mature (composed primarily of Stages 3 and 4). Of course, distinctions can be made within these levels. Stage 1 is truly the child's morality of unilateral absolutes, whereas Stage 2 is close enough to maturity to help explain the cynical streak which persists in much of adult morality. Mature sociomoral thought, in our view, entails the kind of prescriptive ideality that is generated by the achievement of "third-person" perspective-taking on questions of good and right social action with respect to interpersonal relationships (Stage 3) or complex societies (Stage 4). In the context of fundamentally unjust social situations (interpersonal or societal), those who apply this ideality in morally transformational ways (the B orientation) should be considered functionally more mature than those who accept and start from the situation (albeit unjust) in expressing their ideality (the A orientation).

An important contribution to the maturity of normative sociomoral reasoning is also made by the theory-defining level of formal ethical philosophy. Specifically, the systematic coherence, precision, and overall lucidity of one's ethical reasoning is enhanced through the study and practice of ethics on a formal-theoretical level. As Brandt (1959) wrote:

> There is enrichment of personal insight to be gained from the study of normative ethics. Familiarity with the ethical tradition should make us see more features or aspects of problems of choice, aspects easy to overlook. Merely the explicit formulation of principles about obligations should make us more sensitive to those obligations. It should make us less liable to be deceived by selfish ethical reasoning in ourselves or others. It should make us more perceptive in our moral assessment of ourselves and our motivation. (p.14)

Certainly, those whose naturally mature sociomoral thought (defined by Stages 3 and 4) is enriched by ethical philosophy are in some sense "more" mature than those who have never examined and clarified their ethics from a properly philosophical perspective. Operationally speaking, for example, it is possible that participation in college ethics classes may augment one's use of the "B" restructuring orientations (the research should be done). Nonetheless, we do not see that it makes any sense to characterize the use of ethical philosophy as a higher natural developmental stage, any more than it would make sense to characterize the use of a systematic philosophy of language or mathematics as a higher natural stage in language or logical development (see Gibbs, 1977, 1979a). Indeed, that seems now to be a strawman position, since Kohlberg in his latest writing (Kohlberg et al., Note 1; Kohlberg & Shulik, Note 9) dismisses Stage 6 as a naturalistic construct and emphasizes the "operational" rather than philosophical features of Stage 5 (the problem is that it is then hard to see any difference between the "operational" Stage 5 and the B-oriented justifications at Stage 4). Nonetheless, we believe that Kohlberg's identification of a philosophical "theory-defining level of discourse" represented an important advance, and we have included justifications at this level in the reference manual (Chapters 5 through 12)--even though the sociomoral reasoning at this level is not given Piagetian stage status.

USING

THE

MANUAL

As reported in Chapter 2, it is feasible to train oneself in SRM assessment and then to use the SRM for research purposes on the basis of this self-training. SRM assessment skill is not accomplished overnight; we estimate the process to require at least thirty hours of study and practice. Although one could conceivably accomplish the self-training of assessment skill in one week, the more typical--and more advisable--distribution of the work is over a span of four to eight weeks. (Such a time span is comparable to that required for, say, ego-developmental assessment training in terms of the widely used 1970 Loevinger and Wessler Sentence Completion Test.)

SELF-TRAINING: THREE PHASES

Self-training is accomplished in three phases: (1) familiarization, (2) norm-response assessment, (3) protocol-response assessment. The accomplishment of assessment skill will also entail study of the latter sections of this chapter.

Phase 1: Familiarization

Preliminary to actual scoring practice is the attainment of familiarity with the SRM instrument and with the basic ideas of SRM assessment. The two basic parts of the SRM instrument are the questionnaire and the reference manual. The questionnaire is found in Appendix A, and the reference manual is comprised of Chapters 5 through 12. Chapter 3 is an important auxiliary to the reference manual and provides an overview of the stages and aspects specified in it. The SRM questionnaire is used to elicit reflective sociomoral thought, the developmental level of which is then assessed using the reference manual. Specifically, certain justificatory responses elicited by the questionnaire are matched to whatever is the closest "criterion" justification in the appropriate section of the manual. The criterion justifications (CJs) are essential or skeletal forms of stage-significant sociomoral reflection (cf. Kohlberg et al.'s "Criterion Judgments," Chapter 2). Not all features of the CJs are equally important in the matching process. **Portions of the CJ which are in boldface are specifically crucial in determining the stage significance of the CJ and must be essentially evidenced in the questionnaire if a match to the CJ is to be considered.** On the other hand, portions of the CJ which are in parentheses, although natural to the CJ and facilitative of its meaning, need not be evidenced in the data for a match to occur.

It is not surprising that fairly close matches between questionnaire justifications and CJs are often possible, since the CJs were derived through a process of induction as well as deduction. Specifically, although the CJs are deductive constructs systematically related to the Kohlberg moral stages, they are also inductive constructs empirically derived from a fine-grained analysis of extensive cross-sectional data (see Chapter 2). Since the CJs also rest upon the more than twenty years of longitudinal and cross-sectional data collection embodied in the Kohlberg instrument, it is understandable that one encounters few theoretically scorable but unmatchable responses in most research projects.

The SRM questionnaire, then, is used to collect data which are then scored by matching the data to the reference manual. The eight chapters of the reference manual correspond to the eight sections of the SRM questionnaire. These corresponding chapters and sections commonly refer to eight "normative values," or "norms," to which sociomoral reflection is addressed. As noted in Chapter 2, a norm is a socially valued and morally prescribed action, e.g., saving a life (life norm) or obeying the law (law norm). Norms can be thought of as sociomoral truisms, since it is ordinarily taken for granted that one should save a life or obey the law. Persons are capable of reflecting on and justifying such normative values, however, especially when the norms are placed in conflict. A conflict between two equally truistic values, e.g., life and law, is of course the essence of the dilemma and the secret of the dilemma's power to provoke structurally significant reflection (cf. Chapter 2). The SRM questionnaire (whether Form A or Form B) has two "problems" or dilemmas: Problem 1 elicits responses of five norms, and Problem 2 elicits responses on the remaining three. Each norm is covered on the questionnaire by one, two, or three questions, and there is an approximate correspondence between the sequence of the questions and the order of the norms.

After sufficient scrutiny of the early chapters (especially Chapter 3), Chapters 5 through 12 (the reference manual), and the SRM questionnaire (Appendix A), you should be ready to move on to norm-by-norm practice scoring (phase 2), followed by practice-scoring of whole protocols (phase 3).

Phase 2: Scoring by Norm

SRM scoring work begins with massed practice on each norm. Eight norm exercises with answer keys (Appendix B) provide the opportunity for the concentrated development of assessment skill with respect to each sector of the questionnaire and reference manual. Each norm exercise is comprised of 30 sample responses. These responses, taken verbatim mainly from our construction sample data (see Chapter 2), were judged to be of generally average difficulty and to be heuristic for developing assessment skill. You should work through the exercises consecutively, noting your assessment of aspect (with the CJ letter, if any, in parentheses) and stage level for each response idea encountered (note that some responses may be unscorable).

The first expertise needed in response rating pertains to the distinction between scorable and unscorable responses. A scorable unit of reflective sociomoral thought is any normative-value justification which is equally consistent with no more than three adjacent developmental levels (e.g., Transition 2/3, Stage 3, Transition 3/4) in the reference manual and which is not explicitly disavowed by the respondent. The major operational feature of this definition is the stipulation that the justificatory response be consistent with only three or fewer adjacent stage or transitional levels. In assessment work, one encounters responses (e.g., comments, tautologies, and fragments) which seem to relate to CJs which span more than three adjacent levels--if they relate to the CJs at all. Indeed, these responses are "justifications" only in the loosest sense. The identification of scorability or unscorability is so important that an entire section is provided (later in this chapter) to assist you in making these identifications. The first rule of scorability, then, is as follows.

Rule 1: If a response unit is nondiscriminative across more than three adjacent developmental levels, the response should be considered unscorable.

Put positively, the rule is that a response is scorable if it is, for example, discriminative of a particular stage or transitional level (as established by the CJ to which it is matched). What if, however, the response is equally consistent with two adjacent levels? Or three adjacent levels? For such cases, the following two rules apply.

Rule 2: If a response unit is nondiscriminative across three adjacent levels, the rater should match the response to the intermediate level (unless the rater can conclude that the lowest or the highest level is actually slightly more appropriate).

Rule 3: If a response unit is nondiscriminative across two adjacent levels, the rater should match the justification to the higher of the two levels (unless the rater can conclude that the lower level is actually slightly more appropriate).

Not all of the 30 responses comprising a norm exercise will necessarily be found to be scorable. On the other hand, certain of the responses may yield more than one scorable unit of justification. This raises a question: just what is a "unit" of sociomoral data? That is an important question, one which we have attempted to answer formally in Chapters 2 and 3. A scorable idea may be established with a few words or may on occasion take a paragraph to express. Indeed, you will encounter instances (discussed in the training materials) where the boundaries of the idea are essentially problematic, i.e., where one can adopt either a molar or a molecular definition of the response unit. Fortunately, the specification of the unit is ordinarily not problematic, and scorers typically become sensitive in similar ways to the areas of scorability in a response as they work their way through the training materials. Even in those instances where the size of the unit is open to individual judgment, the highest structural level typically is not affected by the unit definition used. It is our impression that a clear grasp of the stage aspects (articulated in Chapter 3) promotes one's ability to identify response units.

Four steps comprise the process of matching justifications to CJs as you work your way through each set of norm exercise responses.

1: Familiarization and screening. Read the opening discussion and "montages" for the appropriate norm chapter in order to gain some familiarity with the stage-related themes, distinctions, and justifications pertinent to that norm. Then read through the first response in this light. Try to gain a sense of the prospectively scorable idea units that seem to be entailed in the response or at least to identify those portions of the given response which are probably unscorable. Response units which are definitely unscorable (see

"Types of Unscorable Responses," this chapter) need not be considered further.

   2: Estimation. Identify the possible stage or transition levels of the justification and make a preliminary estimate. Do this mainly through inspection of the "montages" which follow the opening discussion. A montage is an eclectic or summary justificatory argument which spans the aspects of a specified stage or transitional level. The montages are as comprehensive as possible--short of losing their flow--with respect to the levels they represent. The purpose of the montages is to convey something of the "atmospheres" and nuances of the various levels of sociomoral reflection. The montages should be used to enable you to identify the possible stage levels pertinent to a given response unit and to establish a preliminary assessment of the response's possible level.

   3: Evaluation of estimate. The next step is either to confirm or to adjust your estimate. Although the montages are usually sufficient to permit a preliminary estimate, they are also usually too abbreviated or truncated to support a confident assessment of stage level. (Indeed, the CJ details exist precisely because it was not possible to make the montage representation exhaustive.) To evaluate your estimate, then, turn to the pages in the reference chapter where the CJs pertinent to the estimated stage level are provided. CJs at a given stage are organized mainly by aspect (see Chapter 3). They are also organized, however, in terms of whether they typically address the "important" or "not important" side of the evaluation questions for that norm, and in terms of whether their content relates to either Form A or Form B, Form A only, or Form B only.

   Although occasionally one finds a verbatim correspondence between a protocol response and a CJ, typically some judgment is required in the identification of that CJ which is closest to the meaning of the response idea. Be careful, as you seek to infer the optimal conceptual match, not to read into a protocol response meanings which may not necessarily have been intended. Stay as close as possible to the denotative meaning of the response. Four specific operations facilitative of one's inferential work can be identified.

   1. Inverse matching. This is a match across a difference in valence (important vs. not important), e.g., where a "not important" response justification can be matched to a conceptually analogous "important" CJ idea.

   2. Transverse matching. This is a match across a difference in form or other referential content, e.g., where a Form A protocol justification can be matched to a typically Form B CJ idea (listed in the manual under Form B).

   3. Transposition. This is the recomposition of a syntactically jumbled response into a coherent form, using as many of the respondent's words as possible. Caution is especially warranted when you are engaged in transposition work, since this operation can easily result in misrepresentation. A carefully done transposition, however, can facilitate the matching work by making clear the essential idea evident in the subject's response. Jumbled responses not amenable to transposition are word salads (see "Types of Unscorable Responses," this chapter).

   4. Completion. This is the interpolation of a clearly intended word or phrase in order to render intact an otherwise complete response. Incomplete responses whose completions are open to interpretation are fragments (see "Types of Unscorable Responses," this chapter).

Concrete instances of all four of these operations will be encountered as you work through the training materials.

By engaging in a certain amount of inferential work vis a vis the manual, then, your original montage-based estimate can be evaluated. Contained within the montage are parenthetical numbers which refer to the aspect to which various parts of the montage belong. Some scorers find it helpful to study the aspect system (Chapter 3) well enough to be able to classify the response material by aspect and to use that tentative classification to guide the evaluation process. In any event, you will often find that a relevant-sounding portion of a montage will indicate an aspect which, upon examination, may contain a CJ providing a close fit. Again, however, caution must be advised: it is always possible that a given match, although close, can be superseded by another prospective match at a different level that is even closer (unless the given match is a verbatim one). For this reason, assessment of your estimate should include not only inspection of the CJs associated with the estimated level but also inspection of similar-sounding CJs at other levels, especially those which may have been noticed during estimation (Step 2). Also, the opening discussion of the chapter may have alerted you to important interstage similarities and distinctions which bear upon the response at hand.

4. Citation. As a result of the evaluative process of Step 3, you should eventually be able to specify an aspect and CJ which best fit the response idea (or unit) and which indicate a stage designation which may (or may not) be the same as that of your original estimate. Occasionally, a response idea intrinsically seems to encompass two or even three CJs at a given level. All pertinent aspect numbers should be written down, along with CJ letters in parentheses where there is more than one CJ per aspect. This also applies to cases where Rules 2 and 3 have been invoked: all CJ referents, at all pertinent developmental levels, should be cited. Especially where multiple citations have been necessary, it may be helpful to write out next to the respective citations the pertinent portions of the response.

The above four steps should be followed until all 30 sample responses comprising the first norm exercise have been rated. Then you should check the accuracy of your ratings by referring to the annotated answer key. If you think you have performed quite well, you may be disappointed. We have rarely seen a perfect performance, and most of our trained and self-trained raters (Chapter 2) achieved no better than half correct on the first norm exercise (with progressive improvement on subsequent exercises and especially on the Appendix C protocols, however). In any event, the important concern at this point in the self-training should be not so much with your percentage of correct citations as with how much you learn from those which are in error. The annotations associated with the keyed answers provide explanations which take into account the commonly made mistakes on a particular item, for the purpose of drawing an instructive lesson for the learner. The annotations should be read even where they pertain to citations that confirm your own designation, since it is always possible that you were right for the wrong reason. Only after coming to understand why the keyed citations indicate the best match should you consider yourself prepared to move on to the next norm exercise. After working through all eight norm exercises in this phase, you are ready to move to the next phase of self-training.

Phase 3: Scoring Protocols

Having accomplished extensive massed practice by norm, you should now be in a position to score whole protocols. Thirteen sample protocols, taken verbatim mostly from our test-retest, parallel-form, and intervention samples, are provided in Appendix C, along with annotated answer keys. You should work thoughtfully through this material in a fashion similar to that of the phase-2 work sequence: Familiarize yourself with the data, estimate stage, evaluate the estimate, and specify a citation. Duplicate 13 copies of the rating form (Appendix A) for use in recording your assessment. Then, after each protocol exercise, check your answers with the key for the purpose of learning from your successes and failures. As part of this work, you will be learning to compute overall protocol ratings (see next section, "Rules for Computing Protocol Ratings").

Although the sequence of steps entailed in scoring protocols is essentially the same as that followed in assessment by norm, enough elaborations are entailed to warrant an adaptation of the four norm-scoring steps to the context of protocol scoring. The following procedural sequence is applied successively to the eight norms of a given protocol.

1. Familiarization and screening. The first step is to read through all of the subject's responses to the given norm questions. For the first norm, Affiliation (Marriage and Friendship), the pertinent material consists of responses to questions 1b, 2b, and 3b. (The "b" designation is not used in the Appendix training material, since the "a" evaluation and "b" justification responses have been integrated to save space.) In studying the material, try to gain some sense of the ideas involved, i.e., of the various areas of prospective scorability. You may also be able to identify obviously unscorable response material (study again "Types of Unscorable Responses," this chapter), which need not be considered further. Also, justifications written by the subject in irregular places on the questionnaire (e.g., after an "a" question) should not be scored. Note, however, that everything else which might prove scorable should be retained.

Also as part of the familiarization step, you should refresh your memory of the relevant portions of the reference manual by looking through the chapter containing the discussion, montages, and CJs for the norm at hand.

2. Estimation of highest level. Since only the highest or most mature developmental level evidenced in the norm material will be used for the overall protocol rating, your preliminary estimate should orient to the highest levels that may be represented in the response material. You should establish the foundation for this estimate mainly through inspection of the montages: by this means, identify the various stage levels that are possibly involved in the material or at least the general developmental vicinity of the material (this range may be most readily defined by process of elimination, that is, by excluding the levels which do not seem to be involved). Then, within this stage vicinity, you should select the highest level as your estimate. It occasionally happens that a highest-level justification for a norm will have to be estimated from an "irregular" source, i.e., from a CJ contained in a norm other than the one at hand. Here is where your practice on all of the norms may be helpful, since it may alert you to the possible need for this kind of search. Discussion of this kind of activity is provided in the next step.

3. Evaluation of estimate. As in the previous phase of work, there is the need to confirm or to reassess one's preliminary estimate by reference to the specific CJs pertinent to that estimate, as well as those at higher developmental levels which may actually provide a closer fit to the response idea. Note that even if a higher-level CJ provides a match which is only as close as one at the originally estimated level, the rating for the norm will need to be adjusted to the higher adjacent level (in accordance with Rule 3).

Keep in mind that you may need to engage in an irregular evaluation of your estimate. In other words, one must occasionally resort to inspection of CJs belonging to norms other than the primarily pertinent norm in order to evaluate a higher-level estimate. It may also happen that reference to an irregular or foreign CJ can serve to support or bolster the accuracy of one's within-norm assessment, as when both norms "have it," but the CJ of the foreign norm "says it better." Note, however, that foreign-norm sources for evaluation should be considered only after you have ascertained that none of the within-norm CJs is sufficient to support an accurate assessment of the response idea as the one which represents the highest level for the norm. Although allowance for irregular use of the manual maximizes its applicability, an overreadiness to resort to foreign-norm references will harm the reliability of the measurement.

4. Citation. Specify on a copy of the official rating form (Appendix A): (a) the question number associated with the given response material; (b) the specific aspect number (with CJ letter in parentheses where applicable) or numbers which indicate the closest match to the idea tentatively identified as the highest level for the norm; and (c) the developmental level indicated by the citations, using Rule 2 or 3 if necessary. As with the norm-exercise citations, you may wish to indicate (under Comments) the portions of the response that are referents for the specific citations.

Although you can safely ignore response justifications which are clearly at a lower stage level than that of the justification matched and cited, justifications which are estimated as at the same level should also be rated using the above four-step process. This is a precaution, taken in light of the fact that many of the distinctions across adjacent levels are rather subtle, and an underevaluative error in one's estimate of supposedly same-level material is entirely possible. It is important for the sake of both reliability and validity to confirm, then, that one has correctly identified the highest level for the norm by ascertaining that none of the remaining estimated material is actually at a higher level than that of the previously cited justificatory response. Indeed, during this practice phase using the training protocols in Appendix C, you should identify and score all of the justificatory responses available in the data.

After completing the above rating activity for the relevant norm material, circle the highest stage level indicated for the norm. Where there are several citations at the same level, circle the citation in the top row of the norm. (Highest-stage norm ratings in the Appendix C answer keys are underlined rather than circled.)

This general procedure is then applied to each of the next seven norms. Also, where a subject has made reference to a response on a previous norm, e.g., by writing "same as above," scoring the previous response under the norm at hand is allowable. You may wish to attach colored and labeled index tabs to the first pages of the reference chapters; such tabs help one to find and retain the appropriate norm criteria. After establishing ratings for all eight norms in the protocol, you will have a maximum of eight circled ratings. If fewer than five of the eight norms have been found to have any scorable material, we recommend that the protocol be omitted from the data analysis (we have found that such a small structural sampling is not likely to yield a reliable overall score). An overall protocol rating is then derived from the norm ratings using the procedure described in "Rules for Computing Protocol Ratings" (next section).

   To illustrate the application of the preceding four steps, consider the following Form A, Norm 1 material, taken verbatim from a construction sample protocol (to save space, the decision responses are deleted, and evaluation responses are merely indicated in the questions).

1. It is **very important** for a husband to do what his wife asks, even if he isn't sure whether it's the best thing to do because: **It is very important that his wife get the drug because she is dying. Why can't the druggest let him pay for it on a monthly basis? I think the druggest is being Selfish and Greedy.**

2. It is **not important** for a husband to steal to save his wife, even if he doesn't love her because: **Well if he doesn't love her than why should he take the risk of being caught? Besides he can marry the one he does love after she is gone.**

3. It is **not important** to do everything one can, even break the law, to save the life of a friend because: **Again why should he take the risk of getting caught? He shouldn't, let someone else do it.**

   1. Familiarization and screening. Familiarizing ourselves with the material vis a vis the appropriate chapter in the reference manual (Chapter 5), we see that the norm response does entail scorable material. We may notice that there is nothing among the montages which at all relates to the Question 1 idea of letting the husband have the drug "on a monthly basis." Indeed, checking the "Unscorability" section, we see that such suggestions for avoiding the dilemma fall under the category of "practical suggestions" and are unscorable. We may also notice a repetition of the concern with the risk of getting caught, entailed in Responses 3 as well as 2.

   2. Estimation of highest level. With continued reference to the Chapter 5 montages, we can infer that the various responses are in the general vicinity of Stages 2 and 3, or possibly Transition 3/4. Certainly there is no material suggestive of any ideas at Stage 4 or Stage 1. Our attention is attracted to the 2b suggestion that the druggist is "being Selfish and Greedy," since a reference to the druggist as "terribly selfish" is found in the Stage 3 montage and a reference to the druggist's "greed" is found in the Transition 3/4 montage. Let us say that we estimate the highest level as Transition 3/4.

   3. Evaluation of estimate. The particular aspect number associated in Transition 3/4 with the druggist's "greed" is Aspect 6. Turning to Transition 3/4 Aspect 6 among the CJ listings, we locate a 6(d) suggestion that "her life is more important than this druggist's greed." The response idea that the druggist is "greedy" seems less complex than this CJ, since there is no articulation in the response of an evaluative superordination of the woman's life as "more important than" the druggist's greed. Are there alternative match possibilities at other levels? There is no reference at all to personal attributes of the druggist among the Stage 4 CJs, confirming our impression from the Stage 4 montage that Stage 4 is not relevant. At Stage 3, however, there is a reference to "selfish" in the montage which directs us to Aspect 4, where we find in 4(g) a perfect match ("the druggist is being selfish or greedy"). Hence, we revise our estimate from Transition 3/4 to Stage 3, which offers a

CJ that is less complex and closer to the idea found in the response material. Note, however, that if the Transition 3/4 CJ had been judicable as equally close to the response justification, then the original estimate of Transition 3/4 would have been retained in accordance with Rule 3.

4. Citation. On the rating form, we specify Question 1b, Aspect 4(g), and Stage 3 in the appropriate columns, for our first citation. Since we see that nothing among the remaining response ideas can be estimated as at Stage 3 (we can confidently estimate the concern with the risk of getting caught to be lower than Stage 3), we need not repeat the four-step procedure with other material on this norm. (Remember that during the training phase, however, all response ideas are scored for the sake of assessment practice. In this case, the four-step assessment procedure would result in two other matches: one to Stage 2 Aspect 6b, and another to Stage 2 Aspect 6d.) If we have satisfied ourselves that we have indeed accurately identified the highest developmental level of thought for the norm, then we so indicate by circling the specified stage level citation, in this case Stage 3. The same procedure would then be applied to the remaining seven norms of the protocol, after which the overall protocol rating would be computed.

RULES FOR COMPUTING PROTOCOL RATINGS

For most purposes, our concern in research is not so much with the individual norm ratings per se as with their contribution to the overall assessment of the subject's level of reflective sociomoral thought. In SRM assessment, there are two primary indices which are derived from the norm ratings: the modal stage rating, and the Sociomoral Reflection Maturity Score (SRMS). A secondary index which is useful for certain purposes is the global stage, which is derived from the SRMS. Since all three indices (modal, SRMS, global) were described in Chapter 2, we will focus in this chapter on the procedure for computing them. This procedure entails ten steps and can be conveyed through an illustration.

Suppose that we have established the following set of highest-level norm ratings for a protocol:

Affiliation	3	Conscience	2/3
Life	2/3	Family Affiliation	3
Law & Property	3/4	Contract	4
Legal Justice	3/4	Property	3/4

Overall ratings for the protocol are computed by following these steps:

1. Ascertain that at least five norms have yielded developmental ratings. Protocols yielding fewer than five scorable norms should be eliminated from the data analysis. In the example, all norms show ratings.

2. Ascertain the stages represented in the norm ratings. In the example, Stages 2, 3, and 4 are represented, but not Stage 1.

3. Assign two points to each norm rating. Where a norm rating entails a pure stage, that stage will be credited with both points. In the case of a Transitional Level rating, one point is allotted to each of the adjacent

stages, e.g., one point to Stage 2 and one point to Stage 3 for a Transition 2/3 rating.

4. Taking sweeps through the norm ratings, add and total the points credited to the lowest represented stage, and then the next lowest, and so on. Enter each sum on the appropriate line in the lower left-hand corner of the rating form. In our example, these sums are as follows:

Stage: Weightings

1	0
2	2
3	9
4	5

Since Stage 1 was not evident in any norm rating, it received zero points. Stage 2 receives a weighting of two points, the sum of its single-point credits from the Transition 2/3 ratings on Life and Conscience. Stage 3 picks up a total of nine points: four from the pure Stage 3 ratings on Affiliation and Family Affiliation; plus three from its inclusion in the three Transition 3/4 ratings given to Law (and Property), Legal Justice, and Property; and two from its inclusion in the two Transition 2/3 ratings for Life and Conscience. Finally, Stage 4 gets a five-point weighting: two points for the pure Stage 4 rating on Contract, and three points for the sum of its one-point credits on Law (and Property), Legal Justice, and Property.

5. Identify the modal stage, i.e., the stage which has received the greatest weighting. In the example, the modal stage is Stage 3 (since its weighting of nine points is greater than any other weighting). In the case of a tie for modal stage between two adjacent stages, the modal stage is designated as the intermediate level (e.g., a tie for modal stage between Stage 3 and Stage 4 would result in a Transitional 3/4 designation). In the (rare) case of a tie across three adjacent stages, the intermediate stage would be designated modal stage. A protocol entailing a nonadjacent tie cannot be used in modal stage data analysis (since the intermediate stage in the nonadjacent case is by definition nonmodal). For many research analyses, the problem of low intermediate-level cell frequency can be handled by grouping those infrequent cases with the upper adjacent stage cases (e.g., a Transition 2/3 modal stage instance could be grouped with Stage 3 cases). Enter the modal stage or level in the appropriate space in the upper right-hand corner of the rating form.

6. Compute the sum of the weighting points. In the example, the sum is 16, which is the maximum number of points possible (two points per norm rating times eight norms). Of course, it is possible to have a sum less than 16 if certain of the norms did not yield any scorable data. Note that an odd numbered point total, or a point total greater than 16, is necessarily erroneous. In such cases, the point assignments should of course be checked, and the error corrected. It is also wise to form an impressionistic estimate of the appropriate SRMS level by inspection of the relative weightings for each of the stages involved. A computed SRMS which departs drastically from the impressionistic estimate should be checked before it is accepted.

7. Multiply each weighting by the stage with which that weighting is

associated. In the example:

Stage:	Weightings		Product
1	(x) 0	=	0
2	(x) 2	=	4
3	(x) 9	=	27
4	(x) 5	=	20
	16		51

8. Sum the products obtained in Step 7. In the example (see above), the product sum is 51.

9. Divide the product sum by the point total, and multiply by 100 to obtain the SRMS. Logically, the SRMS can range from 100 (perfect Stage 1) to 400 (perfect Stage 4). In the example, the product 51, divided by the sum 16, equals 3.19. This number multiplied by 100 yields an SRMS of 319. Where a TR or a TP has also been noted alongside a numerical norm rating, this fact is noted as supplemental information on the protocol. Where a protocol has evidenced a preponderance of orientation A or B among its norm ratings, you should also note this fact on the rating form.

10. Compute the global stage. The global stage rating for a protocol is a qualitative summary label which represents the developmental vicinity in which an SRMS can be located. The SRMS point range of 100 to 400 is divided into segments comprising a seven-level scale that is represented as follows: 100-125 = Stage 1; 125-149 = Major-Minor Transition 1(2); 150-174 = Major-Minor Transition 2(1); 175-225 = Stage 2; 226-249 = Major-Minor Transition 2(3); 250-274 = Major-Minor Transition 3(2); 275-325 = Stage 3; 326-349 = Major-Minor Transition 3(4); 350-374 = Major-Minor Transition 4(3); and 375-400 = Stage 4. The global rating for the SRMS given in the example above, then, would be Stage 3, since 319 falls within the range of 275-325 on the SRMS scale. Note that transitional-level ratings are dichotomized into two possible subclassifications by the criterion of whether the SRMS is closer to the lower or to the upper stage involved; where the SRMS indicates an equal net presentation of higher and lower stage usage, e.g., 250, the higher stage is granted majority status, 3(2) for the example of 250.

The uses of the SRMS and the modal or, for certain purposes, global stage ratings complement one another. Many types of research analysis can benefit from the use of both a relatively quantitative, continuous index (the SRMS) as well as a relatively qualitative, discontinuous index (the modal rating). For example, the data of an intervention or enhancement experiment can be studied in terms of both: an interval-scale technique (e.g., analysis of variance) analyzing the significance of the experimental groups' degree of change vis a vis that of the controls (for which the SRMS index would be used); and an ordinal-scale technique (e.g., chi-square), analyzing the relative frequencies of qualitative stage change vs. no change across the groups (for which modal stage would be used).

TYPES OF UNSCORABLE RESPONSES

As noted, a normative justification that is scorable is one that is (a) of some stage-discriminative value, i.e., consistent with no greater than three adjacent levels (as judged in light of the reference manual); and (b) not rejected or explicity disavowed by the respondent. Failure by either of these criteria alone is sufficient for classification of a response as unscorable. A response may be quite specifically matchable by level, yet if it is rejected as inadequate by the subject, it does not qualify for scorability (since the rejection indicates that the idea may be beneath the best ideas of which the subject is capable). Conversely, a response that is quite strongly espoused can nonetheless be of negligible value as a source of structural information--and hence be unscorable--if its meaning can be interpreted at the level of either, say, Stage 2 or Transition 3/4 (since there are more than three adjacent levels involved: Stage 2, Transition 2/3, Stage 3, and Transition 3/4). In practice, SRM responses are rarely rendered ineligible because of a disavowal (this is less rare on the MJI, where an active interviewer can provoke a subject to reject a previous justification). We encountered one case of a parenthetical comment by a respondent to the effect that what he had just written "sounds socialist." This is not quite a case of disavowal, however, since the respondent may have still held to this view despite the voluntary comment as to its socialist overtones. The application of an ascriptive term with an unmistakably devaluing or pejorative connotation, however (e.g., if the respondent had written that the stated justification was "ridiculous"), would be sufficient for identification of the material as disavowed and therefore unscorable. One actual instance of a disavowal was provided by a subject who had justified the importance of "helping one's spouse" (Affiliation norm) by appeal to "the love you would feel" (scorable as Stage 3), and who then added: "but if you based love on the things another person will do for you, that's not important at all." Since this latter thought (pertaining to the Stage 2 idea of instrumental advantages) is explicitly devalued, it is considered unscorable in light of the disavowal criterion (it is lower in stage than the previous response anyway).

Also as noted, the typical reason for unscorability is nondiscriminability. The judgment of whether a response idea is unscorable by this criterion can sometimes be difficult, since it is not always readily determinable whether a justification relates equally to CJs which define a span of more than three adjacent levels. Often, however, one will encounter areas of the response material which can be confidently identified (after some self-training) as insufficiently discriminative, since they bear virtually no relation to any of the montages or CJs. Indeed, it is dubious whether such response units can even be termed "justifications," since they may provide no substantive support for the evaluations they ostensibly justify. These insubstantial responses fall into one (or more) of the following nine categories.

1. Bare valuations. These are responses which scarcely more than echo the value contained in the evaluation question, i.e., which impart essentially no information other than a reaffirmation of the value already evaluated in the previous part of the question (where "very important," "important," or "not important" is circled). For example, a respondent who had evaluated the question, "how important is it for children to help their parents, even when their parents have broken a promise," as "very important," justified the evaluation by writing: "It is important to help your parents." The response is in essence simply an echo of the question, which asks the reasons for the importance of helping your parents. Note, however, that had the subject written "you should always help your parents," the response would then contain some elements not reducible to the question and hence would be eligible for scoring (as Stage 1).

It is clear that a mere assertion of a value, then, does not constitute a justification. As another example, a response which "justifies" the importance of saving a stranger's life (Life norm, Form A) by stating that "it is a life" or that "a stranger's life is important" has merely specified or highlighted the value already referred to in the question. Again, however, any kind of substantive elaboration, e.g., "you should care about even a stranger's life," or "saving a life is more important than obeying the law," can convert the bare valuation into a scorable unit of reflective thought. Also, certain Stage 1 CJs can scarcely be distinguished from bare valuations. Hence, you should always check the Stage 1 CJs on a norm before dismissing a response as a "bare valuation."

2. Tautologies. Closely related to the bare valuation is the tautologous response. Although a tautology also contains little substantive information or meaning, it often gives an impression of significance until analyzed. Consider the following material:

It is **very important** for parents to keep their promises about letting their children keep money: **Because saying that you can do something and then saying you can't is like breaking a promise.**

The respondent has merely defined breaking a promise, a word already entailed in the question. A similar tautology is the justification of keeping a promise (Contract norm) by the statement, "because a promise is a promise." Although a substantive meaning may be intended here (perhaps that one must be true to one's word, a scorable thought), we cannot be sure. As with the bare valuation, there is, strictly, nothing to score.

3. Comments. Most writers of tautologies probably presume that they have provided a meaningful justification. It will also occasionally occur, however, that a respondent will quite deliberately offer merely a comment rather than a response, e.g., a criticism of the question. Since comments by definition fall outside the realm of justificatory responses, they are obviously unscorable. Below is an instance.

It is **important** for judges to send people who break the law to jail because: **Sentence does not give enough detail to flatly agree or disagree.**

4. Fragments. Having the same effect as tautologies are fragments—grossly incomplete responses, e.g., a sentence containing a subject but no predicate ("because a promise is"). Fragments are usually the result of neglectful haste and seem especially to afflict younger subjects' performances.

It is important to keep in mind that nearly complete responses whose meaning can be readily established are not to be considered fragments. For example, the suggestion that it is not important to help one's wife if one doesn't love her because "then he can rid her" is more than a fragment since one reasonably interprets and completes the response to mean: "then he can [get] rid [of] her."

5. Word salads. Such responses are essentially jumbled combinations of fragments. For example, consider the following response, taken verbatim from a construction sample protocol:

It is **not important** to do everything one can, even break the law, to help a friend because: **A isn't important to him afraid is to do nice thing for him not bad thing.**

The above response is a word salad because its words are so randomly tossed together that attempts to discern the intended meaning with any confidence are futile. Again, however, the word salads are the only hopeless cases. Less severe cases, where a transposition of the material can establish a coherent idea, should not automatically be considered unscorable.

6. Disclosures or anecdotes. Occasionally, the rater will encounter a value "justification" which consists of information as to what the respondent would do if confronted with the dilemma circumstances in real life or a digression into a similar episode in real life with which the respondent once had to deal. An example of this category is provided by a subject who justified the importance of not stealing from others (Law and Property norm) with the observation: "I didn't like it when someone did that to me." It is important to note, however, that a personally referenced response that is nonhistorical may be scorable, e.g., "I wouldn't like it if someone did that to me" (Transition 2/3 Aspect 1).

7. Bare opinions. Ostensibly justificatory responses which in fact merely assert an opinion as to what action should or would be taken in the situation are unscorable. An example follows:

It is **very important** to do everything one can, even break the law, to help a friend because: **If nobody helped him I would help.**

8. Practical suggestions. Another alternative to reflective justification sometimes used by a subject is a recommendation of a practical action which could be taken to ease or eliminate the dilemma. Practical suggestions are understandable since dilemmas are almost by definition uncomfortable situations to contemplate. Nonetheless, such responses provide no value justifications and hence no scorable material. Below is an example of a practical suggestion from a Form A protocol.

It is **important** to do everything one can, even break the law, to help a friend because: **You can go out and collect the money that he needs.**

9. Exhortations. This type of response relates to an evaluated normative value by urging an action. Consider the following verbatim example:

It is **not important** for children to help their parents because: **I'm sick of the same old—"Respect your parents even if they're wrong." This has been drugged into us from little on. If they're wrong, stand up to them! You don't have to agree because they're your biological parents.**

The respondent exhorts children to "stand up to" their parents but never quite justifies that exhortation. The respondent's rejection of the idea of unquestioning respect can be viewed as a disavowal.

GUIDELINES

We conclude this chapter with the presentation of some guidelines for use of the manual, specifically, for SRM stage assessment work and for administration of the SRM questionnaire.

SRM Assessment

1: Self-Monitoring. As noted earlier, the most important dimension of self-training is your self-improvement through study of the answer key annotations--especially the annotations of those items you rated inappropriately. The absolute percentage of response units correctly scored is of secondary importance, although a persistent percentage on the norm exercises of less than 50 should be cause for concern. Do check to make sure that your percentage correct is generally improving as you work through the norm exercises. An uncertain or adverse trend should be cause for greater diligence in your study of the answer key annotations. You should also monitor trends in your performance as you work through the 13 practice protocols. You should assess not only your percentage of correct norm ratings, but also your overall performance on the protocols, in terms of modal stage, SRMS (number of points defining the rating discrepancy), and global stage. On both types of exercises, it is also helpful to determine whether you are tending to overrate (or underrate) the stage levels of the responses. You should also determine whether you are tending to overscore in the sense of scoring responses that are in fact unscorable (or to underscore, to commit the "false negative" error of failing to score responses that are in fact scorable).

2. Citations. Citing a CJ on the rating form documents the basis in the reference manual for a particular stage rating. This documentation facilitates self-training efforts, as well as corroborative efforts in preparation for interrater reliability. Also, following through with the specification of a citation guards against perfunctory scoring work. In general, the better you understand the stage aspects (and more specifically, the CJs), the better you understand the stages and the more accurate your scoring will be. Divergences in aspect (CJ) citations should therefore be studied with an eye toward gaining a more precise understanding of the stages.

On the other hand, there is no special importance to citations in their own right. Stage agreement with an answer on a key is counted as correct even if your citation is different from the answer key citation. In other words, citations have no direct effect on the protocol rating. After one has completed self-training and gained criterion levels of scoring reliability, some discretion in the use of citations is acceptable. For example, where one has developed extensive SRM scoring experience and is quite certain of a particular match (perhaps a quite common one), the pro forma act of finding and recording the citation number may not be worth the time.

3. Interrater Reliability. An essential component of any research project using a production measure is the attainment of satisfactory interrater reliability. Two prospective raters who have worked through the SRM self-training materials should independently score 20-30 randomly selected protocols from the pertinent research data. The respective protocol ratings should then be compared in order to determine interrater reliability. In our judgment, minimal standards for acceptable interrater reliability are as follows:

100 percent	modal stage agreement within a one-stage interval
67 percent	exact modal stage agreement
.70	SRMS correlation
25 points	mean absolute SRMS discrepancy
80 percent	global agreement within a one-third interval
50 percent	exact global stage agreement

Where prospective research project raters are inexperienced, it is advisable
for them to score a few protocols in advance to establish, through open comparison and discussion, their corroborative potential.

SRM Administration

   1: Time and mode of administration as a function of age of subjects. For
most subject populations, the SRM can be group-administered without the need
for question-by-question oral administration. The instructions are self-
explanatory, and most subjects can complete the questionnaire within 45 min-
utes. For group administration to subjects younger than 12 (i.e., grade school
classes below the sixth grade level), it is advisable to read the instructions, dilemmas, and each question aloud. Partly because the tester must then
wait for the slowest respondent to complete each question, the step-by-step
scoring procedure takes slightly over an hour for children under 12. This procedure may also be necessary for subject populations with reading problems.
With some special populations, administering the questionnaire over two sessions (one for each dilemma) may be advisable. We have successfully adminis-
tered the SRM to grade school classes as young as the fourth grade but do not
consider its use to be appropriate for earlier grades.

   2. Tester activities during testing. Especially with groups of younger subjects, it is advisable to walk around among the subjects as an encouragement
for them to remain task-oriented. It is easy to make sure, as you scan the
papers, that subjects are in fact writing down responses. If you are asked the
meaning of a word in the questionnaire, give a simple and straightforward dic-
tionary definition, without special interpretation. Requested spellings of
words can be written directly on the subject's questionnaire for the subject
to copy in writing the response.

Norm 1:

AFFILIATION

(MARRIAGE AND FRIENDSHIP)

The Affiliation norm pertains to relationships in general and to the marital relationship in particular. It is an appropriate norm for tracing the evolution of friendship conceptions, as well as of marriage as an institution entailing contractual obligations. At Stage 1, relationships are conceptualized in unequal and unilateral terms (e.g., the husband should help his wife because "she might be an important person" and because "she told him to"), and affiliative helping is supported by appeal to the associated positive label which can thereby be gained (you should help "to be nice"). As affiliative thought moves toward Stage 2, the appeals reflect not only status but also possible concerns of need (you should help because the other person might be your **"best** friend," implying either a status importance, Stage 1, or a need-based value, Stage 2). Stage 2 conceptualizes the relationship in egalitarian terms but focuses upon the respective needs and preferences of the individuals involved and on the exchanges and possible advantages which can thereby ensue. Friendships are appreciated not for their status but rather for their quasi-economic value as possibly scarce commodities (the person to be helped "might be his **only** friend," or in general "friends are hard to replace").

Transition 2/3 reflection encompasses not only individualistic but also possibly mutual and empathic elements. The Stage 2 preferential term "likes" gains adverbial emphasis ("he may like her a **lot"**) or is supplanted by the verb, "loves," suggesting a beginning relationship orientation; and the preferential "doesn't want her to die" (Stage 2) gives way to the possibly interpersonal "doesn't want **to lose** her." Similarly the concern with one's friends shifts from whether it is one's **only** friend to whether it is a **good** friend, and the concern with the other person's need becomes more affiliative (from she "needs to get better" to she "needs [his] **help").** The appeal to exchanges becomes more hypothetical and mutual from "she may return the favor" or "she may have helped him" to "she **would** help him," or at least the temporally continuous "she **helps** him"). It is not until Stage 3 however, that the mutual and truly interpersonal perspective comes to the fore. The appeal is not simply to love as an affiliative motive ("he loves her") but rather to love as an enveloping sentiment (he would help **"out of** love") which should be interpersonally expressed **("to show** that he loves her"). Also, "good" friend is supplanted by "close" friend, a specifically relationship-oriented term.

The empathic element in Stage 3 justification is evidenced in suggestions that the husband would not want **to see** his wife die in pain (without the empathic "to see," the suggestion simply entails Stage 2 preferences, as is the

case with **"he doesn't like it when** she is suffering" or "she just **wants to get
rid of** her pain"). Also, the Transition 2/3 suggestion that "you **would want** to
be helped" is replaced at Stage 3 by a more ideal or aspirational element
("you **would hope** or **expect** to be helped").

Transition 3/4 marks the emergence of a perspective on love as functionally
necessary for the affiliative relationship (marriage "depends on" or is "based
on" love; or, "they cannot have a relationship if they don't trust or love
each other"). There is also a concern not simply with the "closeness" of the
friendship (Stage 3) but more precisely with the **level of** the friendship--a
structural phrase suggestive of the systems perspective of Stage 4. A straight
Stage 4 rating is assigned to references to marriage partners or friends as
part of a working "team" or to marriage or friendship as an institution which
requires cooperation (a more specifically functional concept than love or
trust per se).

The Affiliation norm can also provide the context for tracing the evolution
of the concept of obligation. Whereas obligation derives from authority at
Stage 1 (he should help because "she told him to"), obligation at Stage 2
derives from fair deals: there may be the suggestion that the husband should
help his wife because he "shouldn't have gotten married (in the first place if
he didn't want to help her)." Obligation at Stage 3 derives from shared normative expectations ("when you marry, it is supposed to be in sickness and in
health" or "that's what friends are for"). The direct reference to the husband's "vow" or to what he "owes" or "is responsible for" is suggestive of
Stage 4 contractual responsibility and hence is rated Transition 3/4. At Stage
4, there are references not just to the marital vow but explicitly to the husband's obligation vis a vis the vow (he **"must live up to"** the vow); and not
simply to his being "responsible" for her but more directly to his **responsibility** (noun form) **qua** husband.

Occasionally, one finds a focus not on obligation but on rights, specifically on the property right of the druggist (Form A) or doctor (Form B). An
incipient conception of the drug-owner's property right is even evidenced at
Transition 1/2 ("the drug doesn't belong to you"; cf. **"you shouldn't** take what
doesn't belong to you," Stage 1). The property right as a concrete and unconstrained freedom is specified at Stage 2 (the drug-owner "worked for" or
"earned" the drug and "can do what he wants" with it). Empathic role-taking is
implied in adverbial emphases in Transition 2/3 ("worked **hard** for it") and is
then fully evidenced at Stage 3 (e.g., "sacrificed"). Stage 4 marks the abstract and general reference to "respect" for and nonviolation of the druggist's or doctor's right to property.

The affiliation question pertaining to helping a wife "even if the husband
doesn't love her" often provides a cutting edge for differentiating between
orientation A and orientation B thinkers, at least on Form A. Unlike orientation A, orientation B generally affirms the value or quality of human life
even in the absence of love and may refer to property or law as relatively
less important than life. The Stage 2 orientation B justifications may assert
that "she has just as much right to ask him to save her life" as he does to
ask <u>her</u> to do things for <u>him</u> and that if he doesn't want to help her "then he
shouldn't have gotten married to her in the first place." At higher levels of
orientation B, an unloved life is explicitly recognized as a value in its own
right: as nonetheless "precious" and "more important than **obeying** the law" at

Stage 3 and as "sacred" and "the basis for laws anyway" at Stage 4. In contrast, the absence of love encourages evaluations against the importance of helping for orientation A. The absence of love makes affiliative aid nonsensical at Stage 2 orientation A, where the respondent may even point out that once the wife dies the husband "could marry someone else he likes better." Stage 3 orientation A evaluates helping in the absence of love as unimportant since then there would be no relationship, "she would **mean** nothing to him." Stage 4 orientation A appeals to one's relationship to **society,** centering on the point that if the husband is subsequently caught and jailed "he would not be able to fulfill his responsibilities to society."

Various other distinctions across levels also need to be kept in mind during assessment work. Seemingly minor additions or changes in phrasing can signify differences in stage level. For example, a simple reference to the wife or friend being "sick" is rated as Transition 1/2, but a specification that she **needs** to get better is Stage 2; and a possibly interpersonal suggestion that she needs "his help" is Transition 2/3. Whereas the reference to whether you "know her" enough to help is Transition 2/3, a specified reference to whether you know her **feelings** well enough is Stage 3. Also, whereas a suggestion that helping could "mess up" the husband's life is Stage 2, the same point as an element in an interpersonal context ("she would not want him to mess up his life for her") is Stage 3. A particularly close distinction is between the Stage 3 justification for affiliative aid even if the husband doesn't love his wife because he should still be "human," and the Transition 3/4 recommendation that he should still be **humane** (possibly implying a refined compassion for humanity). In general, whereas Stage 3 already evidences a generalized caring for life ("she is still a human being," or "it is still a human life"), Transition 3/4 specifically directs prosocial conduct to "humanity" or to "your **fellow** human beings," suggesting a conception of a larger social whole. Whereas an appeal to one's **convictions** is Transition 3/4, an appeal to the more character-oriented term "integrity" is Stage 4.

Some distinctions may make a difference of more than an entire stage. For example, whereas a reference to the wife or friend as an "important person" is rated as Stage 1, the suggestion that she may be "important **to him**" is Transition 2/3 (since it implies at least a pragmatic, and possibly an empathic, concern). References to God may be at Stage 1 (don't steal to help because "God doesn't like it"), Stage 2 ("maybe God wants it this way"), Transition 2/3 ("God must have wanted things that way"), Transition 3/4 .(e.g., "Heinz has no right to question God's will"), or Stage 4 ("human law may not be in accordance with God's law"). Whereas the suggestion that the husband should help because "he needs to" is Stage 2, the personal-values-based suggestion that he should help **if he feels** he has to" is rated Transition 3/4 (Type R, relativism of personal values). Obviously, attention to these distinctions is crucial to the accuracy of one's assessment.

THE MONTAGES

Stage 1 (Unilateral and Simplistic)

Helping one's spouse or friend is **important** because: "She told him to (1), and she is his wife (2). She might be an important person (3), and he should be nice to her. After all, he will be sad if she dies (4)." But it is **not important** because: "Your parents don't like it when you steal, and you are told not to (1). A nice person shouldn't steal, because **you shouldn't** take what doesn't belong to you. It is wrong (4), and if you steal you would go to jail (5)."

Transition 1/2

Helping one's spouse or friend is **important** because: "It might be your **best** friend (1) who is very sick (3)." But it is **not important** because: "The drug doesn't belong to you (2). If you steal it, you will get into trouble, might be blamed, or **could** go to jail (3)."

Stage 2 (Exchanging and Instrumental)

Helping one's spouse is **important** because: "She may have done him favors, and if he helps her she may return the favor. Besides, she has as much right to ask him for something as he has to ask her. If he doesn't want to help her, he shouldn't have gotten married to her in the first place (1). She should be equal (2). Also, he may **like** his wife and **want** to help her (4), since she needs the drug. If you **needed** to, you'd steal, too (5). All she wants to do is **get rid** of her pain (4, Form B). You should help her, especially if she could get you out of jail later (6). By taking the drug, you'd also be getting even with the druggist (1, Form A)." But it is **not important** because: "He is the one, not she, who would have to go to jail for this (2), and he wouldn't want to go to jail. Besides, maybe God wants it this way (4). Also, remember that the druggist/doctor worked for that drug (3). And you don't know what you're getting into when you steal. You're taking a risk, and stealing isn't worth it because it doesn't get you anywhere. Why do it if you don't love her, since you can let her die and marry someone else (6)?"

Transition 2/3

Helping one's spouse or friend is **important** because: "Husbands and wives should help **each other,** and you **would want** to be helped (1). This may be a **good** friend, whom he may **like a lot** or **enough** to help; and if he **loves** his wife he **would** surely want to help her (5) because he doesn't want **to lose** her (4). Even if he doesn't love her, he may still care about her (5). He feels sorry for her because she needs **help** (6), and if you were he you'd steal, too, since you'd have a good reason (5). He would be putting her out of her misery because she is **in** pain and can't stand it (6, Form B). This is important **for her.** He shouldn't **just** let her die (8), and if he doesn't help his conscience will **bother** him (10). And if it is for a friend, that's special because having a friend is great (7)." But it is **not important** because: "The druggist/doctor worked **hard** for that drug (2). Besides, if Heinz/Mr. Jefferson is caught he'll be no help to his wife or friend anyway (6). And a friend is not as important **to you** as your wife is (7). If people steal, the world will be a dangerous mess (9)."

Stage 3 (Mutual and Prosocial)

Helping a spouse or friend is important because: "He would be **close** to her or would be a **true** friend. She has shared her life with him, and he would certainly **expect** her to help him (1). He knows her **feelings** well enough (2) and would want to end her **suffering** (2, Form B). If he loves her, he **should** help her to **show** his love (4). Besides, this druggist is being terribly selfish (4,

Form A). Even if he doesn't love her, loyalty doesn't always involve love, and marriage is supposed to be in sickness and in health (3). He would still be **human** and **should** care for her (4); after all, she is still a human being; life is precious, and saving a life is more important than **obeying** the law (5). That way, he would have peace of mind. Otherwise, how could he live with himself (6)?" But it is **not important** because: "If she really loves him she wouldn't ask him to break the law (1) and ruin his life for her (2). Also, if he doesn't love her he wouldn't be doing it **out of** love anyway (4). Besides, the druggist may have sacrificed to make the drug (3, Form A), and if people steal there will be chaos (3)."

Transition 3/4

Helping one's spouse or friend is **important** because: "marriage is **based on** trust and love; you have to be **able to** depend on **one another** (1). The husband did make a vow, and there should be a **bond** of love or friendship. He is **responsible** for her (5) and should respect her (6). After all, everyone should have the right to live (4, Form A) or to die without suffering (4, Form B). He should have **humane** feelings for **another** human being (6), since her life is more important than this druggist's **greed** (6, Form A). But of course, it does **depend on** the **circumstances,** on the **level of** friendship (2), on whether he **really** loves his wife (6), and on what he believes is right (7)." But it is **not important** because: "There must be law or order (3)."

Stage 4 (Systemic and Standard)

Helping one's spouse or friend is **important** because: "He should engage in the **cooperation** which is **required** for a working marriage (1) and **must live up** to his wedding vows as well as God's law. That's his responsibility (3). After all, life is **sacred** and is certainly more important than **property** (2)." But it is **not important** because: "If people steal there would be no organization or predictability to society (5). One should not violate another's rights (2), and once you do, then who could say when stealing is O.K. and when it isn't? You have no right to break the law just because you disagree with it (5). Your integrity is at stake here (7)."

STAGE 1:

Absolute and Simplistic

1: Unilateral Authority

Helping one's spouse or friend is **important** because:

she told him to (do it); (or **not important** because) you are told not to steal, or because God or your parents don't like it.

2: Status

Helping one's spouse or friend is **important** because:

a. it's his wife or friend.

b. she might be an important person or might own a lot of furniture.

3: Rules

Helping one's spouse or friend is **not important** because:

you shouldn't steal or take what doesn't belong to you.

<u>Note.</u> "He shouldn't steal" is unscorable.

4: Labels

Helping one's spouse or friend is **important**:

<u>a.</u> (in order) to be nice; (or **not important** because) a nice person shouldn't steal.

<u>b.</u> (because) he will be sad (if she dies).

<u>c.</u> (but it is stealing; (or but breaking the law) is **bad** or **wrong**

<u>Note.</u> Qualified justifications, e.g., "Even for a dying person it is wrong to steal," are unscorable. Also, specific assertions of **illegality**, e.g., "It's against the law," are unscorable.

5: Punitive Consequences

Helping one's spouse or friend is **not important** because:

he will or would go to jail, or might get punished or killed.

TRANSITION 1/2

1: Status--Needs

Helping one's spouse or friend is **important** because:

it might **be** your **best** friend.

<u>Note.</u> "**If** it's your best friend" is unscorable.

2: Labels--Freedoms

Helping one's spouse or friend is **not important** because:

the drug doesn't belong to you, or it is the druggist's/doctor's.

3: Labels--Advantages

Helping one's spouse or friend is **important**:

Form A

(so that) she won't die; (or because) she is (very) sick or ill.

<u>Note.</u> "(In order) to save her" is unscorable.

4: Punitive Consequences—Advantages

Helping one's spouse or friend is **not important** because:

a. he will or might get into trouble or be **blamed, will** or **would** get **caught,** or **could** go to jail.

b. if you're in jail you can't do anything.

STAGE 2:

Exchanging and Instrumental

1: Exchanges (a, b, c = Orientation B)

Helping one's spouse or friend is **important** because:

a. he married her; (or because otherwise) he shouldn't have gotten married (in the first place).

b. she has (just) as much right to ask him to save her life or do things for her (as he does to ask her).

c. she may have **helped** him or done him favors.

Form A

d. the druggist is (trying to) rip him off; (or in order) to get even (with the druggist).

2: Equalities

Helping one's spouse or friend is:

a. (**important** because) he should be equal; (or **not important** because she shouldn't (try to) boss him around.

b. (**not important** because) he is the one (not she) who would (have to) go to jail.

3: Freedoms

Helping one's spouse is **not important** because:

the druggist/doctor worked for it; (or because) people have earned their things or can do what they want (with their things).

4: Preferences

Helping one's spouse or friend is:

a. (**important** if) he **wants** to help her; (even if he doesn't love her because) he may still **want** to help her; (or **not important** because) he might **want** her to die.

b. (**important** if) you **like** your wife; (because) he **likes** his friend as much as his wife; (or **not important** if he doesn't love her because) he may like someone else (instead).

c. (**important** because) she wants him to (get the drug).

d. (**important** but) he'll have to decide to do either what he wants or what she wants.

e. **important/not important** because) he wants him to get well; (or because) he should want him to live or doesnt' want him to die.

f. (**not important** because) he doesn't or wouldn't **want** to go to jail.

Form A

g. (**important** because) she wants to live.

Form B

h. (**important** because) he **doesn't like it when** she is suffering.

i. (**important** because) she wants to die (without pain), wants to **get rid of** her pain, or doesn't want to go through the pain.

j. (**not important** because) he wants her to live longer or shouldn't want to kill her.

k. (**not important** because) she should want to live.

l. (**not important** because) maybe God wants it this way.

5: Needs

Helping one's spouse or friend is **important** because:

a. he has to; (or because) if you **needed** to, you'd steal it, too.

b. she **needs** the drug; (or if) the friend is hard up or bad off.

Note. Echoes of Question 3 ("the friend can get no one else to help") are unscorable.

c. they may have children who **need** her; (or because) the children **need** food or shelter.

Form A

d. he might be his **only** friend; (or because good) friends are hard to replace.

e. she **needs to** get better, or she **needs** him to help her.

6: Advantages (b, c, d, e = Orientation A)

Helping one's spouse or friend is:

a. (**important** because) she **may** or **will** help him (some time); (or **important** if) she could get you out of jail or return the favor.

b. (**not important** because) he shouldn't take the risk, would be cautious, or doesn't know what he's getting into; (because) **if** he is caught he'll get in trouble or go to jail.

Note. "He shouldn't risk his life" is unscorable.

c. (**not important** because) stealing isn't worth it or gets you nowhere; (because) it would mess up his life; (or but) it depends on whether the friend is worth going to jail for.

Note. "(**Not important** because) he might lose his life" is unscorable.

d. (**not important** if he doesn't love her because) then why do it?; (or because then) stealing would be stupid, or he could marry someone else (after she dies).

Form B

e. (**not important** because) she will die in a few months anyway.

TRANSITION 2/3

1: Exchanges--Relationships

Helping one's spouse or friend is **important** because:

a. she **helps** him or **would** (probably) help him; (because) you **would want** to be helped; (or **not important**) if she **wouldn't** help him.

b. (because) spouses or friends (should) help **each other.**

2: Freedoms--Normative Expectations

Helping one's spouse or friend is **not important** because:

the druggist/doctor worked **hard** for that drug.

3: Preferences--Empathic Role-Taking

Helping one's spouse or friend is **important** because:

she **really** wants it.

4: Preferences--Relationships

Helping one's spouse or friend is:

a. (**important/not important** because) he doesn't want **to lose** his wife or friend.

Form B

b. (**not important** because) once she dies he'll never see her again; (or because) he'd want to spend the time she has left with her.

5: Preferences--Prosocial Intentions

Helping one's spouse or friend is:

a. (**important** because) he **loves** his wife or should want to **help** her; (because) if he (really) loves her, he **would** want to help her; if he knows her
well enough or if it is a **good** friend; (or because) he may **really** like his
friend, or like his friend **a lot** or **enough.**

Note. "**(Not important** because) he shouldn't do it if he doesn't love her"
is unscorable, particularly in response to Question 2 which posits that he
"doesn't love her."

b. (**important** even if he doesn't love her because) he must at least like
her, or may still care about her, or might (still) care a lot; (or **not important** if he doesn't love her because then) he (probably) doesn't care or
isn't concerned about her, or may love or care about someone else; (or because) there would not be the motivation.

c. (**important**) if you have a good reason.

d. (**not important** because) God **must have** wanted things like that.

6: Needs--Empathic Role-Taking

Helping one's spouse or friend is **important** because:

a. if you were Heinz/Mr. Jefferson, you'd steal, too.

b. he feels sorry for her.

c. she needs (his) **help, really** needs it, needs it **badly** or is desperate;
(**not important** because) if he's caught he'll be no **help** (to her anyway);
(or because) **he won't help anyone by** getting in trouble.

Form B

d. he would be putting her out of her misery; (or because) she is in pain
or can't stand the pain.

7: Advantages--Relationships

Helping one's spouse or friend is **important:**

a. having a friend is great, or friends are special.

b. (if she is a **good** friend.)

c. (but your friend isn't as important **to you** as your wife is.

Form A

<u>d.</u> (so that) she will trust or love you.

8: Advantages--Empathic Role-Taking

Helping one's spouse or friend is **important**:

<u>a.</u> (because) it is important **for her**.

<u>b.</u> (even if he doesn't love her because) he shouldn't **just** let her die.

<u>Note.</u> "He shouldn't let her die" is unscorable.

<u>c.</u> (because/but) it would be hard on him (if/when she dies).

9: Advantages--Normative Expectations

Helping one's spouse or friend is **not important** because:

(if people steal) the world would be dangerous, a mess, or in bad shape.

10: Advantages--Intrapersonal Approval

Helping one's spouse or friend is **important** because otherwise:

his conscience will **bother** or keep **hounding** him.

STAGE 3:

Mutual and Prosocial

1: Relationships (f = Orientation A)

Helping one's spouse or friend is:

<u>a.</u> (**important** because) he would be or feel close; (or because) your wife is **the one** you love or a **loved** one.

<u>b.</u> (**important** for the sake of) the relationship; (or because) she has shared her life with him, or has been his companion.

<u>c.</u> (**important**) if you are a **real, true,** or **close** friend; (or but) it depends on the relationship or how **close** the friend is.

<u>d.</u> (**important** because) you **would expect** her/him to help you, or **would hope** the other person would help you; (or because) you should follow the Golden Rule.

<u>e.</u> (**important** but) if she loved him she would not ask him (to break the law); (but) she is asking too much or should understand (that he would have to commit a crime); (or but) a (true) friend would not put you on the spot (by asking you to do such a thing).

f. (**not important** if he doesn't love her because then) she would **mean** nothing to him.

g. (**not important** because) you should have trust or faith in God (instead).

2: Empathic Role-Taking

Helping one's spouse or friend is **important**:

a. (because he doesn't want **to see** his wife or friend in pain.

b. if you know her **feelings** well enough; (or because otherwise) she may be crushed or feel unloved.

c. if the friend is desolate or has no one.

d. (but) she would not want him to ruin his life or jeopardize his future (by going to jail).

e. (because otherwise) the children will **suffer**.

Form A

f. (because) he wouldn't want **to see** his wife or friend die.

Form B

g. (in order) to end her **suffering**; (or so that) she won't **suffer**.

h. (so that) she will die knowing that he helped her.

i. (because) he would feel tortured (seeing her die in pain).

j. (but) he wouldn't be able to bring himself to kill her.

3: Normative Expectations (c = Orientation A)

Helping a spouse or friend is **important**:

a. (because) when you marry, it's supposed to be in sickness and in health; (because) they married to share life together; (because) a husband should love his wife; (or even if he doesn't love her because) loyalty doesn't always include love.

b. (because) that's what friends are for.

c. (but if people steal) there will be chaos.

Form A

d. (but) he tried to be decent.

e. (but) the druggist may have sacrificed (to make the drug).

4: Prosocial Intentions

Helping one's spouse or friend is **important**:
a. (because) it is for a **loved** one or for her **sake**.

Note. "It is for her" is unscorable.

b. (because) he **should** be sympathetic, **should** care, or would give of him-self; (or because) of his emotions or feelings.

c. (in order) to **show** that he loves her or that he doesn't want to lose her.

d. (because) if he (really) loves her he **should** help her.

e. (even if he doesn't love her because) he must have loved her at one time; (because) he would still be **human** or **should** care about her; (because) he would still think of her as a friend; (or **not important** if he doesn't love her because then) he wouldn't be doing it **out of** love, wouldn't **really** care, or would be doing it for selfish reasons or **just** to steal.

f. (because) he shouldn't (just) **watch** her suffer.

Form A

g. (because) the druggist is being selfish or greedy.

Form B

h. (but) the doctor knows best.

Note. "(Because) the doctor will take care of it" is unscorable.

5: Generalized Caring (Orientation B)

Helping one's spouse or friend is **important**:

a. (even if he doesn't love her because) she is still a human being.

Form A

b. (because) life is **precious**.

c. (even if he doesn't love her because) it is still a (matter of) a human life or a person's life, or a life is (still) at stake.

Note. "It's her life," "it's a life," or "it's a person" is unscorable.

d. (because) saving a life or a loved one is more important than **obeying** the law; (or because) saving a **life** is worth the punishment.

Note. "A life is a life," "a life is more important than anything," or "a life is more important than the law" is unscorable.

6: Interpersonal Approval

Helping one's spouse or friend is **important** so that:

he could have peace of mind, be proud, or feel good (inside); (or because otherwise) he would feel guilty or have it on his conscience, or couldn't live with himself.

TRANSITION 3/4

1: Relationships--Societal Requirements

Helping one's spouse or friend is **important** because:

a. marriage or friendship is **based on** trust; (because) they should be **able to** depend on **one another**;   (because) they may have **built up** a good relationship; (or because) they cannot have a relationship if they do not trust each other.

b. marriage or friendship depends on love or caring.

2: Relationships--Procedural Equity

Helping one's spouse or friend is **important** but:

a. it **depends on** the **circumstances, case,** or **situation**; (or **not important**) because one should not steal, no matter what the **circumstances.**

Note. "Sometimes it's important to break the law" is unscorable. Also, "one should not steal, no matter what" is unscorable.

b. it depends on the **level of** friendship.

3: Normative Expectations--Societal Requirements

Helping one's spouse or friend is **not important** because:

there must be law or order.

4: Normative Expectations--Basic Rights/Values

Helping one's spouse or friend is:

Form A

a. (**important** because) everyone has the right to live.

b. (**important** because) the druggist has no right to say who lives and who dies.

c. (**not important** because) Heinz has no right to make a decision of life or death, or to question God's will; (or because) he should not play God.

Form B

d. (**important** because) everyone should have the right to decide whether to end her or his life (to avoid terminal suffering).

e. (**not important** because) Mr. Jefferson has no right to help her die or to destroy a human life.

5: Normative Expectations--Responsibility

Helping one's spouse or friend is **important**:

a. (because) he made a vow; (because) of what he promised or said when they got married; (because) that is part of getting married; (because) he **is responsible** (for her); (or because) of the **bond** of friendship.

Note. "(But) the marriage vows didn't say he had to steal for her" is unscorable.

b. (because) he owes her his devotion.

c. (but) it depends on whether he is willing to pay the penalty; (or but) he should accept the consequences.

6: Prosocial Intentions--Basic/Rights Values

Helping one's spouse or friend is **important**:

a. out of respect; (or because) he should respect her or him.

b. (because) you should have **humane** feelings or should have compassion for **another** human being or your **fellow** human beings; (or because) he should care about humanity.

c. (but) it **depends on** whether he **really** loves his wife [Type R, relativism of personal values].

Form A

d. (because) Heinz should fight this injustice; (because) the drug should be used to save lives, not make someone wealthy; (or because) her life is more important than this druggist's **greed**.

Note. "(Because) her life is more important than anything" is unscorable.

7: Prosocial Intentions--Standards of Conscience

Helping one's spouse or friend is **important**:

if he feels he has to or that the issue is important to him; (but) you have to do what you believe is right; (but) one should follow one's conscience or convictions or use one's own judgment; (but) that is a personal decision; (or but) one shouldn't go against one's own will or compromise one's beliefs or values [Type R, relativism of personal values].

Note. "If he is sure it is the right thing to do," "(but) he should have his own opinion," or "(but) it is his opinion that counts" is unscorable.

STAGE 4:

Systemic and Standard

1: Societal Requirements

Helping one's spouse or friend is **important** because:

a. he should or (someone) must be the head of the house, the leader, or the one in charge.

b. marriage partners are part of a team; (or because) a friendship requires or must be based on **cooperation** or **respect.**

c. human law may not be in accordance with higher law or with God's law.

2: Basic Rights/Values (b, c = Orientation B)

Helping one's spouse or friend is:

a. (**not important** because) one should not **violate** another's rights, or should **respect** the druggist's/doctor's property right.

Form A

b. (**important** because) life is **sacred.**

c. (**important** because) life is more important than **property** or **society,** or should be the basis for laws anyway.

3: Responsibility (c = Orientation A)

Helping one's spouse or friend is:

a. (**important** because) of his commitment, responsibility, duty, or obligation; (or because) he **must live up to** his (marital) vow.

b. (**important** but) he **must** be willing or should be **prepared** to accept the consequences; (or but then) he should accept responsibility.

c. (**not important** because) if caught and jailed he would not be able to fulfill his responsibilities to society.

Note. The response, "(**not important** if he doesn't love her because then) he isn't responsible," is unscorable.

4: Character

This aspect is not typically evidenced on this norm.

5: Consistent Practices

Helping one's spouse or friend is **not important:**

<u>a.</u> (because if people steal) there would be no organization or predictability (to society).

<u>b.</u> (because then) who could say when stealing is O.K. and when it isn't?

<u>c.</u> (because) people should not take this issue or the law into their own hands; (or because) you don't have the right to break a law just because you disagree with it.

6: Procedural Equity

This aspect is not typically evidenced on this norm.

7: Standards of Conscience

Helping one's spouse or friend is **not important** because:

one's integrity or self-respect is at stake.

6

Norm 2:

LIFE

This norm provides an optimal context for tracing the evolving conception of life as a right or value. We will first discuss this development in terms of Form A justifications for saving a stranger's life, and then in terms of Form B justifications for "living even when you don't want to," although the basic developmental trends are common to both forms. The Form A life question is generally more effective than is that of Form B in making possible a differential assessment of A vs. B orientation. Whereas Orientation A evaluates saving the life of a stranger as relatively unimportant, Orientation B upholds the importance of saving the stranger because anyone's life has value and importance. Orientation B at Stage 2 represents an extension of the Stage 2 concern with strict equalities to include strangers ("everyone should have a chance to live"). Stage 3 Orientation B responses may indicate that "you shouldn't just care about your friends" and that any life is "precious" and important enough to break the law for." Stage 4 Orientation B emphasizes the "sacredness" of life as a value that "should be the basis of written laws"; society may be critiqued in this light ("a society in which one must steal to save a life is unjust in the first place"). The theory-defining level of Theoretical Principles formulates this justification philosophically ("the right to life takes precedence over the right to property").

In contrast, the value of life is not even addressed by the A orientation. Stage 2 Orientation A finds saving a stranger almost incomprehensible ("why help someone you don't know?"). Similarly, Stage 3 Orientation A sees little point to helping since there is no relationship and "you would have no feelings for a stranger." At Stage 4, Orientation A centers on the illegality that may be entailed in saving a stranger's life and emphasizes one's responsibility to uphold society's laws.

Form A justifications for negative evaluations of the importance of saving a stranger's life are also informative as to the conception of life at different levels. At Stage 1, saving the stranger's life may be rejected on the grounds, for example, of a simplistic rule against "going near strangers." The conditional anticipation that the stranger "could grab you" is expressed at Transition 1/2. The nonutility of saving the stranger for one's self-interest is the focus of Stage 2 justifications, whereas at Transition 2/3 there is a possible relationship value (the stranger is "not as important **to you**") which becomes explicitly expressed at Stage 3 (you "wouldn't feel attached" to the stranger). A possibly responsibility-oriented concern with the lack of any "bond" of friendship with the stranger is rated Transition 3/4, the highest level which can be discriminated among the negative justifications.

On Form B, life is conceptualized as having value for the person, for others or society, and for God. At Stage 2, life is valued as long as it offers advantages and opportunities (you could still "do things" or "live long" as a cripple), and because the alternative would mean a deprivation of these opportunities (you wouldn't know "how things would have turned out" or "what would have happened"). At Transition 2/3, the Stage 2 appreciation of life as a pragmatic opportunity extends to an expression of valuing in terms of enjoyment ("we should enjoy life **while we can**"). There is also an anticipation of emotional improvement, "you could become happy later," which could be introduced as either an attitude conducive to new advantages (Stage 2) or as an appreciative value such as enjoyment per se (Stage 3). A direct prescription to "enjoy life" reflects on intrinsic valuing that is rated Stage 3, as is a disapproval of self-pity. Transition 3/4 relates the question of emotional well-being to the "perspectives" which individuals may have on life and usually supports the importance of living even when you don't want to because "your views may change." Transition 3/4 may also involve going beyond the Stage 3 disapproval of self-pity to prescribing a need for "courage" or "will"; these attributes are prosocially expressive but are also associated with a dedication to standards or ideals (Stage 4).

One's life may also be conceptualized as a value in relation to other people or to society (especially on Form B). At Stage 2, there is the suggestion that one take into account others' preferences (other people "want you to live") or needs ("the husband still needs her"). Transition 2/3 justifications are still possibly instrumental but also reflect a bit more emotional depth (others "love you," "don't want to **lose** you,", or would be upset"). Needs may still be referred to, but in a context suggestive of mutual role-taking ("she **should realize that** her husband still needs her"; or, "the children still need **to be taken care of**").. The concern for others becomes more directly empathic at Stage 3: e.g., "loved ones would suffer." Finally, at Stage 4, the life value is related to **society**: life, even if not desired, remains a "responsibility" or an "obligation" because "we all have a role to play in society," for the sake of society's "survival" or "progress."

One evolving theme mainly evident on Form B pertains to the valuing of life in religious terms. At Stage 1, God is conceived as a unilateral authority who quite directly acts in the world to cause life and death (e.g., "we should live until God kills us"). By Stage 2, there is the suggestion that one should accommodate to the pro-life preferences or interests attributed to God ("God wants people to live"). Similar-sounding but more deterministic suggestions can be relationship-based (Transition 2/3: "That must be what God wants for us") or oriented to divine rights or prerogatives (Transition 3/4: "that is the Lord's will"). At Stage 3, life is valued as "precious" in light of its status as a "gift" which we, in our relationship with God, should "appreciate." There is also at Stage 3 an explicit reference to finding a "purpose" for living (cf. the less specific Transition 2/3: "we were created to live"). Transition 3/4 marks the extension of God beyond the mutualistic context to a conception of God as a decision-maker whose jurisdiction over questions of life and death should be respected: "We cannot question God," or "we should not take it upon ourselves to decide life's worth." Where a Stage 4 framework is involved, this justification will usually include a reference to life as "sacred" (cf. "precious," Stage 3).

Certain discriminations on the Life norm are particularly subtle. For example, a slight elaboration can sometimes change the level of the rating, although usually only by one or two levels. A simple reference to the stranger's "need" to live is Stage 2, whereas a suggestion that the stranger needs **your help** (somewhat more interpersonal) is rated at Transition 2/3, and a reference to the stranger's being **in** need (e.g., a state or condition of neediness) is Stage 3. A simple reference to what the dying woman or others "want" is Stage 2, but a suggestion that the woman **really** wants to live rather than die (a possibly interpersonal orientation which recognizes underlying intentionality) is Transition 2/3. Whereas a simple suggestion that not living or helping to live would result in a disadvantageous situation ("there wouldn't be many people left") is rated Stage 2, the incipiently interpersonal suggestion that "you would be lonely" is Transition 2/3. Finally, an unelaborated suggestion that life is "priceless" is Stage 3, but a reference to the difficulty of measuring the value of one person's life as against another's reflects an orientation to Stage 4 consistent practices.

THE MONTAGES

Stage 1 (Unilateral and Simplistic)

Saving a stranger's life or living even when you don't want to is **important** because: "(Form A) The stranger might be an important person (2), and you should save her to be nice (4). (Form B) We should live until God kills us (3)." But it is **not important** because: "Stealing is bad (4), and you would go to jail (5). (Form A) You should never go near strangers (3), unless you are a firefighter or a hospital person (4)."

Transition 1/2

Saving a stranger's life or living even when you don't want to is **not important** because: "You **could** go to jail or get into **trouble** (1). (Form A) The stranger might tell the police or could grab you. Besides, you would be **blamed** if she dies (1)."

Stage 2 (Exchanging and Instrumental)

Saving a stranger's life or living even when you don't want to is **important**: "If you want to (4), and you should because otherwise there won't be many people left (6). (Form A) The stranger may save **your** life someday if you help (1). Everyone has just one life and should have the chance to live (2). The stranger may want to live (4) and will probably thank you by doing you a favor (6). (Form B) Even if you don't want to live, you can still have some fun (6), and other people may want you to live (4). After all, the woman's husband still needs her even if she is crippled (5), and she shouldn't die until God wants her to (4). A cripple can still have a long life, and if she kills herself she won't find out what would have happened in her life (6)." But it is **not important** because: "(Form A) You are the one, and not the stranger, who would have to go to jail (2). You shouldn't butt into the stranger's business (3), and, besides, for all you know the stranger is just faking in order to trick you. Why help someone you don't know? (6). (Form B) She just wants to die (4), and she doesn't have to live if she doesn't want to (3)."

Transition 2/3

Saving a stranger's life or living even when you don't want to is **important** because: "(Form A) The stranger **would** do it for you (1). He needs **your help**

badly (5), and could become a friend once you save him (6). Besides, if no one saves anyone, the world would get to be a lonely place (6). (Form B) She wouldn't want her husband to decide to die and leave her (1). People were created to live, not to kill themselves (2). Others love you and would be **upset to lose** you (3), and there may be children who need to be **cared for** (5). **Deep down** she still wants to live (2), and you should enjoy life **while you can** (6). Besides, you could become happy later (2)." But it is **not important** because: "(Form A) The stranger is not as important **to you** as your friend. After all, you don't **even** know the stranger (6)."

Stage 3 (Mutual and Prosocial)

Saving a stranger's life or living even when you don't want to is **important** because? "Life is precious (5). (Form A) It is horrible to watch someone **in** need suffer (2), so saving the stranger is the human thing to do (4). Saving a life is important enough to **break** the law for (5). After all, if he doesn't do it, it will be on his conscience (6). (Form B) Life is a gift we should appreciate (1). Besides, we should be concerned about the feelings of loved ones (2). We should enjoy life (4) and can find some purpose to live for if we try (3). You shouldn't just feel sorry for yourself (4). But it is **not important** because: "(Form A) You wouldn't feel attached or close to the stranger (1). Besides, there is a point when being a good person has to end (4)."

Transition 3/4

Saving a stranger's life or living even when you don't want to is **important** because: "(Form A) We are all human beings, and should have compassion on a **fellow** human being (5). After all, a person's life is worth more than greed (5), and this druggist should not be in control of someone's life (2). (Form B) We have no right to kill ourselves (2) and should not abuse life (5). You can make it if you have the courage; if you just quit, it's a cop-out (4). Besides, your views about the value of life may change (5)." But it is **not important**: "It depends on the situation, of course (3). This is an emotional, not a legal matter (4), and each person must follow his or her own judgment (6). (Form A) The husband has no **bond** of friendship with the stranger (1). He should not play God and try to make a decision of life or death (2)."

Stage 4 (Systemic and Standard)

Saving a stranger's life or living even when you don't want to is **important** because: "God's laws take priority over human law (1). Life is sacred, and everyone can make a contribution (2). (Form A) People **must** feel responsible for others (3). Saving life is more important than society's need for law and has a higher priority than **property** rights, because the law should serve first the right to life. Indeed, a society in which you must steal to save a life is itself unjust in the first place (2). Besides, you must save the stranger's life, because you can't measure the value of another person's life (5). (Form B) Even a crippled person is still useful and can be productive, because we all have a role to play in society (3)." But it is **not important** because: "You have an obligation to obey the law (3) and should not compromise your integrity (7)."

Theoretical Relativism (TR)

Saving a stranger's life or living even when you don't want to is **important: "(Form A) If Heinz considers the right to life to be greater than that of the established laws of society"; or, "(Form B) Because although by the standards of society mercy-killing may be wrong, by Mr. Jefferson's standards as an individual mercy-killing could be morally right."

Theoretical Principles (TP)

Saving a stranger's life or living even when you don't want to is **important** because: "(Form A) The **right** to life supersedes the **right** to property"; or because "(Form B) The right to decide one's life or death should be part of the social contract."

STAGE 1:

Unilateral and Simplistic

1: Unilateral Authority

Living even when you don't want to is **important** because:

God doesn't like it (if you kill yourself).

2: Status

Saving a stranger's life is **important** because:

the stranger might be an important person; (or) if the stranger is someone important.

Note. "But it depends on who the stranger is" is unscorable.

3: Rules

Saving a stranger's life or living even when you don't want to is:

<u>a.</u> (**not important** because) stealing is against the law.

Form A

<u>b.</u> (**not important** because) you should never go near a stranger, or should not help strangers.

Form B

<u>c.</u> (**important** because) we should live until God kills us.

4: Labels

Saving a stranger's life or living even when you don't want to is:

<u>a.</u> (**not important** because then) you are stealing, or stealing is bad or wrong.

Form A

<u>b.</u> (**important**) to be good or nice.

<u>c.</u> (**not important** unless) you are a firefighter, policeman, or hospital person.

5: Punitive Consequences

Saving a stranger's life or living even when you don't want to is **not important** because:

<u>a.</u> you will or would go to jail, or might get punished or killed.

Form B

<u>b.</u> the stranger could be bad, or could grab, hurt, or kill you.

Transition 1/2

1: Punitive Consequences—Advantages

Saving a stranger's life or living even when you don't want to is:

<u>a.</u> (**not important** because) you **will** or **would** get **caught** or **could** go to jail or get into **trouble**.

Form A

<u>b.</u> (**important** because otherwise) you would or might be b**lamed** (if she dies); (or **not important** because) the stranger could tell the police.

STAGE 2:

Exchanging and Instrumental

1: Exchanges

Saving a stranger's life is **important** because:

the stranger may return the favor, or might save your life (some day).

2: Equalities (a = Orientation B)

Saving a stranger's life is:

<u>a.</u> (**important** because) everyone should have a chance to live, or just has one life.

<u>b.</u> (**not important** because) you are the one (not the stranger) who would (have to) go to jail.

3: Freedoms

Saving a stranger's life or living even when you don't want to is **not important** because:

Form A

<u>a.</u> you shouldn't butt in or stick your nose into someone else's business; (or because) it's not Heinz's problem.

Note. This criterion justification is not applicable to other norms.

Form B

b. if she doesn't want to live, she doesn't have to.

Note. "You can't make someone stay alive if they don't want to" is unscorable.

4: Preferences

Saving a stranger's life or living even when you don't want to is **important:**

a. if you want to.

Form A

b. (because) the stranger (is a person who) wants to live; (or **not important** because) the stranger may want to die.

Form B

c. (because) she should want to live, or you should try to live as long as possible; (because) if I were she I would want to live; (or **not important** because) all she wants to do is die.

Note. "Because I want to live" is unscorable.

d. (because) someone might want her to live, or other people want her to live; (or because) God wants people to live.

e. (because) we should die when God wants us to (not when we want to).

5: Needs

Saving a stranger's life is **important** because:

Form A

a. the stranger needs to live.

b. you (still) need to live.

c. her husband (still) needs her.

6: Advantages

Saving a stranger's life or living even when you don't want to is:

a. (**important** because otherwise) there would be no one or not many people left.

Form A

b. (**important** because) the stranger will thank you or might do you a favor (some day).

c. (**not important** because) the stranger could be a **crook**, faking, or tricking you.

d. (**not important** because) why help (someone you don't know?) or that would be stupid; (because) you shouldn't go to jail for someone you don't know; (or because) you shouldn't take the risk.

Note. The noninterrogative and unelaborated "you don't know him" is unscorable. Also, "(but) you shouldn't risk your life" is unscorable.

Form B

e. (**important** because) you (still) have many things you can do, can (still) have fun, or may (still) have a few reasons to live; (because then) there is no reason to die; (or because) you can help yourself.

f. (**important** because) you don't know that death is better; (or because otherwise) you'd never know how your life would have turned out or what would have happened.

Note. "(Because) you might be cured" or "she might walk again some day" is unscorable.

g. (**important** because) you only live once, or you would have a longer life (if you are only crippled rather than dying).

TRANSITION 2/3

1: Exchanges--Relationships

Saving a stranger's life or living even when you don't want to is **important** because:

Form A

a. the stranger **would** do it for you, or I **would want** the stranger to help me; (or **not important** because) the stranger (probably) **wouldn't** do it for you.

Form B

b. she **wouldn't want** her huband to do that to her or to leave her.

c. (even if crippled) she should thank God she's alive.

2: Preferences--Prosocial Intentions

Saving a stranger's life or living even when you don't want to is:

Form A

a. (**not important** because) that **must** be what God wants.

Form B

b. (**important** because) God put people here to live; (or because) people were created to live, or were not put on Earth to kill themselves.

c. (**important** because) she **really** (still) wants to live, or **deep down** she wants to live; (or because) you could become happy later, or see the good things in life.

Note. "(**Important** because) later you could be glad you're alive" is unscorable.

3: Preferences--Relationships

Saving a stranger's life or living even when you don't want to is **important** because:

a. someone might love you; (because) others love or care about you or don't want to **lose** you; (or because) she is special to her husband.

Form A

b. someone (probably) **loves** the stranger.

4: Preferences--Empathic Role-Taking

Living even when you don't want to is **important** because otherwise: the husband would be upset.

5: Needs--Empathic Role-Taking

Saving a stranger's life or living even when you don't want to is **important** because:

Form A

a. the stranger needs **your help** or **someone** to **help** or **needs** the drug badly; (or **not important** because) **God** will **help** the stranger.

Form B

b. she **should realize that** her husband still needs her.

c. the children would still need to be **cared for** or taken **care** of.

6: Advantages--Relationships

Saving a stranger's life or living even when you don't want to is **important** because:

Form A

a. the stranger could become a friend; (or **not important** because) the stranger is not as important **to you** as your wife or friend); (or **not important** because) you don't **even** know the stranger.

Note. "The stranger is **not important**" is unscorable.

b. (otherwise) you would be alone, or the world would be a lonely place.

Form B

<u>c.</u> she should enjoy life **while she can.**

STAGE 3:

Mutual and Prosocial

1: Relationships (c = Orientation A)

Saving a stranger's life or living even when you don't want to is:

Form A

<u>a.</u> (**important** because) how would you feel if you were dying (and someone wouldn't help you?); (because) what if you were the stranger?; (or because) you **would hope** for or **expect** the stranger to save your life.

<u>b.</u> (**important** because) you might become **close** friends.

<u>c.</u> (**not important** because) you wouldn't feel attached to, would have no feelings for, or would not be close to a stranger; (or because) the stranger doesn't **mean** as much to him.

Form B

<u>d.</u> (**important** because) life is a gift, or we should appreciate or be **thankful** for (the) life (God gave us).

2: Empathic Role-Taking

Saving a stranger's life or living even when you don't want to is **important** because:

Form A

<u>a.</u> (**important** because) you wouldn't want to see someone die; (or because) it's horrible to watch someone suffer.

<u>b.</u> (**important** because) the friend is in (a time of) need.

Form B

<u>c.</u> you should be concerned about (the feelings of) others, or shouldn't hurt people (who love you); (because they should **realize that** there are people who love them; (because otherwise) loved ones would suffer; (or **not important**) if loved ones couldn't bear to see you in pain.

<u>Note.</u> "Hurting others" is rated Stage 3 on the Life norm because in this context it almost always connotes **emotional** hurt.

3: Normative Expectations

Living even when you don't want to is **important** because:

there is still some **purpose** (for you to live), or you may find something to live for; (or because) you can still do something with your life or live a **full** life.

4: Prosocial Intentions

Saving a stranger's life or living even when you don't want to is **important** because:

Form A

<u>a.</u> it is the **human** or compassionate thing to do; (or **not important** because) there is a point when being a good person has to end.

Form B

<u>b.</u> you may become less bitter or depressed, or accept your condition.

<u>c.</u> you shouldn't just feel sorry for yourself, or feel ashamed.

<u>d.</u> you should enjoy life (as best you can).

5: Generalized Caring (Orientation B)

Saving a stranger's life is **important** because:

<u>a.</u> life is precious or priceless.

<u>Note.</u> "A life is worth living" is unscorable.

Form A

<u>b.</u> a life is important enough to **break** the law for, or is more important than **money.**

<u>Note.</u> "A life is more important than anything" is unscorable.

<u>c.</u> you should care for everyone, or shouldn't just care about your wife or friends; (or because) it is **still** a person or a human life, or **even** a stranger is a person.

<u>Note.</u> "It's important to help anyone," "it's a life," "it's a person," or "someone is dying" is unscorable.

6: Intrapersonal Approval

Saving a stranger's life or living even when you don't want to is **important** because:

Form A

<u>a.</u> (otherwise he would feel guilty, would have it on his conscience, or would not be able to live with himself; (or **not important** because) if the drug didn't work (and made her die), Heinze would feel terrible (knowing he killed someone).

Form B

b. you should feel good about yourself.

TRANSITION 3/4

1: Relationships--Responsibility

Saving a stranger's life is **not important** because:

there is no **bond** (of friendship with the stranger).

2: Normative Expectations--Basic Rights/Values

Saving a stranger's life or living even when you don't want to is **important** because:

Form A

a. no one should die because they are poor, or everyone has the right to live.

b. the druggist should not be in control of someone's life; **(not important** because) Heinz shouldn't play God or try to make decisions of life and death; (or **not important)** because (maybe) that is the Lord's **will.**

Form B

c. we cannot question God, or should have faith in God's wisdom; (but) we should not take it upon ourselves to decide life's worth, or have no right to kill ourselves; (or because) we cannot control life.

Note. "God will always see you through" is unscorable.

3: Normative Expectations--Procedural Equity

Saving a stranger's life is **important** but:

it **depends on the situation** or **circumstances.**

Note. "But sometimes the law should be broken" is unscorable.

4: Prosocial Intentions--Character

Saving a stranger's life or living even when you don't want to is **important:**

a. (but) this is an emotional or moral, rather than a legal, matter.

Form B

b. (because) you must have courage or should have the will (to live or keep on going); (or because otherwise) it's a cop-out.

5: Generalized Caring—Basic Rights/Values

Saving a stranger's life is **important** because:

<u>a.</u> you should respect life.

Form A

<u>b.</u> a person's life is more important than (satisfying this druggist's) **greed;** (because) we are all human beings; (because) you should have compassion on a **fellow** or **another** human being; (or because) you should care about society or humanity.

Form B

<u>c.</u> we should not abuse life.

<u>d.</u> you should see the positive aspects of life; (or because) your views (about the value of life) may change.

<u>e.</u> you can still lead a **fulfilling** life.

6: Intrapersonal Approval—Conscience

Saving a stranger's life or living even when you don't want to is **important** but:

<u>a.</u> a person should follow his or her own judgment [Type R, relativism of personal values].

Form B

<u>b.</u> people should be allowed or have the right to decide whether to end their own lives.

STAGE 4:

Systemic and Standard

1: Societal Requirements

Saving a stranger's life or living even when you don't want to is **important** because:

<u>a.</u> life is a higher law, or God's law takes priority over human law.

Form A

<u>b.</u> people must help **each other.**

2: Basic Rights/Values

Saving a stranger's life or living even when you don't want to is **important** because:

a. life is sacred.

b. everyone has something to offer (society), or can make a contribution.

Form A

c. saving lives is the spirit of the law, or should be the basis of written laws; (because) saving life is more important than society's need for law, or has a higher priority than **property** (rights); (or because) the law should serve first the right to life.

d. laws were **made** to protect the **rights** of **all.**

e. a society in which one must steal to save a life is unjust (in the first place).

f. laws can be changed; (or because) publicity or controversy (from Heinz's stealing the drug) could lead to an improvement in, or reform of, society.

Form B

g. a crippled person is still useful, or can be productive; (because) it's through each person's life or contribution that there will be advances or progress; (or) for the sake of society or survival.

3: Responsibility

Saving a stranger's life or living even when you don't want to is:

a. (**not important** because) one has an obligation or duty to obey the law.

Form A

b. (**important** because) one has a responsibility, obligation, or commitment to any human being; (or because) poeple **must** feel responsible for others.

Note. "(**Not important** because) the stranger isn't your responsibility or obligation" is unscorable.

c. (**important** but) one must accept responsibility (for one's actions).

Form B

d. (**important** because) we all have obligations or responsibilities (to society), or a role to play (in society); (or because) we should (choose to) accept (the) responsibility (of doing the best we can in life).

4: Character

This aspect is not typically evidenced on this norm.

5: Consistent Practices

Saving a stranger's life is **important** because:

who is to say that the life of one is "worth" more than the life of another?; (or because) you can't measure the value of another person's life.

6: Procedural Equity

This aspect is not typically evidenced on this norm.

7: Standards of Conscience

Saving a stranger's life or living even when you don't want to is **not important** because:

one should not compromise one's integrity.

THE THEORY-DEFINING LEVELS:

Sociopolitical Philosophy

TR: Theoretical Relativism

Saving a stranger's life or living even when you don't want to is **important:**

Form A

a. if Heinz considers the value of the individual's right to life to be
greater than that of the established laws of society; (or because) although
by the standards of society stealing is wrong, by Heinze's standards as an
individual, stealing to save a life could be morally right.

Form B

b. (because) although by the standards of society mercy-killing may be
wrong, by Mr. Jefferson's standards as an individual, mercy-killing could
be morally right.

TP: Theoretical Principles

Saving a stranger's life or living even whn you don't want to is **important** because:

Form A

a. the **right** to **life** supersedes or transcends the **right** to **property**; (or
because) material values are meaningless when put prior to individual human
worth.

Form B

b. autonomy or the right to decide one's life or death should be part of
the social contract, or is a **basic human right.**

7

Norm 3:

LAW AND PROPERTY

Justifications for obeying the law and not stealing frequently appeal to the consequences of breaking the law (for the group, the self, or others), and to the functions which laws serve for people. One of the main lines of evolution pertains to consequences for the group. At Stage 2, the group consequence is conceptualized as a generalized concrete disadvantage ("there would be nothing left to steal, no money, everyone would be in jail"). Transition 2/3 introduces the idea of general protection and safety and implies an incipient concern with the prospect of antinormative confusion (the world would be "a wreck," a "mess," or "in bad shape"). A straight Stage 3 rating is reserved for direct references to the results of widespread violations of normative expectations (things would "fall apart," there would be "chaos," it would be "crazy"). The normative concern at higher levels is structured by concepts of consistent functioning. The appeal at Transition 3/4 is explicitly for "order," "control," and the prevention of "lawlessness." There is the suggestion that with general lawlessness the world would be "at war" (implying structured conflict), in contrast to the simpler concept of danger evident in the 2/3 suggestion that the world would be "full of crime." Transition 3/4 functional concerns fully blossom at Stage 4. Instead of the 3/4 appeal to the value of "order" (either order with reference to prosocial intentions, Stage 3; or order with reference to societal organization, Stage 4), there is a direct suggestion at Stage 4 that laws keep **"society** in order," i.e., maintain smooth social functioning. Where "order" is the main reference at Stage 4, it is represented as a valued <u>outcome</u> generated by laws (laws **make possible** order;" or, "society is based on laws").

Positive references to group welfare also assume different forms according to stage. Group welfare is understood in terms of diffuse "happiness" at Stage 3. Transition 3/4 marks an intimation of a concern with broader functional advances (laws "make life **better"**). By Stage 4, there is a conception of general societal benefits generated by laws (laws are for the "common good" and "the advancement of society").

Consequence justifications can also refer to consequences for the self. At the lowest levels, these consequences are conceptualized as physical and punitive ("you might be punished, **put** in jail, killed, or **put** in the hospital;" Stage 1); quasi-physical but inevitable and punitive ("you **will** be caught, be found out, go to jail, or end up in jail" Stage 1); or quasi-physical but still implicitly punitive (trouble, blame; Transition 1/2). By Stage 2 the punitive connotations have disappeared, and the "consequences" are construed as benefits or liabilities resulting from the calculations of a self-interested individual (obey the law "so you can get farther in life; because otherwise "you're taking a risk," or the person you steal from "would get mad at you"). If the usually punitive term "trouble" is used, it is found at Stage 2 in the context of prudential calculation (obeying the law is important **"if you know** you would get caught or in trouble"), pragmatic liabilities (stealing "just causes trouble"), or unfair disadvantage ("he would be the one, not she, who would get in trouble").

At levels beyond Stage 2, the referents for self "consequences" become more internal. A quasi-external, possibly still pragmatic justification is that your conscience would "bother" you if you steal; by Stage 3, the consideration is more intrinsic (your having stolen would be "on your mind"). The corresponding Stage 4 consideration implies not simply a self disapproval but also a set of internal standards which one must live up to in order to judge oneself worth of "self-respect."

Another line of evolution in Law and Property addresses the functions that law serves for people. At Stage 2, it is suggested that without law there would be uninhibited or undeterred self-interested actions (people "would be stealing, killing, and getting away with things"). At Stage 3, antisocial conduct is referred to in a context of clear disapproval ("people could **just** kill anyone or steal anything"; "we wouldn't be civilized"). At higher levels, laws are represented as personally valuable aids to conduct or character (laws should be a "guide" by which to "keep order in our lives"; or, a goad to our better judgment so that we can have "self-control" or do not "lose sight of right and wrong"). By Stage 4, the idea of law as a guide has become explicit as a necessity for the functioning of society ("self-control is important for **society"**).

Somewhat specific to the property question (5b) is a concern with the importance of working rather than stealing. At Stage 2, this concern is expressed in the form of an appeal to the concrete rights or freedoms of persons who may have "worked for their things." At the next higher levels, more empathic concerns may be implied ("worked **hard** for their things", Transition 2/3) or directly expressed ("sacrificed or worked **so hard** for their things," Stage 3). There is also the Stage 3 normative prosocial expectation that we "should work for **our** things" or "shouldn't take advantage of others." The broader and possibly societal concern with the loss of a "motivation to work" is pegged Transition 3/4; discriminatively Stage 4 is the specific concern that widespread theft could destroy the "incentive to invent new drugs" beneficial to society.

It is interesting to trace the evolving ways in which role-taking appeals are used in Law and Property reflection. At Stage 2, moral reciprocity is understood in terms of quid pro quo exchanges and can be applied to positive evaluations of the importance of obeying the law ("the laws will help us if we help them") or to the fairness of legal sanctions ("once you break a law you must pay for it"). The role-taking appeal at Transition 2/3 is more hypothetical but still expressed in terms of preferences ("you **wouldn't want** someone to take your things"). By Stage 3 the appeal is oriented to feelings and mutualities of expectation ("how would you feel . . .?"; you would "expect" or "hope" that the other person wouldn't take your things). The overall perspective implied by Stage 3 expands at higher levels such that the role-taking is applied not just to dyadic relationships but to the relation between the personal claims or circumstances and the functions of the larger social whole. Thus there is a Transition 3/4 suggestion that, after all, "laws aren't perfect," a concern with procedural equity which becomes discriminatively clear with the Stage 4 specification of the **impossibility** of perfect or adjustment-free laws ("laws **cannot** take into account every circumstance"). Similarly, there is an emerging concern with the obligations owed by the individual to society, a concern which is possibly already evident in the Transition 3/4 prescription that a person be **"willing** to accept the penalty" for wrongdoing and which reaches its full power in the Stage 4 guarded allowance for lawbreaking acts of deliberate conscience so long as one is **"prepared** to accept the consequences."

Finally, there is an evolution in the concern with the consequences **for others** if laws are broken. At Stage 2, the concern is simply with the needs of another person (obeying the laws is important because "someone else who can pay may need it" or not important because "his wife needs it"). By Stage 3, the concern with others has become more empathic or socioemotional (obeying the law is important because people can be "attached to" or "sentimental over" property). Transition 2/3 thoughts are, of course, intermediate. For example, obeying the law is important because otherwise "you could hurt someone" (either physically, Stage 2 or emotionally, Stage 3). At Transition 3/4 Type R, Stage 3 prosocial intentions are relativized as subjectively defensible values (obeying the law is important or not important depending on, for example, whether you "feel" your love outweighs the law). Concern for others at higher levels is also expressed in terms of respect: one should respect others' property (Transition 3/4); indeed, one "has a **responsibility** to respect others' property" and "should **respect** the **rights** of others" (Stage 4). An appeal to **universal human rights** is at the theory-defining level (Theo-retical Principles).

Obeying the law may be evaluated as unimportant especially on Form A in view of the druggist's objectionable behavior. At Stage 2, the concern is simply to "get even" with the druggist, whereas at Stage 3, dismay is expressed at the druggist's "greed" or "selfishness." This concern at higher levels is related to the value of life: it is suggested at Transition 3/4 that the druggist is **inhumane** (not simply inhuman, Stage 3) because he is placing the satisfaction of his greed over human lives and is in effect making a "decision of life and death" which is not his prerogative. By Stage 4, life has become a basic right which should be protected by law "over property."

Finally, several miscellaneous stage discriminations should be discussed. Not breaking the law because of one's pragmatic interests ("it would just cause trouble," Stage 2) should not be confused with a relativistic appeal to subjective (if possibly pragmatic) **values** (you **"may feel** it's not worth the trouble," Transition 3/4 Type R). There are also subtle distinctions between appeals to pragmatic preferences ("someone you **like** may go to jail," Stage 2), preferences or prosocial intentions ("someone you **love** may go to jail," Transition 2/3), and discriminatively prosocial intentionality (unless you are acting **out of** love or for a **loved** one," Stage 3). On Form A, an appeal to the wife's "needs" is rated Stage 2 only if explicit; "without the drug she'll die" is rated Transition 1/2. A prescriptive appeal to "act according to one's values" is rated Transition 3/4 (Type R), whereas a clearly standards-oriented concern with the individual's **higher** values (vis a vis "human law") or **internal laws** is Stage 4.

MONTAGES

Stage 1 (Unilateral and Simplistic)

Obeying the law or not stealing is **important** because: "The law is there for you to follow (1). You should always obey the law and shouldn't take other people's things (3). Stealing is a bad thing to do, and you're not nice if you steal. You should obey the law to be good (4). If you steal, then those people **will** steal your things. You **will** be found out and might be **put in** jail (5)."

Transition 1/2

Obeying the law or not stealing is **important** because: "Other people's things don't belong to you (1), and if you steal, you will be called a criminal (3). You will get in trouble and **could** go to jail (4)." But it is **not important** because: "That druggist is mean (2, Form A), and if she doesn't get the drug she'll die (3, Form A).

Stage 2 (Exchanging and Instrumental)

Obeying the law or not stealing is **important** because: "The laws will help us if we help them. If you **do** break a law, you **have to** pay for it (1). Besides, you **don't want** people to steal your things. If the husband steal, he would be the one--not his wife--who would have to go to jail (2, Form A). No one wants to go to jail, even if it is for someone you **like** (4). Stealing gets you nowhere, and **if you are caught** you will get in trouble. The person you steal from would get mad, and eventually there would be nothing left to steal. People would be killing and getting away with things (6). Besides, maybe the druggist is poor and needs the money (Form A, 5). You should remember that it was the druggist who worked to make the drug, so he can do whatever he wants with it (Form A, 3). But it is **not important** because: "The druggist is stealing from him, so why shouldn't he steal back (1)? Besides, his wife needs the drug (5)."

Transition 2/3

Obeying the law or not stealing is **important** because: "You **wouldn't want** people to steal your things (1). Besides, the other person may have worked **hard** for what he has (2). If people break the law, someone you **love** might go to jail (3), someone could be hurt (5), the world would be unsafe, a mess, and full of crime (6), and your conscience would **bother** you (8). So you shouldn't steal unless you need the drug **badly** (4)."

Stage 3 (Mutual and Prosocial)

Obeying the law or not stealing is **important** because: "Then the world would be **happier.** After all, how would you feel if somone took your things? You **would expect** others not to steal from you (1). You should realize that people often work **so hard** and feel sentimentally attached to their property, and it causes a hardship in many ways to steal their things. After all, the druggist may have sacrificed to make this drug--even though you can understand how the husband, too, would feel (2). But still, if everyone stole, the world would be crazy, the country would fall apart, and there would be chaos (3). People could **just** kill anyone or steal anything. It is selfish and despicable to take advantage of others (4). Earning money instead of just stealing gives you a feeling of pride. Remember, you're only hurting yourself by stealing (6)." But obeying the law is **not important** because: "The druggist is being selfish and **inhuman,** and Heinz will have to be the same way the druggist is (4, Form A).

Transition 3/4

Obeying the law or not stealing is **important** because: Laws make life **better** (1). Obeying the law shows your trustworthiness (2). A law can be changed if it is wrong (3), and admittedly laws aren't always fair. There can be exceptions for special cases (4). Clearly, for example, this druggist shouldn't be greedy **when a life is involved** (9, Form A). But laws are important for the sake of order and harmony in society. Without them, there would be no harmony and the world would be at war (5). Laws are made for the people, and if people don't follow them there would be no **point** in having them. For example, the motivation to work and earn money would be lost, and there would be no respect for one another's property (6). The laws should serve as a guide to encourage self-control and greater awareness of right and wrong (8). You should respect the law and have no right to take something just because you **think** you need it (9). Of course, you should act according to your values and make your **own** decision (10), but then you should be **willing** to accept the penalty (7)."

Stage 4 (System and Standard)

Obeying the law or not stealing is **important** because: "Laws **make possible** order in society. Without laws, there could be no organization or predictability (1). The law is for the common good and protects people's rights, including the right to property. If everyone were to steal these drugs, there could be no incentive for people to invent new drugs that help humanity (2). Besides, you have a **responsibility** to respect others' property. This is one of the obligations that go along with the privileges of living in society. If you do steal, you have to be **prepared** to accept responsibility for your actions, especially since stealing violates God's law as well as human law (3). That way you won't lose others' respect (4), not to mention self-respect (7). After all, people **cannot** break the law whenever they feel justified, because any theft can be rationalized (5). Nonetheless, laws **cannot** always be fair or appropriate for every particular circumstance; you do **have** to judge each case individually (6). Sometimes, one must follow God's law or one's own **internal laws** (3). This case makes the point that the laws should be protecting life before property (2, Form A)."

Theoretical Relativism (TR)

Obeying the law or not stealing is **important:** "If one takes the legal standpoint, or believes in the rules of society, rather than the values of the individual."

Theoretical Principles (TP)

Obeying the law or not stealing is **important:** "In order to protect **universal human rights,** or so that everyone can be assured of the **right** to life or liberty."

STAGE 1:

Unilateral and Simplistic

1: Unilateral Authority

Obeying the law or not stealing is **important** because:

the law is (there) for you to follow; (or because) the Bible says don't steal.

Note. "'Don't steal' is one of God's Commandments" is unscorable.

2: Status

This aspect is not typically evidenced on this norm.

3: Rules

Obeying the law or not stealing is **important** because:

a. you are supposed to, should (always) obey the law; (because) you must obey or have to follow the law; (or because) no one should steal or break the law.

Note. "You should obey the law no matter what" is a pseudo-Stage 1 response and unscorable, but "you should obey the law no matter what **the circumstances**" is scorable as Transition 3/4.

b. **you shouldn't** take other people's things.

Note. "It isn't fair to take other people's things" is unscorable.

4: Labels

Obeying the law or not stealing is **important.**

a. (in order) to be good; (or because otherwise) it's not nice.

Note. "(Because) stealing is mean" is unscorable.

b. (because) it's the law; because stealing is bad, wrong, or a sin; (or because otherwise) that's stealing.

Note. Qualified assertions, e.g., "stealing is bad, even if for a good cause," are not scorable at Stage 1. Also, assertions of illegality, e.g., "it's against the law," are unscorable.

5: Punitive Consequences

Obeying the law or not stealing is **important** because otherwise:

a. you **will** or **would** be caught, be found out, go to jail, or end up in jail; (or because otherwise) you will or might be punished, or could be **put** in jail, killed, or **put** in the hospital.

b. (then) they **will** steal your things.

TRANSITION 1/2

1: Labels--Freedoms

Obeying the law or not stealing is **important**:

a. (because) it isn't yours or doesn't belong to you; (or because) it's theirs.

b. (unless) they have something that's yours.

2: Labels--Exchanges

Obeying the law or not stealing is **not important** because:

Form A

the druggist is mean.

3: Labels--Disadvantages

Obeying the law or not stealing is **important**:

a. (because otherwise) he will or might be called a criminal.

Form A

b. (but) if he doesn't steal the drug, his wife will die.

4: Punitive Consequences--Disadvantages

Obeying the law or not stealing is **important**:

(so that) you won't get **caught,** get in trouble or be blamed; (or because otherwise) you **could** go to jail, or they **might** steal your things or get you.

STAGE 2:

Exchanging and Instrumental

1: Exchanges

Obeying the law or not stealing is **important** because:

a. the laws will help us if we help them.

b. you **don't want** your things stolen; (or because) if you don't steal from others, they shouldn't steal from you.

c. if you don't follow the law you go to jail; once you break the law you **must** pay (the price); (otherwise) you **have to** pay (for your crime); (or but) you can steal if you can take it (when they get even).

Note. "If you break the law you should be punished" or "you should pay the consequences" is unscorable.

Form A

d. (but) the druggist was stealing from him; (or but) why shouldn't he steal back?

2: Equalities

Obeying the law or not stealing is **important** because:

he (not she) would get the blame or trouble, or would be the one to go to jail.

3: Freedoms

Obeying the law or not stealing is **important** because:

they may have worked for or earned their things, or paid for what they have; (or because) they can do whatever they want with their property.

4: Preferences

Obeying the law or not stealing is **important:**

a. (because) you wouldn't want to go to jail, they want their things, or no one wants to go to jail; (or because then) someone you **like** might go to jail.

b. (because) you might not want to (steal or break the law); (or because) there may be a good law (that you don't want to break).

c. (unless) it is for someone you **like**.

Form A

d. (but) if you were dying, you would want to get the drug, too.

Form B

e. (but) you don't like it (that she is suffering).

5: Needs

Obeying the law or not stealing is **important:**

a. (because) you might not need to (steal or break the law); (because) someone else (who can pay) may need it; (unless) you need the drug; (or but) his wife or friend needs it.

Form A

b. (because) the druggist could be poor.

c. (but) the stranger needs to get better.

6: Advantages

Obeying the law or not stealing is **important:**

a. (so that) you can get farther in life; (because) stealing gets you no-where, isn't worth it, or just causes trouble; (because otherwise) you would get a (criminal) record; (or but) it depends on whether the friend is worth going to jail for.

b. (unless) you can get away with it.

c. (because otherwise) you're taking a risk or **might** get **caught;** (because) **if you are caught** you will get in trouble; (or) **if you know or think** that you will get caught or in trouble.

d. (because otherwise) they will not like you, or could get mad.

e. (because otherwise eventually) there would be nothing left to steal, or no money; (or because otherwise) everyone would be in jail, or there would be no one left to break the law.

f. (because otherwise) everyone will be stealing or killing, or people will be getting away with things; (or because otherwise) there would be trouble.

Note. "(Because then) people will do what they want" is unscorable.

Form B

g. (because if she takes the drug) she could (just) wind up with more pain.

<h3 style="text-align:center">TRANSITION 2/3</h3>

1: Exchanges--Relationships

Obeying the law or not stealing is **important** because:

You **wouldn't want** people to steal your things; (or because) I **wouldn't want** it done to me.

2: Exchanges--Empathic Role-Taking

Obeying the law or not stealing is **importnat** because:

the other person (may have) worked **hard** or **long** (for what she has); (or because) that could have been all the person has.

3: Preferences--Prosocial Intentions

Obeying the law or not stealing is **important** because otherwise:

someone you **love** might go to jail; (or unless) it is for someone you **love.**

4: Needs--Empathic Role-Taking

Obeying the law or not stealing is **important** unless:

you **really** need it or need the drug **badly.**

5: Advantages—Prosocial Intentions

Obeying the law or not stealing is **important:**

(because) you could hurt someone; (unless) it wouldn't hurt anyone; (or unless) you could help someone (by breaking the law).

6: Advantages—Normative Expectations

Obeying the law or not stealing is **important:**

<u>a.</u> (because) the laws (were made to) protect people, or make things safer; (or because otherwise) the world would be dangerous, or (innocent) people would or might be **hurt.**

<u>Note.</u> "Because the laws were made for a reason" is unscorable.

<u>b.</u> (so that) things would be peaceful; (because otherwise) things would be a mess, wreck, or shambles, or would be in bad shape; (or because otherwise) the world would be full of crime.

<u>c.</u> (because otherwise eventually) **people would think** that you don't get caught (if you steal).

<u>d.</u> (because otherwise) it would be hard to live or get along in the world, or the world wouldn't be worth living in.

7: Advantages—Prosocial Intentions

Obeying the law or not stealing is **important** unless:

it is for someone you **love**

8: Advantages—Intrapersonal Approval

Obeying the law or not stealing is **important** because otherwise:

your conscience will be affected or would **bother** you.

STAGE 3:

Mutual and Prosocial

1: Relationships

Obeying the law or not stealing is **important** because:

<u>a.</u> **we should treat others the way we would like to be treated;** (because) you **would expect** others not to steal from you, or others **expect** the same from you; (or because otherwise) how would you feel?

<u>b.</u> (then) things would be easier or nice for everyone; (because) then the world or people would be **happier;** (or because otherwise) **life** would be **unhappy.**

2: Empathic Role-Taking

Obeying the law or not stealing is **important**:

a. (because) they feel attached to or sentimental over their things; (because) it might **mean** a lot to them; (or because) they (may) have worked **so hard** for their things.

b. (because) of the hardship stealing causes.

c. (but) you can understand how the husband would feel.

Form A

d. (because) the druggist (may have) **sacrificed** to make this drug.

e. (but) you can't **just sit there and** let her die.

Form B

f. (but) you wouldn't want **to see** someone in pain.

3: Normative Expectations

Obeying the law or not stealing is **important** because:

a. we should work for or deserve **our** things.

b. (otherwise) the world would be confusing or would go crazy; (because otherwise) the country would be in havoc or would fall apart; (or because otherwise) there would be chaos.

4: Prosocial Intentions

Obeying the law or not stealing is **important**:

a. (so that) you will be a better person, or can be a good citizen; (or because otherwise) we wouldn't be civilized, the world would be a rotten place, or people could **just** kill or would **just** steal.

Note. "(Otherwise) everyone would be doing all kinds of things" is unscorable.

b. (because) it is selfish, cruel, callous, or despicable to steal; (because) you shouldn't take advantage of others; (or because) you shouldn't want what others have.

Note. "(Because) stealing is mean" is unscorable.

c. (unless) you are acting **out of** love or for a **loved one.**

d. (but) not everyone can obey the law all the time.

Form A

e. (but) the druggist is (being) greedy, selfish, or **inhuman;** (or because)

Heinz has to be the same way the druggist is.

5: Generalized Caring

Obeying the law or not stealing is **important** but:

Form A

a life is **at stake,** or is more important than **obeying** the law.

6: Intrapersonal Approval

Obeying the law or not stealing is **important** because:

<u>a.</u> (then) you can be proud or have a good feeling inside.

<u>b.</u> (otherwise) you are only hurting yourself, or it will be on your mind.

TRANSITION 3/4

1: Relationships--Basic Rights/Values

Obeying the law or not stealing is **important** because:

laws make **life better.**

2: Relationships--Character

Obeying the law or not stealing is **important** so that:

you **can be** trusted by others, or will show that you are trustworthy.

<u>Note.</u> "(Because otherwise) you couldn't trust anyone" is unscorable.

3: Empathic Role-Taking--Basic Rights/Values

Obeying the law or not stealing is **important** because:

the laws can be changed (if they are wrong or unfair).

4: Empathic Role-Taking--Procedural Equity

Obeying the law or not stealing is **important** but:

<u>a.</u> laws aren't perfect or always fair; (or but) some laws have flaws.

<u>b.</u> there can be exceptions or special **cases/situations;** (but) it **depends on** the **circumstances;** (or but) this is a moral or emotional rather than a criminal issue.

<u>Note.</u> "This is special," "it depends," or "(but) sometimes it's best to steal" is unscorable.

5: Normative Expectations-- Societal Requirements

Obeying the law or not stealing is **important:**

a. (so that there is order (in society); (in order) to control society, or to prevent lawlessness or anarchy; (so that) we can **live in** peace; (or because otherwise) the world would be at war or things would get out of hand.

Note. "(Because otherwise) there would be no law" is unscorable.

b. (because) we need to work together or have harmony (in society).

6: Normative Expectations--Basic Rights/Values

a. (because) laws are made by the people or the majority.

b. (because) laws are **made** for the **people** or **public;** (or because) laws were **made** to help us or for our own good.

Note. "(Because) laws are for our own good," "laws are there to help us," or "laws are made to be followed" is unscorable.

c. (because) property or the law should be respected, or we should respect one another's property.

d. (because) stealing is wrong in the eyes of the law or society, or is a violation of morality.

e. (because otherwise) there would be no **point** in having laws.

Note. "(Because) that's what laws are for" is unscorable, since it could also have Stage 1 significance ("the law is for you to follow"). Also, "(because) then there would be no laws" is unscorable.

f. (because otherwise) people would not be motivated to work or earn money.

Form A

g. (but) **in this case** a life is **at stake.**

7: Normative Expectations--Responsibility

Obeying the law or not stealing is **important** unless:

you are **willing** to accept the risk or penalty; (or **not important** but) people should have good judgment, or should know how far they can go (in breaking the law).

Note. "If you get caught, you should pay the consequences" is unscorable.

8: Prosocial Intentions--Societal Requirements

Obeying the law or not stealing is **important** because:

the laws should be a guide, or should keep order in our lives; (because) people should not just do what they want to or feel like (all the time), cannot always have what they want, or must have patience; (because) people need self-control or should not act impulsively; (or because otherwise) people will steal even if they don't have to, get out of control, think stealing is O.K., or lose sight of right and wrong.

Note. "(Because then) people will do what they want" is unscorable.

9: Prosocial Intentions—Basic Rights/Values

Obeying the law or not stealing is **important** because:

a. you should respect the law.

Note. "You should (always) respect others" is unscorable.

b. you have no right to take something just because you **think** you need it.

c. (otherwise) there would be no caring, or people would just be looking out for themselves.

Form A

d. (but) the druggist is **inhumane,** should not withhold a life-saving drug, or should not be greedy **when a life is involved.**

10: Prosocial Intentions—Standards of Conscience [Type R]

Obeying the law or not stealing is **important:**

a. (because) you **may** not **value** the other person's life enough to ruin your life, or **may feel** it is not worth the trouble or sacrifice; (but) one should act according to one's values; (or but) it depends on his morals.

b. (but) you must make your **own** decision, or **may feel** you must break the law or that your love outweighs the law; (or but) saving a **life** may be more important **for you** than obeying the law.

STAGE 4:

Systemic and Standard

1: Societal Requirements

Obeying the law or not stealing is **important:**

a. (in order) to keep **society** together or things in order, or to **make possible** order (in society); (because) society or civilization needs or is based on laws, or **must** have order; (because) the law is the backbone or basis of society; (or because otherwise) there would be no structure, organization, or predictability, **society** would be (in) chaos, or the **system would break down.**

b. (because) honesty, character, or self-control is important for **society.**

c. (because) the right to property **must** be protected or respected.

2: Basic Rights/Values

Obeying the law or not stealing is **important:**

a. for the common good or the advancement of **society;** (or) for the benefit **everyone** or the **whole.**

b. (because) laws are made to help (protect or build) **society;** (or because) otherwise) society could not work smoothly, function, or survive, or there would be no society.

c. (because) the law protects people's rights; (because) you should **re-spect** the **rights** of others; (or because) stealing **violates** another person's **rights.**

d. (because) changes can be made **within the system** or **through the proper channels.**

e. (because otherwise eventually) there would be no encouragement or incentive for the invention of new drugs.

f. (but) society is responsible for criminals or crime.

Form A

g. (but) the laws should protect lives before property.

3: Responsibility

Obeying the law or not stealing is **important:**

a. (because) you have a **responsibility** to respect another's property; (or because) of one's duty (as a citizen).

b. (because) one has obligations as well as privileges (in society); (because) you must accept the restrictions along with the benefits of laws; (or because) the law is an agreement.

c. (because) stealing violates God's law as well as human law; (because) laws are based on God's law or common morality; or if the law is in accordance with God's law.

d. (unless) you are **prepared** to accept the consequences, or will accept **responsibility** or be held accountable (for your actions); (or as long as) one realizes or understands the legal implications.

4: Character

Obeying the law or not stealing is **important:**

a. (so that) you don't lose others' respect.

b. for the sake of character.

5: Consistent Practices

Obeying the law or not stealing is **important** because:

people **cannot** or **must not** break the law whenever they feel justified or for emotional reasons; (because) theft can be rationalized by anyone who steals; (because) people's standards are inconsistent, or there are too many individual beliefs or subjective values; (or because otherwise) everyone would go off in different directions or there would be people taking the law into their own hands.

6: Procedural Equity

Obeying the law or not stealing is **important** because:

<u>a.</u> the law **cannot** always be fair, appropriate, or right (for a specific situation); (because) laws **cannot** take into acount every case or circumstance, or **cannot** be more than simplistic rules; (or because) you **cannot** generalize, or each case **must** be judged individually.

<u>b.</u> (because) some laws are made for the good of the few or reflect the tyranny of the majority.

7: Standards of Conscience

Obeying the law or not stealing is **important:**

<u>a.</u> for the sake of self-respect or one's integrity or self-esteem.

<u>b.</u> (because) stealing degrades you.

<u>c.</u> (but) one must (also) follow one's **internal laws** or **higher values.**

THE THEORY-DEFINING LEVEL:

Sociopolitical Philosophy

TR: Theoretical Relativism

Obeying the law or not stealing is **important:**

if one takes the legal standpoint, or believes in the rules of society (rather than the values of the individual).

TP: Theoretical Principles

Obeying the law or not stealing is **important:**

(in order) to preserve or protect **universal human rights;** (so that) everyone can be assured of the **right to** life or liberty.

8

Norm 4:

LEGAL JUSTICE

The Legal Justice norm provides a good context for tracing the evolution of the concepts of deterrence and of role responsibilities. Deterrence is not evident among Stage 1 justifications, which emphasize retributive reasons for punishment. At Transition 1/2, there is the thought that punishment is important so that the husband "won't do it again," which may presume that punishment automatically or "immanently" (Piaget, 1932/1965) brings forth this outcome (Stage 1) but which may also already reflect a concern with pragmatic deterrence (Stage 2); hence the Transition 1/2 rating. Where "do it again" is elaborated in a way suggestive of a concern with bad behavior as a habit ("will **keep on** doing the **same** thing" or "will do it over **and over**"), the rating is straight Stage 2. A Stage 2 rating is also given to concrete anticipations of generalized lawbreaking ("everyone will be doing it"). Transition 2/3 marks an implicit expectation that the punishment will be educative (e.g., so that the lawbreaker "will **know** not to do it again")--although the concern here could still be pragmatic. Another Transition 2/3 suggestion is that without punishment the husband "would steal again for **someone he knows or loves**" (either for the sake of a future exchange, Stage 2, or for the sake of a relationship, Stage 3). Straight Stage 3 ratings are assigned where there is an appeal to discouraging well-intentioned wrongdoing on future occasions (e.g., "otherwise he might steal again **out of** love or for a **loved one**") or to preventing widespread violations of normative expectations ("everyone would be committing crimes since they wouldn't have to pay for them by going to jail," or "there would be chaos"; cf. Stage 4: "**exceptions** would lead to chaos").

At higher levels, the concern is with judicial practices such that one must consider the effect of precedent from the husband's case upon other cases and on society. At Transition 3/4, this concern is already discernible ("people would break the law and use his **case** as an excuse; c.f. Stage 3: "the excuse would become common"). Stage 4 marks a discriminatively clear expression of the justification, e.g., "the laws have to be consistently enforced to avoid setting a dangerous precedent." Similarly, at Transition 3/4 there is a concern that "people cannot break the law whenever they feel **dissatisfied**" (either because such dissatisfaction is antisocial, Stage 3, or because such dissatisfaction is a subjective and therefore unjustifiable reason for breaking the law, Stage 4). By Stage 4, the thought has consolidated into an objection to the potential subjectivity or rationalizing quality that could develop among reasons for lawbreaking ("people cannot break the law whenever they feel **justified**"). Also, the concern with "order" at Transition 3/4 is specifically related to the functioning of society ("to keep society in order") at Stage 4.

Justifications for punishment by appeal to role expectations or obligations refer either to the judge or to the husband/lawbreaker. Stage 1 conceptions of the judge's role are constraint-oriented ("the judge has to send people to jail; it's a rule"), sometimes backed up by an appeal to punitive consequences ("if the husband isn't punished, the judge **will** go to jail, or could be **punished**"; c.f. Transition 1/2: "he will get into **trouble**"). There is no corresponding justification at Stage 2, but at Stage 3 one finds an appeal to normative expectations of rightful conduct for a judge ("that is what is expected of judges," or "judges are supposed to give sentences to people **who deserve them**"). Higher levels relate role expectations for the judge to the framework of law and society. Transition 3/4 asserts that "a judge's job is to uphold the law" and appeals to the need for impartiality, albeit in a stereotyped way (the judge "shouldn't play favorites"). By Stage 4, the appeal is explicitly to the judge's "responsibility," to his or her having accepted the "position" or having **"sworn** to uphold the law," and to the necessity for impartial judgment ("the judge **must not** be influenced by his feelings or biases").

The focus in Legal Justice may also be on the obligatory implications of the husband's having broken the law. At Stage 1, this focus is simply on the transgressive act itself as constituting a self-evident reason for punishment (he "stole," or "did something wrong"). By Stage 2, the husband's having broken the law is construed as a voluntary act that is not necessarily objectionable but which entailed a risk that should be accepted by the lawbreaker (e.g., "he knew he was taking a risk"). Accepting punishment as part of an implicit "deal" is expressed in the cliche one sometimes hears among correctional inmates: If you can't do the time, don't do the crime. The general idea of punishment as an outcome which the lawbreaker should accept is also found at higher levels. At Stage 3, the appeal is to the husband's presumed prior awareness of wrongdoing ("he knew it was wrong"). At Transition 3/4, there may be a direct prescriptive suggestion that the husband **"should** accept the consequences," or "should be willing to pay the penalty," as well as a justification of punishment "as an example to people that if you break the law you must pay the penalty." By Stage 4, the prescription regarding the husband has become specifically obligatory ("he **must** accept the consequences"), emphasizing the conscious and deliberate nature of the decision to break the law (he broke the law "of his own free will" or "because of his convictions"). Stage 4 justifications for punishment may emphasize the idea of a balanced obligation to society ("the sentence may show people that there are responsibilities as well as rights").

Considerations addressed to the husband's actions, personality, or character may be used as justifications for either punishment or leniency. The evolving justification for punishment in terms of this theme assumes that jail will be ameliorative for the husband (or for lawbreakers in general) in some way. At Transition 1/2, punishment is often evaluated as **very** important because, it is felt, a stiff jail sentence will "teach him a lesson" and "set him straight." There seems to be a simple assumption that a punishment which is severe enough will inevitably or automatically cause expiation and reform (Stage 1), but there may also be a **quid pro quo** retaliatory element (Stage 2). At Transition 2/3, the appeal instead is to instilling "regret" in the sense of either a conclusion that wrongdoing isn't worth the risk (Stage 2), or a remorse for antisocial conduct (Stage 3). Stage 3 indicates an expecta-

tion of personality reform (they can **realize** they've done wrong" or **"learn
from their mistakes"**). Transition 3/4 is assigned where the concern with
prosocial reform also implies a possible concern with promoting a potential
for productiveness or societal contribution (jail may be important "if that
way the person may be rehabilitated"). Stage 4 ratings are reserved for
discriminatively clear expressions of this thought ("if they can learn to
become productive, or to contribute to society").

References to the husband's actions, personality, or character may also be
used in an exculpatory way. At Stage 1, the justification may consist simply
of a reference to an unqualified positive label (e.g., "the husband is nice";
cf. Stage 3: "the husband **tried** to be decent or nice"). At Stage 2, Heinz's
action is excused on the ground of pragmatic necessity ("he needed the drug,"
"didn't have enough money"), or of external accommodation (she "kept asking
him to do it," or he "was only doing her a favor"; cf. Stage 1: "she told him
to do it"). A reference to the husband's having "helped" or "saved" his wife
is scorable as Transition 2/3 if there is an elaboration implying that the
reference to helping possibly reflects prosocial intention ("he was **only trying** to help," or **"just** wanted to save his wife"; cf. Stage 2: "he **wanted** to
save his wife"). The Stage 3 rating is reserved for discriminatively clear
expressions of underlying prosocial intention: he stole "for her **sake," "out
of** love," or "for a **loved one"** (cf. Transition 2/3: "for someone he **loved";**
and cf. Stage 2: "for someone he **liked").** It may be suggested at Stage 3 that
the husband's underlying prosocial intentions were obscured by his emotional
burdens ("he must have been under great strain and wouldn't have stolen ordinarily"). At Transition 3/4, the concern with prosocial intentions may be
extended in the scope of its referent ("he did it for humane or humanitarian
reasons"; or, "this was an emotional **issue")** or may be used as a subjective
validator of the ethical rightness of the action ("he **felt** it was right, or
was doing what he **thought was** right"). At Stage 4, the scope is explicitly
societal (the husband "is not a threat to society") and may relate the
husband's actions to the dictates of a "higher" or "personal" law.

Although the role expectations (or, at Stage 4, contractual responsibilities) described earlier may support punishment for the husband, role-taking
considerations as applied to the judge's role are usually directive of leniency. Stage 2 features a pragmatic role-taking (**"if the judge needed the drug,**
he would have taken it, too"), which at Transition 2/3 becomes possibly empathic ("the judge would have stolen, too," or, "might feel sorry for him").
Role-taking at Stage 3 entails a discriminatively empathic expression (the
judge "would understand," "should have a heart," or "should put himself in the
husband's place"). By Stage 4, leniency through role-taking is recommended as
an option within the framework of the judicial function ("the judicial system
should be flexible," or, "the judge can use discretion").

A related evolution pertains to the appeal to motive or circumstance as the
criterion for leniency. A Transition 2/3 rating is given to the suggestion
that the judicial decision depends on the "reasons" or "motives" for wrongdoing (the "reasons" may be pragmatic, Stage 2, or prosocially expressive,
Stage 3; higher-level referents are unusual). The suggestion that the sentence
"depends on the circumstances" is rated Transition 3/4 since there is an implication of a concern with considerations of judicial practice and precedent. Stage 4 marks an obligatory prescription to make an equitable exception
in the husband's case ("the judge **must** recognize special circumstances") or a
suggestion that the laws, as they are applied, need to be fine-tuned ("the
law **cannot** always apply appropriately").

THE MONTAGES

Stage 1 (Unilateral and Simplistic)

Sending lawbreakers to jail is **important** because: "He stole the drug and it
is bad to steal (4). The judge has to send people to jail, since it's a rule
(3) that bad people get locked up (5). After all, maybe Mrs. Jefferson was an
important person (2, Form B). If the husband isn't sent to jail, the judge
could get **punished** (5)." But it is **not important** because: "She told him to do
it (1), and he is nice (4)."

Transition 1/2

Sending lawbreakers to jail is **important**:   "So he won't do it again (1).
Besides, punishment could teach him a lesson and set him straight (2). After
all, if the husband isn't sent to jail, the judge will get in **trouble** (3). But
it is **not important** because otherwise: "his wife **would** have died (1, Form A)."

Stage 2 (Exchanging and Instrumental)

Sending lawbreakers to jail is **important** because: "The husband decided to
break the law and was taking a risk--he was caught, so now he goes to jail
(1). Besides, the druggist has a right to complain (3, Form A). If the husband
isn't sent to jail, he'll steal again for someone he **likes** (4). He'll **keep**
doing the **same** things, again **and again.** Then everyone will be doing it, fig-
uring they can get off easy. There'd be more stealing and killing (6)." But it
is **not important** because: "He was only doing her a favor (1). She kept asking
him to do it. Besides, he **wanted** to help her (4), since she needed the drug.
If the judge **needed** the drug, he would have taken it, too. After all, the husband has enough trouble as it is and doesn't need any more (5). Remember that
his wife could have died without the drug (6)."

Transition 2/3

Sending lawbreakers to jail is **important**: "To make them regret it, so
they'll **know** not to do it again. After all, the husband should have known
better (1). He should go to jail like any other lawbreaker, because otherwise
it wouldn't be fair to other lawbreakers; if he isn't punished, then others
would have to be let free (2). And the husband will steal again for someone
he **loves** (6). Laws do protect people and make things safer. Otherwise, people
not punished would persuade others to break the law (8)." But it is **not important** because: "He **loved** his wife and **just** wanted to help her (3). She was **in**
pain, and he was only putting her out of her misery (4, Form B). It depends on
the motives, but the husband had a **good** reason since he was **only trying** to
help (5). Besides, if he goes to jail then he couldn't see his wife (7, Form
A)."

Stage 3 (Mutual and Prosocial)

Sending lawbreakers to jail is **important** because: "Otherwise the world
would be an unhappy place. Judges are supposed to give the sentence people **deserve.** There is no excuse for wrongdoing, and hard criminals shouldn't get off
easy--if they do, there will be chaos (3). Also, the husband must have known
that what he did was wrong, and a sentence may help him **learn** from his mistake. Otherwise, he may steal again for a **loved one** (4)." But it is **not important** because: "The judge should understand and put himself in the husband's

place (2). The husband didn't want to see her in pain, (2, Form B). The husband had good intentions, since he was stealing for her sake. He must have been under great strain and is not a common criminal (4). He tried to be decent but was the victim of the selfish druggist (4, Form A). Indeed, he showed that his wife's life was worth more than obeying the law (5, Form A). Surely, the suffering he has gone through has been punishment enough (6)."

Transition 3/4

Sending lawbreakers to jail is important because: "That's what laws are for. The laws must be enforced if there is to be order (2). The husband should accept the consequences, and should be punished as an example that if you break the law you must pay the penalty. Otherwise, without the laws as a guideline people wouldn't think twice about breaking the law. So the judge shouldn't play favorites for the husband—it's the judge's job to uphold the law (4). If the husband isn't punished, people would use this case as an excuse to break the law and will steal whenever they feel dissatisfied (5). For example, they could murder and claim mercy-killing (5, Form B). Besides, the judge and the law should be respected. Jail may be the place for rehabilitation (6). But it is not important because: "The sentence should depend on the circumstances of the particular case, and the judge should realize what an emotional issue this case was (1). The husband acted for humane reasons, and leniency may promote caring and compassion in society (6). After all, Heinz was the victim of the druggist, who would actually let others die for the sake of a profit (6, Form A). He acted with her consent (7) and felt that what he was doing was right (8). Remember that this was a life or death situation (10, Form A)."

Stage 4 (Systemic and Standard)

Sending lawbreakers to jail is important because: "Laws are needed to protect society and must be enforced even if a particular law is unfair (1). Laws were created to protect rights and help society (2). Besides, the judge has sworn to uphold the law and has the responsibility to enforce it. The husband must accept the consequences and be held accountable. After all, if you live in society, you must be willing to accept its restrictions (3). The laws have to be consistent. People cannot break the law whenever they feel justified, and exceptions will only lead to chaos—society couldn't function then in an orderly fashion. The judge must go by the law rather than his feelings (5)." But it is not important because: "The husband may have made contributions to society (2). Society should value life (2, Form A), which is more important than property. The judge must recognize extreme circumstances, since the law does not always apply appropriately. The judge should use discretion and temper justice with mercy (6), especially since Heinz was responding to a higher law (7, Form A)."

Theoretical Principles (TP)

Sending lawbreakers to jail is important but: "The right to life takes precedence over the right to property."

STAGE 1:

Unilateral and Simplistic

1: Unilateral Authority

Sending lawbreakers to jail is:

a. (**important** because) it says "don't steal" in the Bible, or he didn't get permission (to take the drug).

b. (**not important** because) she **told** him to do it.

2: Status

Sending lawbreakers to jail is:

Form A

a. (**not important** because) maybe Heinz's wife is an **important** person.

Form B

b. (**important** because) maybe Mr. Jefferson's wife was an important person.

3: Rules

Sending lawbreakers to jail is:

a. (**important** because) the judge has to (send people to jail), or it's a rule; (or because) judges should never let people go free.

Note. "The judge has a job to do" is unscorable.

b. (**not important** because) he has to go to jail.

4: Labels

Sending lawbreakers to jail is:

a. (**important** because) he stole the drug, took something that wasn't his, or did something wrong or bad.

Note. (**Important** because) "he shouldn't be **stealing**" is unscorable. Also, an explicit assertion of illegality, e.g., "he committed a crime," is unscorable.

b. (**important so that**) bad people won't kill.

c. (**not important** because) he is nice or good.

5: Punitive Consequences

Sending lawbreakers to jail is **important**:

a. (so that) bad people are locked up.

b. (because otherwise) the judge could get **punished** or **will** go to jail.

Form B

c. (because) he killed her, so the judge should kill him.

Note. "(Because) he killed her" is unscorable.

TRANSITION 1/2

1: Labels--Advantages

Sending lawbreakers to jail is **important**:

a. (so that) he won't do it again, or won't steal any more; (or because otherwise) he will or might do it again, or do something else.

b. (because) if Heinz hadn't stolen it, his wife **would** have died.

Form B

2: Punitive Consequences--Exchanges

Sending lawbreakers to jail is **important** because:

punishment or jail will or could set him straight; or will be good for him; (in order) to teach him a lesson; (or **not important** because) he may have already learned his lesson.

3: Punitive Consequences--Advantages

Sending lawbreakers to jail is **important** because otherwise: the judge will or could get in **trouble**.

STAGE 2:

Exchanging and Instrumental

1: Exchanges

Sending lawbreakers to jail is:

a. (**important** because) if you are caught you go to jail; (because) he was taking a chance or risk; (because) he chose to steal or decided to break the law; (or because) he should or must pay for what he took.

Note. "(Because) if you break the law you should be punished" is unscorable.

b. (**not important** because) he was only doing her a favor.

Form A

c. (**not important** because) the druggist was nasty or was asking for it.

2: Equalities

This aspect is not typically evidenced on this norm.

3: Freedoms

Sending lawbreakers to jail is:

Form A

a. (**important** because) the druggist has a right to complain.

Form B

b. (**not important** because) he was forced (into it); (or because) she persuaded him to do it, or kept asking him to do it.

4: Preferences

Sending lawbreakers to jail is:

a. (**important** because otherwise) he might steal again for someone he likes.

b. (**not important** because) he **wanted** to help her, or stole for someone he — liked.

c. (**not important** because) it wasn't his fault, or he did what she wanted; (or because) he didn't mean it or didn't want to (break the law).

Form A

d. (**not important** because) he wanted to save his wife.

e. (**not important**) if that is what the druggist wants.

5: Needs

Sending lawbreakers to jail is:

a. (**not important** because) she needed the drug, or he had to do it; (or **important** because) someone else might have needed that drug.

b. (**not important** because) if the judge **needed** the drug, he would have taken it, too.

c. (**not important** because) the husband has enough trouble, or doesn't need any more hassles.

Form A

d. (**not important** because) Heinz was poor or didn't have enough money; (or because) the druggist wanted more money than Heinz had; (or **important** because) he didn't have to (do it if she was just sick).

Form B

e. (**important** because) he didn't have to, or she was going to die anyway.

6: Advantages

Sending lawbreakers to jail is:

a. (**important** because otherwise) everyone will be free or will be doing it, others will do it, or there would be more stealing, mugging, or killing;

(because otherwise) there would be murderers (walking the streets); (or because otherwise) the person or other people will figure they can steal or get off easy.

Note. "(Because otherwise) people will do what they want" or "punishment acts as a deterrent" is unscorable.

b. (**important** because otherwise) he will do the **same** thing, will **keep** doing it, or will do it over **and over** or again **and again.**

c. (**important** so that) they won't do it again **right away,** won't get into **more** trouble, or won't **go out** or go **back** and steal again; (or so that) they won't be **able to** do it again (soon).

Form A

<u>d.</u> (**important** because) he was just being safe; (or because) his wife **could** have died (without the drug).

Note. (**Important** because) "his wife was dying" is unscorable.

Form B

<u>e.</u> (**important** because otherwise) not many people would be alive.

<u>f.</u> (**not important** because) it was better for her to die without pain.

TRANSITION 2/3

1: Exchanges--Prosocial Intentions

Sending lawbreakers to jail is **important:**

<u>a.</u> (Because) he knew what he was doing, should have known better, or should have realized what he was getting into.

Note. "(Because) he should have thought about it first" is unscorable.

<u>b.</u> (in order) to make them regret it; (or so that) they will **know** not to do it again.

Note. "(Because) he should suffer" is unscorable.

2: Equalities--Normative Expectations

Sending lawbreakers to jail is **important** because:

he should go to jail like any other lawbreaker; (because otherwise) it wouldn't be fair to others (who broke the law and have been punished); (because otherwise) others (who break the law) will think they shouldn't be punished, or would have to be let free.

3: Preferences--Prosocial Intentions

Sending lawbreakers to jail is **not important** because:

Form A

a. he **loves** or **cares for** his wife, or **just** wanted to save her.

Form B

b. he **loved** or **cared for** his wife, or **just** wanted to help her out of her pain.

4: Needs--Empathic Role-Taking

Sending lawbreakers to jail is **not important** because:

<u>a.</u> the judge might feel sorry for him, would have stolen, too, or wouldn't have wanted his wife to die.

<u>b.</u> he was desperate, or **tried** but couldn't get the money.

<u>c.</u> she was **in pain;** (or because) he was only putting her out of her misery or pain.

<u>d.</u> the husband will be needed by the children (if there are children); (or because) the children will need to be taken care of.

5: Needs--Prosocial Intentions

Sending lawbreakers to jail is:

<u>a.</u> (**important** but) it depends on his motives; (or unless) he had a **good** reason or a real cause.

<u>Note.</u> "It's important to know why he did it" or "he did something very important" is unscorable.

<u>b.</u> (**not important** because) he wasn't hurting anyone, was **only trying** to help, or **meant** to **help** her.

<u>Note.</u> **"(Not important** because) he helped her die" or "was helping her" is unscorable.

Form A

<u>c.</u> he was **only trying** to save her.

<u>Note.</u> "He was trying to save her" or "he saved a live" is unscorable.

6: Advantages--Relationships

Sending lawbreakers to jail is **important** because otherwise:

he will steal again **for someone he knows** or **loves.**

7: Advantages--Empathic Role-Taking

Sending lawbreakers to jail is **not important** because otherwise:

Form A

he couldn't see his wife.

8: Advantages--Normative Expectations

Sending lawbreakers to jail is **important** because:

<u>a.</u> the laws protect people; (in order) to make things safer; (or because otherwise) the world wouldn't be safe or would be a wreck or mess, (innocent) people could get hurt, or there would be **more** or a **lot of** crime.

<u>Note.</u> "(Otherwise) what kind of world would it be?" is unscorable.

<u>b.</u> (otherwise) they would persuade **others** to break the law.

STAGE 3:

Mutual and Prosocial

1: Relationships

This aspect is typically not evidenced on this norm.

2: Empathic Role-Taking

Sending lawbreakers to jail is **not important** because:

<u>a.</u> the judge should understand or have a heart, would have some feeling, should put himself or herself in the husband's place, or should take the situation into consideration.

Form B

<u>b.</u> he acted out of pity or empathy, or to end her suffering or agony; (or because) he didn't want **to see** her in pain.

3: Normative Expectations

Sending lawbreakers to jail is **important** because:

<u>a.</u> judges are supposed to give the sentence people **deserve;** (or because) that is what is expected of judges.

<u>b.</u> criminals must be **disciplined;** (or because otherwise) **hard** criminals would get off easily.

<u>c.</u> there is no **excuse** for wrongdoing or breaking the law; (or because otherwise) that **excuse** (for breaking the law) would become common.

<u>d.</u> (otherwise) the country would be berserk, there would be chaos or the world would be an unhappy place; (or because otherwise) everyone would be committing crimes **since they wouldn't have to pay for them** (by going to jail), or wouldn't have anything to lose.

4: Prosocial Intentions

Sending lawbreakers to jail is:

<u>a.</u> **(important)** if they have stolen to benefit themselves; (because otherwise) he would steal again for a **loved one;** (or **not important** because) he stole for a **loved one, out of** love, or for her **sake;** (because) he had good

intentions; (or because) he wasn't stealing for himself, for selfish gain, or just to get rid of her.

Note. "He stole for her" or "for his wife" is unscorable.

b. (**important** because) he knew or must have **known** that it was wrong; (in order) to help them **realize** that they have done wrong; (so that they can **learn** from their mistakes; (or but) he may already **realize** that what he did was wrong.

c. (**not important** because) he must have been under great strain or pressure, or was in anguish; (or because) he wouldn't have stolen ordinarily, or is not a common criminal.

Form A

d. (**not important** because) he had **tried** to be decent or nice; (because) the druggist had no compassion, was greedy, or is the guilty one; (or because) Heinz was the victim of the druggist.

5: Generalized Caring

Sending lawbreakers to jail is **not important** because:

Form A

he saved a **person's, someone's,** or a **human** life, or showed that (his wife's) life is worth more than a jail sentence, or is more important than **obeying** the law.

Note. "He saved a person" or "he saved a life" is unscorable.

6: Intrapersonal Approval

Sending lawbreakers to jail is **not important** because:

he has suffered enough already, or has (probably) punished **himself** enough.

TRANSITION 3/4

1: Empathic Role-Taking--Procedural Equity

Sending a lawbreaker to jail is:

a. (**important**) **depending on** the **circumstances** or the **case;** (but) exceptions may be allowable; (or but) there are too many variables for this to be cut-and-dried or the judge should **evaluate** the case or situation.

Note. "Depending on what he did," "(but) it depends on the judge," or "depending on the crime or how bad it was" is unscorable. Also, an unelaborated reference to "the circumstances" or "case" is unscorable.

b. (**not important** because) this was an emotional or moral **issue.**

2: Normative Expectations--Societal Requirements

Sending a lawbreaker to jail is **important** because:

a. that is what laws are for, you have to have law or order, or the law is the only order we have; (or because otherwise) there would be no sense, point, or value in having laws (if they are not enforced or followed).

Note. "The law was made to be followed" is unscorable.

b. the laws must be enforced (if they are to work).

c. (in order) to keep order or peace (in society); (so that) things don't get out of hand, or deviant behavior doesn't increase; (or because otherwise) there would be no control.

Note. "To deter others from wrongdoing" or "(because otherwise) there would be no law" is unscorable.

3: Normative Expectations--Basic Rights/Values

Sending a lawbreaker to jail is **important** because:

a. judicial leniency is why there is so much crime (in society).

Form B

b. no one has the right to take another's life; (or because) only God should decide such things.

c. widespread mercy-killing could weaken the laws (against mercy-killing).

4: Normative Expectations--Responsibility

Sending a lawbreaker to jail is **important**:

a. (because) he knew the consequences, **should** accept the consequences, or **should** be willing to pay the penalty.

Note. "(Because) that is the price you pay," or "(because) he should take his consequences" is unscorable.

b. as an example (to people) that if you break the law, you must pay the penalty; (so that) people will know that crime doesn't pay, or won't start thinking that stealing is all right; (because otherwise) the law won't be a guideline; (or because otherwise) people will lose sight of right and wrong, or wouldn't think twice about breaking the law.

Note. "(Because then) people would do what they want" or (because otherwise) the law won't be a deterrent" is unscorable.

c. (because) a judge's job is to uphold or enforce the law; (or because) the judge should not play favorites.

Note. "(Because) a judge's job is to protect people" is unscorable.

5: Normative Expectations--Consistent Practices

Sending a lawbreaker to jail is **important** because:

a. people cannot steal whenever they feel **dissatisfied.**

b. people would break the law and use **this case** as an excuse.

Form B

c. people could murder and claim mercy-killing.

6: Prosocial Intentions—Basic Rights/Values

Sending a lawbreaker to jail is:

a. (**important** because) the judge should be respected; (or because other-wise) people would lose respect for the law.

b. (**important**) if the person is misguided, or if that way the person can be rehabilitated; (but) jail does not help the individual, or may do more harm than good; (or **not important** because) he did it for **humane** or humanitarian reasons.

c. (**not important** in order) to set an example for people to be compassion-ate or kind, or to promote caring or good will.

Form A

d. (**not important**) as an example for people to be concerned about human life, or because he saved **another** human life.

e. (**not important** because) Heinz was the victim of circumstances beyond his control, or of one **who would let others die** (for the sake of a profit); (or because) it was the druggist who was responsible for her death.

7: Prosocial Intentions—Character

Sending a lawbreaker to jail is **not important** because:

he acted with her consent.

8: Prosocial Intentions—Standards of Conscience

Sending a lawbreaker to jail is **not important** because:

he felt it was right, or was doing what he **thought** was right [Type R, rela-tivism of personal values].

Note. "(Because) he thought he was doing what was best" is unscorable.

9: Generalized Caring—Basic Rights/Values

Sending lawbreakers to jail is **not important** because:

he saved (the life of) **another** or a **fellow human** (being).

10: Generalized Caring—Procedural Equity

Sending lawbreakers to jail is **not important** because:

this was a life or death situation; (or because) saving a life is more im-portant than the druggist's greed.

Note. "It was a life" is unscorable.

STAGE 4:

Systemic and Standard

1: Societal Requirements

Sending a lawbreaker to jail is **important** because:

a. the law is the backbone of (our) society.

b. the laws are **needed** to protect society.

c. the law **must** be enforced **even if a** (particular) **law is poor or wrong.**

2: Basic Rights/Values

Sending a lawbreaker to jail is:

a. (**important** because) laws help humanity; (in order) to help or protect **society;** (because otherwise) there is no society; if the lawbreaker is a threat to society; (or **not important** because) the husband has not acted against society; (or because) punishment in this case would not be in the public interest.

Note. "(Because) lawbreakers are dangerous" is unscorable.

b. (**important** because) laws were created to protect rights; or for the sake of, or in order to give respect to, property rights; (or so that) the rights of others will be respected or protected.

c. (**important**) if living together (in society) is to have meaning (for people).

d. (**important**) if they can learn to become productive, or to contribute to society (while in jail); (or **not important** because) the person may have worked for the betterment of society, or made a contribution (to society).

e. (**important** because) the sentencing may stimulate reform, or improve the conscience of the community; (or **not important** because) the judge may favorably influence society by giving a lenient sentence, or may make an innovation or improvement in legal justice in justifying leniency.

f. (**not important** because) society is composed of individuals, or the individual should be the basis of society.

Form A

g. (**not important** in order) to recognize or establish the precedent that human life comes before property; (because) a life-saving drug should be available to anyone; (or because) the laws should protect life, or society should value life.

h. (**not important** because) life is sacred.

Form B

i. (**important** because) life is sacred.

3: Responsibility

Sending a lawbreaker to jail is **important**:

a. (because) that is the judge's responsibility; (because) the judge accepted this position or has **sworn** to uphold the law.

b. (because) he broke the law of his own free will or because of his convictions; (because) he **must** (be willing to) accept or realize the consequences, or be held responsible or accountable.

c. (because) if one lives in, accepts, or benefits from society, one has an obligation or must be willing to live by its rules or accept its restrictions; (or because) the sentence may show people that there must be limitations to freedom, or that there are responsibilities as well as rights.

d. (because) anyone who harms another has no right to live in society.

e. (but) society is responsible for criminals or crime.

4: Character

This aspect is not typically evidenced on this norm.

5: Consistent Practices

Sending a lawbreaker to jail is **important** because:

a. the laws have to be consistent, or standards must be upheld; (because) **inconsistencies** or **exceptions** would lead to subjective actions, lawbreaking, or chaos; (in order) to keep society in order, or to avoid setting a dangerous precedent; (or because otherwise) people would take the law into their own hands, or would break the law whenever they feel **justified**.

b. the judge **must** go by law or **must** not be influenced by his feelings, emotions, or biases; (or) if jail is required by law.

6: Procedural Equity

Sending a lawbreaker to jail is **not important** because:

a. the judge **must** recognize exceptions or special circumstances; (because) each case is different or unique, or **must** be considered separately; (because) the law **cannot** always apply appropriately, or there **cannot** be set rules for all cases, (or because) the judge should interpret the law.

b. (because) the judge can give the minimum sentence, should show wisdom, or should use discretion.

c. justice should be tempered with mercy or understanding; (or because) the law or judicial system should or must be flexible or fair.

7: Standards of Conscience

Sending lawbreakers to jail is **not important** because:

Form A

Heinz was responding to a **higher law** or God's law, or was going by a **personal law.**

THE THEORY-DEFINING LEVEL:

Sociopolitical Philosophy

TP: Theoretical Principles

Sending a lawbreaker to jail is **important** but:

Form A

the **right** to **life** comes before or takes precedence over the **right** to **property.**

9

Norm 5:

CONSCIENCE

Many of the sequences discussed in Legal Justice can also be found on Conscience. A distinctive focus of conscience justifications, however, is on the relation of the "lawbreaking out of conscience" factor to judicial decisions. These justifications generally imply certain qualitatively distinct understandings of conscience at the different levels. The Stage 1 evaluation of leniency as not important because the husband's conscience "was only his mind" suggests that the psychological reality of conscience is not understood: the frequently low evaluation of conscience may be because its lack of physical salience (since it is immaterial) gives way in the child's attention to the concrete **act** of having stolen. On the other hand, where "conscience" is embodied figuratively as a voice of unilateral authority, leniency may be recommended ("his conscience told him to do it"). At Stage 2, conscience is understood as a psychologically significant agency; however, the conscience agency is construed as a kind of external adversary force. Leniency may be justified as important because the husband "couldn't help" obeying his "powerful" conscience, or might have been "tricked" by his conscience; or leniency may be seen as **not** important because the husband should learn how to "handle" his conscience. (Note that whereas the authoritarian appeal "he did what his conscience **told** him" is Stage 1, a view of the action as pragmatically understandable—"his conscience **was telling** him to do it"; or "he was **just** doing what his conscience told him"—is scored as Stage 2.)

Conscience continues to be a powerful force at Transition 2/3, but the "power" is construed in terms of a "hounding" or attention-seeking persuasiveness. Thus, leniency may be important because "a conscience can convince anyone into doing anything" and is something "you can't ignore," something which if unattended to "could have driven him into an early grave." By the same structural token of thought, however, conscience may be **unimportant** because "you don't always have to listen to your conscience." By Stage 3, the power of conscience has become self-accepted ("he wouldn't have been able to live **with himself**") and psychological in its nature ("he had a **psychological** problem"; cf. Transition 2/3: "he had a problem") and effects ("he could have gone **insane**"; cf. the more concrete "early grave" reference of Transition 2/3). There is also the concern that punishing the husband may cause people to get a bad impression of conscience ("people would think their conscience is no good or might never listen to their conscience"; cf. the possibly pragmatic Transition 2/3 justification that you "can't ignore conscience" or, alternatively, "don't always have to listen to your conscience"). Conscience may also be seen in unfavorable terms at Stage 3, however. It is pointed out that "conscience isn't always right" since "you could have a selfish conscience." There is also the suspicion of conscience as an easy "excuse" for antinormative conduct which could become "common" if the husband isn't punished (cf. the more outcome-oriented Stage 2 concern with everyone's "getting off easy"). This suspicion further evolves at later levels. Although at Transition 3/4 the dictates of conscience may be granted a certain subjective validity ("he was doing what he **thought** was **right**," Type R; cf. the partially outcome-oriented Transition 2/3 justification for punishment: "if he thinks it is right he'll do it again"), the sense in which the act of conscience was "right" may be juxtaposed against other senses in which it is nonetheless "wrong" ("although he was morally right, he was still legally wrong"; or, "acts of conscience can still be harmful"). Occasionally, "true" conscience is construed at Transition 3/4 as an objective or rational agency which can be undermined (leniency because "one's emotions can get in the way of guidance from one's conscience"). More typically, however, the Stage 3 suspicion of conscience is still manifested at Transition 3/4, although on the level of practices ("law should be the determining factor in sentencing, not conscience"; or "if everyone did what their conscience told them, we'd be in big trouble"). By Stage 4, the framework of procedural precedent and practice is consolidated. For example, those who broke the law out of conscience may be dealt with leniently, provided they can prove they acted "responsibly" or "not arbitrarily."

Conscience at Stage 4 is more typically evaluated negatively, however, because it is seen as a subjective and therefore inadequate basis for action: conscience is "only one person's morality" which may be "wrong from the viewpoint of society" and "too vague to use in court"; "you must have a common standard for judging acts of conscience," so that not just "anything can be **justified**" as right, and so that people are not able to break the law "just because they **think** they have a good reason." The Stage 3 concern with the antisocial features of some consciences ("your conscience isn't always right, you could have a mean conscience") is related at Stage 4 to the functional necessity for the legal institution ("the whole **reason for laws** is that conscience is not always right").

THE MONTAGES

Stage 1 (Unilateral and Simplistic)

Going easy on lawbreakers who have acted out of conscience is **important** because: "The husband did what his conscience **told** him to (1), and it was his conscience (not he) that got bad ideas from someplace. After all, the husband is a nice person (4)." But it is **not important** because: "Your conscience is only your mind (2), and it told you to do something that was wrong (4). You shouldn't steal, because people who steal have to go to jail (3)."

Transition 1/2

Going easy on lawbreakers who have acted out of conscience is **important** because: "If Heinz hadn't stolen it, his wife **could** have died (1, Form A)." But it is **not important** because: "He should be taught a lesson and get set straight (2) so that he won't do it again (1)."

Stage 2 (Exchanging and Instrumental)

Going easy on lawbreakers who have acted out of conscience is **important** because: "His conscience **was telling** him to do it, and he couldn't help it since his conscience was so powerful (3). He might have been tricked by his conscience. Besides, he did **want** to help his wife, and that's what she wanted (4). If the judge **needed** the drug, he would have taken it, too (5); otherwise, Heinz's wife **could** have died (6, Form A)." But it is **not important** because: "He knew he was taking a chance. He shouldn't have blamed it on his conscience (4), but instead should have handled his conscience. You can control your conscience if you try (3), but it's easy to let your conscience take over when you want something (4). The people who talk about their conscience could be trying to lie or trick the judge in order to get off easy. But they'll do the **same** thing again once they're free (6)."

Transition 2/3

Going easy on lawbreakers who have acted out of conscience is **important** because: "They **just** did what their consciences told them (2). He loved his wife and didn't want to **lose** her (2, Form A). He was **only trying** to help someone (3). After all, the judge would have done the same thing (4). Your conscience can be very persuasive, and if you try to ignore it you can be driven into an early grave (5). The husband did have a problem (6), and anyone can make a mistake (7). Of course, it does depend on the pain his wife was in (4). But it is **not important** because: "He should have known better and realized what he was getting into (1). You don't always have to listen to your conscience (5). And if he thinks it is right, he'll do it again and keep on **acting up** (7)."

Stage 3 (Mutual and Prosocial)

Going easy on lawbreakers who have acted out of conscience is **important** because: "The judge should understand that the husband may have had **psychological** problems (2) since he was under such stress in the situation and was only acting **out of** love (4). He surely has suffered enough already (6)." But it is **not important** because: "Sometimes even good people must be reprimanded, and the husband should be punished to let him know that what he did was wrong. After all, one's conscience isn't always right or the best guide (4). Conscience is a poor excuse, and if the judge is easy, then the excuse will become common (3). Then people would think that conscience is no good and never listen to it (5)."

Transition 3/4

Going easy on lawbreakers who have acted out of conscience is **important** because: "The person may have acted **out of** humanity (6), as in life-or-death **cases** (7, Form A). Besides, one's emotions can get in the way of guidance from one's conscience. Or, perhaps he **felt** that what he was doing was **right** (8)." Still, it **depends on** the situation, and regarding **this** situation, the judge should use good judgment (1)." But it is **not important** because: "Otherwise there would be no order (2), and some acts based on conscience can cause more harm than good and be legally wrong (3). The husband should have thought about the consequences before listening to his conscience and now **should** accept those consequences. After all, it is the law rather than conscience that should be the determining factor here, and the judge should **enforce** the law without playing favorites (4). Otherwise people could murder or do anything whenever they were **dissatisfied** and plead conscience (5). Making exceptions would quickly lead to disrespect for the law (6)."

Stage 4 (Systemic and Standard)

Going easy on lawbreakers who have acted out of conscience is **important** because: "One's conscience may be consistent with **the common** morality and may respect life or the quality of life. After all, society should be based on moral values (2). Perhaps the husband can prove that he acted responsibly (4). Remember that the law **cannot** take into account every circumstance, and the judge should interpret the law (6)." But it is **not important** because: "Leniency would set a dangerous precedent (5) which would be harmful for society. If the husband goes to jail, that may even stimulate reform and improve the conscience of society (2). But in any event, the judge has a **responsibility** to enforce the law, and the husband **must** accept the consequences of his actions (3). After all, the whole **reason for laws** is that conscience is not always right. You must have a common standard for judging acts of conscience, because "conscience" is otherwise too vague a defense to use in court (5)."

STAGE 1:

Unilateral and Simplistic

1: Unilateral Authority

Going easy on people who have acted out of conscience is:

a. (**important** because) his conscience **told** him to do it, or he did what she told him to do.

Note. Elaborated versions of this justification, e.g., "(because) **he was right to do what** his conscience told him," are unscorable.

b. (**not important** because) it says "don't steal" in the Bible.

2: Status

Going easy on people who have acted out of conscience is **not important** because:

his conscience was only his mind.

3: Rules

Going easy on people who have acted out of conscience is:

a. (**important** because) you should always do what your conscience **tells** you (to do).

Note. "You should always go by your conscience" is unscorable.

b. (**not important** because) you should not steal.

c. (**not important** because) you have to go to jail.

Note. Qualified rule-like assertions, e.g., **"even if your conscience told you to do it,** you still have to go to jail" or "he **still** broke the law" are unscorable.

4: Labels

Going easy on people who have acted out of conscience is:

a. (**important** because) he is nice or good.

b. (**important** because) something gave his conscience bad ideas.

c. (**not important** because) his mind told him to do something wrong; (because) his conscience shouldn't have told him to do that; (or because) he took something that wasn't his.

Note. Elaborated versions of the justification, e.g., "(because) his conscience should have told him not to steal **no matter what,**" are unscorable.

5: Punitive Consequences

This aspect is not typically evidenced on this norm.

TRANSITION 1/2

1: Labels--Advantages

Going easy on people who have acted out of conscience is:

a. (**not important** because otherwise) he will or might do it again.

Form A

b. (**important** because) if Heinz hadn't stolen it, his wife **could** have died.

2: Punitive Consequences--Exchanges

Going easy on people who have acted out of conscience is **important** because:

he (still) should be taught a lesson; (or because) the punishment could set him straight.

STAGE 2:

Exchanging and Instrumental

1: Exchanges

Going easy on people who have acted out of conscience is **not important** because:

a. he shouldn't have blamed it on his conscience.

b. he was taking a chance or risk, or chose to steal; (because) if you are caught you go to jail; (or because) he should pay for his crime.

2: Equalities

This aspect is not typically evidenced on this norm.

3: Freedoms

Going easy on people who have acted out of conscience is **important** because:

your conscience is powerful; (because) his conscience was forcing or **was telling** him to do it; (because) he couldn't help it or was **just** doing what his conscience told him; (or **not important** because) you should control your conscience, have to (learn how to) handle your conscience, or shouldn't do what your conscience or someone (tries to) tell you to do.

Note. "(Because) conscience is a powerful force for truth" is unscorable.

4: Preferences

Going easy on people who have acted out of conscience is:

<u>a.</u> (**important** because) he was tricked by his conscience, or might not have done it on purpose.

<u>b.</u> (**important** because) he **wanted** to help his wife, or stole for someone he **liked.**

<u>c.</u> (**not important** because) he shouldn't have blamed it on his conscience; (or because then) he will let his conscience take over when he wants or likes something.

Form A

<u>d.</u> (**important** because) his wife wanted to live.

Form B

<u>e.</u> (**important** because) his wife wanted to die.

5: Needs

Going easy on people who have acted out of conscience is **important** because:

<u>a.</u> she needed the drug.

<u>b.</u> if the judge **needed** the drug, he would have taken it, too.

Form A

<u>c.</u> Heinz was (too) poor (to pay).

6: Advantages

Going easy on people who have acted out of conscience is:

<u>a.</u> (**not important** because) they could be lying or trying to trick the judge.

<u>b.</u> (**not important** because otherwise) everyone would (lie to) get off easy, would figure they wouldn't get in trouble or will think they can get away with it; (or because then) no one would be in jail.

<u>c.</u> (**not important** because otherwise) there would be killing or stealing all the time).

d. (**not important** because otherwise) he will **keep on** stealing, or will do the **same** thing.

Form A

e. (**important** because otherwise) his wife **could** have died.

Note. "(Important because) his wife was dying" is unscorable.

Form B

f. (**important** because otherwise) he will **keep on** killing.

TRANSITION 2/3

1: Exchanges--Prosocial Intentions

Going easy on people who have acted out of conscience is **not important** because:

he knew what he was doing, should have known better, or should have realized what he was getting into.

Note. "(Because) he should have thought about it first" is unscorable.

2: Preferences--Prosocial Intentions

Going easy on people who have acted out of conscience is **important** because:

a. they **just** did what their conscience told them, or were **just** following their intuitions.

b. he **loved** his wife.

Form A

c. he didn't want to **lose** his wife.

3: Needs-- Prosocial Intentions

Going easy on people who have acted out of conscience is:

a. (**important** because) he was **only trying** to help someone, or had a **good** reason; (or because) people who act out of conscience help others.

Note. "He helped her" or "he was trying to save a life" is unscorable.

b. (**not important** because) he should have asked for help.

4: Needs--Empathic Role-Taking

Going easy on people who have acted out of conscience is **important** because:

a. the judge would have done the same thing.

b. she might have been **in** a lot of pain; (or but) it depends on the pain.

5: Freedoms--Intrapersonal Approval

Going easy on people who have acted out of conscience is **important** because:

you can't ignore your conscience, or a conscience can convince anyone into doing anything; (because) your conscience can (sometimes) make you do **harsh** or **hurtful** things or send you to an early grave; (or **not important** because) you don't always have to **listen** to your conscience, or (sometimes) you shouldn't **listen** to your conscience.

6: Advantages--Empathic Role-Taking

Going easy on people who have acted out of conscience is **important** because:

he had a problem.

7: Advantages--Prosocial Intentions

Going easy on people who have acted out of conscience is:

a. (**important** because) anyone can make a mistake.

b. (**not important** because) **if he thinks it's right**, he'll do it again; (or because otherwise) he might go on a stealing binge or could keep on **acting up.**

STAGE 3:

Mutual and Prosocial

1: Relationships

This aspect is not typically evidenced on this norm.

2: Empathic Role-Taking

Going easy on people who have acted out of conscience is **important** because:

a. the judge would understand the situation or should have a heart.

b. (some) people would go insane (if they couldn't act to get something off their mind); (because) the pressure can affect your mind or can cause **psychological** problems; (or because) the husband may have been emotionally unstable (when he stole the drug).

3: Normative Expectations

Going easy on people who have acted out of conscience is **not important** because:

a. that's no excuse; (or because) you should think instead about (the fact that you are) breaking the law.

b. (otherwise) the excuse will become common, or others might say they acted out of conscience (after they've done something wrong).

c. there would be chaos or confusion.

4: Prosocial Intentions

Going easy on lawbreakers who acted out of conscience is:

a. (**important** because) he did it for her benefit, cared about her, or acted **out of** love.

b. (**important** because) he was only human, was under stress, or was acting from the heart (and not from the mind).

c. (**important** because) of the situation.

d. (**important** because) if he confesses, he should be forgiven.

e. (**not important** because) you could be a selfish person or mentally ill, or could have a mean conscience, warped mind, or bad intentions.

Note. "Send him to the crazy house" is unscorable.

f. (**not important** because) one's conscience isn't always right, good, or the best guide.

g. (**not important** because) he knew he shouldn't steal; (in order) to let him know that what he did was wrong or that he was breaking the law; (or because sometimes) even good people must be reprimanded.

5: Generalized Caring

Going easy on people who have acted out of conscience is **not important** because otherwise:

people would think their conscience is no good or might never listen to their conscience.

6: Intrapersonal Approval

Going easy on lawbreakers who have acted out of conscience is **important** because:

he wouldn't have been able to live with himself (if he hadn't acted), has suffered enough already or has (probably) punished himself enough.

TRANSITION 3/4

1: Empathic Role-Taking--Procedural Equity

Going easy on lawbreakers who have acted out of conscience is **important** but:

it **depends on** the **circumstances, situation,** or **case;** (or but) the judge should **evaluate** the situation, consider the **particular** situation or **this** situation, or should use good judgment.

Note. "(But) it depends" or "(but) it's up to the judge" is unscorable. Also, an unelaborated reference to "the circumstances" or "the situation" is unscorable.

2: Normative Expectations--Societal Requirements

Going easy on lawbreakers who have acted out of conscience is **not important** because otherwise:

there would be no order, things would get out of hand, or we would be in big trouble.

3: Normative Expectations--Basic Rights/Values

Going easy on lawbreakers who have acted out of conscience is **not important** because:

a. although he was morally right, he was still legally wrong; (because) acts of conscience can still be harmful or inappropriate; (or because) some acts (based on conscience) could cause more harm than good.

b. judicial leniency is why there is so much crime (in society).

4: Normative Expectations--Responsibility

Going easy on lawbreakers who have acted out of conscience is **not important** because:

a. he should have thought about the consequences before listening to his conscience, or should have had better judgment; (or because) he **should** face or accept the consequences, or should be **willing to** pay the penalty.

Note. "(Because) he should have thought about it first" or "he should **pay** the consequences" is unscorable.

b. the law or justice (rather than conscience) should be the determining factor; (because) conscience is irrelevant; (because) the judge should decide the same way whether conscience is brought up or not; (or because) the judge should consider not only conscience but also the crime.

c. (because) the judge should **enforce** the law, or should not play favorites.

5: Normative Expectations--Consistent Practices

Going easy on lawbreakers who act of conscience is **not important** because:

a. (sometimes) your conscience may say to **murder;** (or because otherwise) people could do **anything** and plead conscience.

Note. "Sometimes your conscience may say to kill" is unscorable.

b. people cannot steal whenever they feel **dissatisfied.**

6: Prosocial Intentions--Basic Rights/Values

Going easy on lawbreakers who act out of conscience is:

a. (**important**) if the person acted **out of** humanity or if the act was a **humane** one.

b. (**not important** because otherwise) it will lead to disrespect for the law or authority.

7: Generalized Caring--Procedural Equity

Going easy on lawbreakers who act out of conscience is **important**:

Form A

in life-or-death **cases** or **situations**.

8: Intrapersonal Approval--Standards of Conscience

Going easy on lawbreakers who act out of conscience is **important** because:

<u>a.</u> he **felt** it was **right,** or was doing what he **thought** was **right** [Type R].

<u>Note.</u> "(Because) you should do what your conscience tells you to do" or "(because) he thought it was the best thing to do" is unscorable.

<u>b.</u> one's emotions can get in the way of (guidance from) one's conscience.

STAGE 4:

Systemic and Standard

1: Societal Requirements

Going easy on lawbreakers who have acted out of conscience is **important** because:

The law **must** be enforced, **even if a** (particular) **law is poor or wrong.**

2: Basic Rights/Values

Going easy on lawbreakers who have acted out of conscience is:

<u>a.</u> (**important**) if one's conscience is consistent with society or **the common** morality, or if the act has helped society or was humanitarian; (**not important** because) conscience is only one person's morality, or some acts of conscience may be wrong according to or from the viewpoint of society; (or because) leniency may be harmful to society.

<u>b.</u> (**important**) if one's conscience respects life or the quality of life.

<u>c.</u> (**important** because) society or the judicial system is or should be based on moral values.

<u>d.</u> (**not important** because) the prison sentence may stimulate social or legal reform, or improve the conscience of the community.

3: Responsibility

Going easy on lawbreakers who have acted out of conscience is **not important** because:

<u>a.</u> the judge has a **responsibility** (to enforce the law).

<u>b.</u> a person **must** be responsible for his or her actions, or **must** (be prepared to) accept the consequences.

<u>Note.</u> "The person must take his consequences" is unscorable.

4: Character

Going easy on lawbreakers who have acted out of conscience is **important:**

if they can prove they acted responsibly or not arbitrarily.

5: Consistent Practices

Going easy on lawbreakers who have acted out of conscience is **not important** because:

<u>a.</u> the (whole) **reason for laws** is that conscience is not always right; (because) you must have a common standard or rule for judging acts of conscience; (because) leniency would set a dangerous precedent; (because) the husband should not have taken the law into his own hands; (because) people **cannot do whatever** they want; (or because then) people would break the law whenever they feel **justified** or led by conscience.

<u>Note.</u> "(Because) people shouldn't do whatever they want" is unscorable.

<u>b.</u> "conscience" is too vague (to use in court); or (because) the judge may not be able to determine whether or not the person is mentally fit.

6: Procedural Equity

Going easy on lawbreakers who have acted out of conscience is **important** because:

<u>a.</u> laws **cannot** take into account every circumstance; (because) each case is different; (or because) the judge should interpret the law.

<u>b.</u> (because) the judge should temper justice with mercy; (or because) justice can be accomplished with temperance.

7: Standards of Conscience

Going easy on lawbreakers who have acted out of conscience is **important** because:

Form A

Heinz was responding to a **higher law** or was going by a **personal law.**

Norm 6:

FAMILY AFFILIATION

The evolution of sociomoral reflection on the general normative value of family affiliation can be described in terms of justification for: (1) children helping or obeying their parents; and (2) parents keeping promises to their children. The family affiliation norm juxtaposes the first value against the second by depicting a parent-child situation where helpfulness and obedience is expected from a child despite a broken promise. Evolution through Stages 2, 3, and 4 encompasses an A orientation where helping parents is justified without any effort to deal with the injustice; and a B orientation which addresses the significance of the injustice for the parent-child relationship. Thus, helping one's parents at Stage 2 orientation A is justified by appeal to possible instrumental gain. The A orientation is represented at Stage 3 by appeals to the subservient role that is normatively expected of children; and at Stage 4 by appeal to the child's subordinate position in relation to the entitlements and prerogatives of parental authority. In contrast, Orientation B justifications, supporting the value of keeping promises to one's children, appeal to role-taking considerations: to the contradiction between the parent's privileges and what the parent is demanding that the children do (Stage 2); to how the parents would feel if they were treated in a way which destroys trust in the relationship (Stage 3); and to the unfortunate loss of respect for one's parents which must rightfully result from the abuse of parental authority (Stage 4).

Helping-parents justifications can also be developmentally analyzed specifically in terms of responses to the suggestion in Question 6 that the parent needs the money to pay for food for the family. This supposition directly informs Stage 2 justifications based on preferences ("you would rather eat") and needs ("they need to eat"; or, "your parents may be all you have"). Stage 3 construes the need as a general predicament (it is "an emergency" or "a matter of starvation" or means that "the parents are having hard times") which should elicit understanding (since food is **so** important, and the parents "make mistakes, too"). Stage 4 introduces the consideration of functional necessity: dealing with the predicament constitutes a "priority" which the child **must** understand as occupying "a higher level of importance."

Justifications for the importance of parents keeping their promises may appeal, at various levels, to the consequences of parents breaking their promises for the child or for the relationship. The appeal at Stage 1 is to negative global affect: the child will be "sad," will "feel bad," or may "cry."

By Transition 1/2 this consideration has become merely conditional (the child "may feel bad"; "cry" is Stage 1 even if conditional) and causal (it could make the child feel bad"). At Stage 2, the emotion consequence is given a connotation of disadvantage or retaliation: the child will "get mad" or "won't like" the parent. By Transition 2/3, a relationship orientation is intimated: the child will no longer "trust" the parent (2/3 because the thought could still be strictly pragmatic, e.g., won't trust the parent "to do things for the child"). Once the relationship orientation is clearer (the child won't "have trust in the parent" or "there would be a loss of trust"; note the noun or condition status of "trust"), the thought can be scored Stage 3.

At higher levels, the concern is with trust as a functional necessity (e.g., "children have to be able to trust" their parents; Transition 3/4), even for the sake of society (Stage 4). There is also a concern, at the higher levels, with the kind of model the parent is providing. Transition 3/4 appeals to the importance of "consistency" in the child's upbringing, especially when the child's "character" is "still forming"; hence the parent should be a good "guide," "teacher," or "model." At Stage 4, the specific prescription is that the parents should provide a model of integrity.

Although one of the Family Affiliation questions specifically removes from consideration the story element that the children's money was earned (Question 1), many respondents (especially younger ones) make use of this element anyway on Family Affiliation (use of this assumption is appropriate on Property, where it is re-established). Whereas Stage 2 justifications suggest simply that the child "earned it," Transition 2/3 offers elaborations suggesting a possibility of empathic appreciation of the child's feelings of pride and deservingness (e.g., "she earned it all by herself," or "really wanted to go; cf. the flatly instrumental "wanted to go," Stage 2). By Stage 3, the suggestion that the child "deserves" her reward is explicit, as is the emotionally empathic concern that she will "feel hurt" or "unloved." A relevant concern at higher levels is with adverse effects on the child's character development (Transition 3/4) or, more specifically, on the child's sense of responsibility (Stage 4).

Many of the distinctions on the Family Affiliation norm are rather subtle. Some of these distinctions occur where an elaboration of a justificatory response permits a more discriminative stage assessment for the response. For example, the Transition 1/2 suggestion that parents "can break promises" could be Stage 1 (Unilateral Authority) or Stage 2 (Pragmatic Needs), but the elaborated version, "parents can break promises if they need to" is discriminatively Stage 2. The Transition 2/3 anticipation that the children will be "let down" becomes discriminatively Stage 3 with the empathic addition "by their own parents." The concern with whether the parents will still "love" an unhelpful child (Transition 2/3 because the frame of reference could be that of calculative disadvantages, Stage 2) becomes clearly Stage 3 with an elaboration that conceptualizes the concern in emotional or personal terms (whether the child will feel unloved or will think that the parents don't love him). Also a prescription of love makes possible a Stage 3 rating. Whereas an appeal to not losing trust is Stage 3, an appeal to the functional necessity for not losing trust is Transition 3/4. Also a conceptualization of the Transition 3/4 appeal to "priorities" in terms of positional requirements ("the child must understand priorities") is rated Stage 4. In the opposite direction, the Transition 3/4 concern with children showing "respect" (which could relate to a hierarchy of positional statuses in the family, Stage 4) is demoted to a straight Stage 3 response given an elaboration implying shared role expectations ("children are supposed to respect their parents").

Discriminations generated by significant syntactical alteration are often even more subtle than those which stem from differences in justificatory elaborations. Whereas the suggestion that the child should "thank" the parents is Transition 2/3 (since it could reflect an exchange orientation, Stage 2), the less act-oriented "should **be thankful**" is rated Stage 3 because it connotes the relationship-oriented sentiment of interpersonal appreciation. The justification of helping one's parents in order "to be nice" (which usually reflects a concern with acquiring a positive label, Stage 1) should not be confused with the use of "nice" as a term of social approval for the expression of underlying prosocial intentions (helping the parents is nice **of** the children).

Apart from the elaborative and syntactical kinds, other distinctions are less subtle but nonetheless sometimes trip up raters. On Form B, the thought that the parents "will find out anyway" is Transition 1/2 (since it may connote an assumption of punishment as an inevitability, Stage 1), whereas the point that "if Louise keeps quiet, the mother will never know" is clearly calculative (hence Stage 2). Whereas the suggestion that the parents may have had a "good reason" is Transition 2/3 (since "good" could be meant in a pragmatic sense), the consideration that the parent "may have tried to do the best thing" for the child is rated Stage 3 since the referent of benevolence is clear. (The elaborative qualifier, "in this instance" may prompt a Transition 3/4 rating.) Concerns with the child's self-evaluation shift from a feelings orientation ("the child will feel better about himself," Stage 3) to "self-esteem" (Transition 3/4) to personal dignity ("self-worth," Stage 4). Another set of shifts along these three levels is from normative expectations for helping ("children are part of the family," Stage 3) to a group-oriented declaration ("everyone in the family should help," Transition 3/4,) and finally to a direct appeal to "contribute" to the "family unit" (Stage 4). Finally, simple references to respect ("children should respect their parents," promise-breaking parents "lose their children's respect") are Transition 3/4, but an assertion that the parent must **earn** the child's respect specifically reflects a concern with equitable procedures, Stage 4.

THE MONTAGES

Stage 1 (Unilateral and Simplistic)

Helping one's parents is **important** because: "It's your parents, and parents are grown-ups (2). You should always obey your parents and tell them what you do (3), so that you are good and nice. Then the parents will be happy (4). If you don't help them, you may get spanked (5)." **But keeping promises to one's children is important** because: "Parents should never break promises (3), because if they do their children **will** feel bad or might cry (2)."

Transition 1/2

Helping one's parents is **important** because: "Children should do what their parents tell them to (1). The parents can break a promise (2). Besides, if the children don't help, the parent **may** feel bad or steal to get the money (3). Also, if the children don't help, the parents will find out anyway (4). Perhaps if the children help the parents, the parents won't break a promise again (3)." **But keeping promises to one's children is important** because: "If the parents don't, it could **make** the children sad (3)."

Stage 2 (Exchanging and Instrumental)

Helping one's parents is **important**: "Because the parents do a lot for the children, like pay for things. You owe them a lot and should return the favor (1); that is something you should want to do. Besides, they can take their money back **if they want to** (4). After all, the parents need the money so they can eat (5), and if the children help them, then the parents will help the children later or at least won't bother them. The child could go to the camp or concert another time, and you won't like yourself if you don't help (6)." **But keeping promises to one's children is important** because: "Taking the money back is unfair. The parents want the children to keep their promises, so the parents should keep theirs (1). Children are equal to parents, and children can't break promises, so parents shouldn't, either (2). The child worked for the money (3) and needs it (5). If the parents break their promises, their children won't like them and may get angry (6)."

Transition 2/3

Helping one's parents is **important** because: "The parents **love** their children, **try to** help, and do **so** much. Who brought you into the world, anyway? The children **would want** the parents to help them, and should **thank** the parents by helping (1). **If you love** your parents, you'll help them, and after all, the food is for everyone (4). The parents **really** need the children's **help** (5) and have a **good** reason (6). It will get the parents and children back together for the children to help, and then the parents will still **love** their children (7)." **But keeping promises to one's children is important** because: "The parents don't like it if their children were to break **their** promises (1). After all, the child **went out** and earned the money **all by himself** (2); the child worked **hard** and **really** wanted to go (3). If the parents don't keep their promises, the children will not believe them or count on them for help (7)."

Stage 3 (Mutual and Prosocial)

Helping one's parents is important because: "The parents **are always helping** their children. The children should **think of** how much their parents have done for them and be **thankful**. After all, the children expect the parents to understand when the children break promises, so the children should help, especially for the sake of the relationship (1). The children should also forgive them; after all, parents are only human, and they are **in** need. If you don't help them, they'll feel hurt (2). Besides, children are part of the family and **supposed to** respect their parents (3). It is nice **of** the children to help, but they should also give **out of** love knowing that their parents are only trying to do what's best for them (4). That way, they'll feel better about themselves (6)." **But keeping promises to one's children is important** because: "Otherwise the children will **lose** trust and stop believing in their parents (1). Promises mean a lot to children. If they are let down **by their own parents,** they will **think** that their parents don't love them (2). After all, they did sacrifice and deserve to go (3). Keeping promises will **show** the children that the parents do love them (4)."

Transition 3/4

Helping one's parents is **important** because: "The parent's word should be law (5), and children should respect their parents (6). After all, **everyone in the family** should be willing to help out. That way, the child would learn to share, and the parent would realize how responsible the child is (7). Besides, it would be good for the child's self-esteem (11)." **But keeping promises to one's children is important** because: "It is important to **build** up trust, and children **have to be able** to trust their parents (1). Keeping promises will make for a closer and more harmonious family and prevent loss of respect from the children (2). Although parents do have many responsibilities and sometimes can't keep promises because priorities change (3), they should try because one's word is one's bond (7) and the child is old enough to be treated on an equal basis (8). Yet the child is also still developing and looks up to the parent; the parent should be a good influence so that the child learns honesty and is taught responsibility (9). It is a way of respecting the child (10)."

Stage 4 (Systemic and Standard)

Helping one's parents is **important** because: "The family **must** come before recreational needs, and the child **must** understand priorities (1). Children should **contribute** for the sake of family **unity** (2) and should remember that the parent is in charge. The child should take responsibility toward the needs of the family (3)." **But keeping promises to one's children is important** because: "Parents have an **obligation** to keep their word (3) and to provide an example of **character** for the sake of the child's achievement of self-sufficiency and development as an individual with a **sense of** responsibility (4). Parents must earn their children's respect (6), both for the sake of the parents' self-respect, and so that the child will have a sense of self-worth (7)."

Theoretical Principles (TP)

Helping one's parents is **important** because: "Sometimes the common good requires that a contract be broken." **But keeping promises to one's children is important** because: "All individuals, children no less than parents, have fundamental human rights."

STAGE 1:

Absolute and Simplistic

1: Unilateral Authority

This aspect is not typically evidenced on this norm.

2: Status

Helping one's parents is **important** because:

it's your parents; (or because) the parent is grown up, important, or the oldest.

Note. Any elaborated version of this justification, e.g., "they're **still** your parents," is unscorable.

3: Rules

Helping one's parents is **important** because:

a. **you** should or must (always) obey or help your parents.

Note. Any elaborated version of this justification, e.g., "you should help **in any way you can,**" is unscorable.

Form B

b. you should (always) tell (about what you do); (or because) children shouldn't tell lies.

Keeping promises to one's children is **important** because:

c. parents should never break promises.

4: Labels

Helping one's parents is **important**:

a. (in order) to be nice or good (to your parents).

b. (so that) the parents **will** be happy.

Keeping promises to one's children is **important** because otherwise:

c. the children **will** be sad or feel bad, or may cry.

Form B

Helping one's parents is **important**:

d. Judy lied or did something wrong; (or because) lying or disobeying your parents is bad.

5: Punitive Consequences

Helping one's parents is **important** because otherwise:

the child may get spanked or punished.

TRANSITION 1/2

1: Unilateral Authority—Preferences

Helping one's parents is **important** because:

children should do what their parents tell or want them to do.

2: Unilateral Authority—Needs

Helping one's parents is **important** because:

parents can break a promise.

3: Labels—Freedoms

Keeping promises to one's children is **important** because:

it's the child's money.

4: Labels—Advantages

Helping one's parents is **important**:

a. (so that) the parents won't break a promise again.

b. (so that) the parents won't steal or get into trouble.

c. (because otherwise) the parents **may** feel bad or be sad.

Form B

d. (because otherwise) Judy will or may do it again.

Keeping promises to one's children is **important** because otherwise:

e. it will or could **make** the children sad or unhappy.

5: Punitive Consequences--Advantages

Helping one's parents is **important** because:

Form B

the parents will find out anyway.

STAGE 2:

Exchanging and Instrumental

1: Exchanges (f = Orientation B)

Helping one's parents is **important**:

a. (because) the parents do or have done a lot of things for their children; (because) the parents pay for their children or give the children things; (or because) you owe them a lot.

b. (because) **if** the parents help the children, then the children should help the parents; (because) parents help kids **so** kids should help parents; (or because) the children **want** the parents to help them (so they should help their parents).

c. (because) not everything is fair.

d. (so that) the parents will return the favor or may do things back (for the children).

Keeping promises to one's children is **important** because:

e. taking the money back is unfair.

Note. This criterion justification should not be applied to other norms, where the simple "unfair" reference is nondiscriminative and hence unscorable.

f. (because) the parents want the children to keep their promises (so the parents should keep theirs).

Form B

g. Louise probably did things (their mother didn't know about), and Judy didn't tell (so Louise shouldn't tell either).

2: Equalities

Keeping promises to one's children is **important** because:

children are equal (to their parents); (because) parents should keep promises just like anyone else; (because) if parents don't keep their promises, why should the children?; (or because) children can't break promises, so parents shouldn't either.

Note. "(Because) it is important for anyone to keep his or her promise" is unscorable.

3: Freedoms

Helping one's parents is **important** because:

a. it's the parents' money; (or because) the child didn't earn or was just given the money.

Keeping promises to one's children is **important** because:

b. the child worked for or earned it, or it's the child's money; (or because) she can do what she wants with her money.

4: Preferences

Helping one's parents is **important**:

a. if the child likes her parents or **wants** or **likes** to help them; (or because) children should **want** to help their parents.

Note. "(Because) children should help their parents" is unscorable.

b. (Because) you don't always **get to** do what you want.

Note. "(Because) you can't always do what you want" is unscorable.

c. (because) you would rather eat (than go to the camp or concert).

d. (because) the parents can take money back **if they want to.**

Keeping promises to one's children is **important** because:

Form A

d. Joe wants to go to camp, or may not want to give up the money (to his father).

Form B

e. Judy wanted to go to the concert.

5: Needs

Helping one's parents is **important** because:

a. the parents need it or need the money more (than the children do); (or so that) they can eat.

Note. "Food is important" or "(otherwise) they won't have food and will die" is unscorable.

b. your parents may be all you have.

Keeping promises to one's children is **important:**

c. (because) the child needs the money.

d. (but) parents can break promises if **they need to.**

6: Advantages (a = Orientation A)

Helping one's parents is **important** because:

a. the children may want a favor (later), or may want their parents to help them; (because then) the parents will help them; (so that) the parents will still **like** or talk to the children, or won't bother them; (or because otherwise) the parents won't do extra things for their children.

b. the child could have gone another time.

c. (otherwise) you won't like yourself.

d. (otherwise) the parents will **go out** and steal.

Form B

e. (but) if Louise keeps quiet, their mother will never know.

Keeping promises to one's children is **important** because then:

f. the children will like the parents more; (or because otherwise) the children would rebel or be angry.

TRANSITION 2/3

1: Exchanges--Relationships

Helping one's parents is **important** because:

a. the parents have helped, **try to** help, or **love** their children; (because) the parents do or have given them **so** much, or have brought them up; (or because) if it weren't for your parents, you wouldn't (even) be here.

Note. "Parents help their children" is unscorable (since "help" is so salient in the question).

b. the children **would want** the parents to help them (so they should help their parents).

c. the children should **thank** their parents.

Keeping promises to one's children is **important** because:

the parents **wouldn't** like it (if the children were to break their promises).

2: Freedoms—Empathic Role-Taking

Keeping promises to one's children is **important** because:

the children earned the money **all by themselves;** (or because) the child **went out** and worked or earned the money.

3: Preferences—Empathic Role-Taking

Helping one's parents is **important** because:

a. you don't, wouldn't, or shouldn't want your family to starve.

Keeping promises to one's children is **important** because:

b. Joe/Judy had been excited or looking forward to going; (because) the child wanted to go **badly, really** wanted to go, had worked **hard,** or made plans; (or because) the child was let down or disappointed.

4: Preferences—Prosocial Intentions

Helping one's parents is **important** because:

you **love** them; (because) **if you love them,** you (should) want to help them; (because) the food is for everyone (including the children); (or because) you will be helping yourself and your family.

5: Needs—Empathic Role-Taking

Helping one's parents is **important:**

if parents **really** need it, need it **badly,** or **need help.**

Note. "If the parents have run out of money" is unscorable.

6: Needs—Prosocial Intentions

Helping one's parents is **important:**

if parents have a **good** reason.

Note. "If the parents have an important reason" is unscorable.

7: Advantages—Relationships

Helping one's parents is **important:**

a. (so that) their parents will trust them.

b. (so that) the parents will still **love** their children; (or in order) to get them back together.

Note. "(Because) a family should stick together" is unscorable.

Keeping promises to one's children is **important** because otherwise:

c. the children will no longer believe or trust them; (or because otherwise) the children will stop relying on their parents or may no longer count on their parents (for help).

Note. "The parents' credibility is at stake" is unscorable.

STAGE 3:

Mutual and Prosocial

1: Relationships (e, f, g = Orientation B)

Helping one's parents is **important**:

a. (because) parents sacrifice, go out of their way, **are always helping** (their children) or may deserve help; (because) the parents have (always) supported their children; (because) the children should **realize, think of, look at,** or **remember** how much their parents do or have done for them; (or because) the children should **be thankful,** appreciative, or grateful.

b. (because) the parents understand when the children break promises (so the children should understand); (because) the child **would expect** the parents to help them (so the children should help the parents).

c. if the parents are appreciative; (or but) the parents should be **thankful** (that the child worked so hard).

d. for the sake of the relationship, faith, or trust; (or because otherwise) there is little or no relationship, or it would spoil the relationship.

e. (because then) the parents may (be able to) apologize or admit they made a mistake.

Keeping promises to one's children is **important** because otherwise:

f. the children will **lose** trust or faith, or would stop believing in their parents.

g. parents **would expect** their children to keep their promises (so the parents should keep theirs); (or because) how would the parents feel if the children did that?

2: Empathic Role-Taking

Helping one's parents is **important**:

<u>a.</u> (because) the child should forgive or understand; (because) parents are people, too, are only human, or make mistakes.

<u>b.</u> (because) your parents are having hard times or are **in** need; (or because) that's an **emergency**, a **matter of** starvation, or **whether** they eat or not; (or because) food is **so** important.

<u>Note.</u> "(Because) food is important" is unscorable.

<u>c.</u> (so that) the parents know they are loved or appreciated; (or because otherwise) the parents may feel hurt or unloved.

<u>Keeping promises to one's children is **important** because:</u>

<u>d.</u> promises mean a lot to children; (because) broken promises hurt (a child), are heartbreaking or can cause (emotional) stress; (because then) they are let down **by their own parents** or by ones who should love them; (or because otherwise) the children will be hurt or will **think** that their parents don't love them.

<u>Note.</u> "The children deserve to do what they want" is unscorable.

3: **Normative Expectations (a, b, c = Orientation A)**

Helping one's parents is **important** because:

<u>a.</u> children are **supposed to** or **expected to** honor or respect their parents.

<u>b.</u> children are part of the family (and should help, too).

<u>Note.</u> "Children should help, too" or "you're helping part of the family" is unscorable.

<u>c.</u> parents expect their children to help them (out).

<u>d.</u> the parent may **deserve** help; (or but) Joe or Judy sacrificed or deserved to go to camp or the concert.

4: **Prosocial Intentions**

Helping one's parents is **important:**

<u>a.</u> (because) children should (be ready or willing to) sacrifice, or shouldn't be selfish; (because) children **should** love their parents or give **out of** love; (or because) it is nice **of** the children (to help out their parents).

<u>b.</u> (because) the parent may have tried to do the best thing (for the child); (because) the parent knows best; (or because) the parent may have seen something unfit about the camp or concert.

<u>c.</u> (in order) to show their love; (or so that) the parents will see that the children care.

<u>Keeping promises to one's children is **important** because:</u>

d. it **shows** that the parents love or care for their children; (or because otherwise) it is inconsiderate, cruel, or mean.

Form A

e. the father wants Joe to sacrifice his fun for the father's own fun; (because) it was just for the father's pleasure; (or because) the father is (being) selfish or childish.

5: Generalized Caring

This aspect is not typically evidenced on this norm.

6: Intrapersonal Approval

Helping one's parents is **important** because then:

the children will feel better about themselves; (or because otherwise) you are only hurting yourself.

TRANSITION 3/4

1: Relationships—Societal Requirements

Keeping promises to one's children is **important** because:

a. a promise is based on trust; (in order) to **establish** or **build** (up) trust; (or because) there should be a **bond** (of trust).

b. children **have to be able to** trust their parents, **need to feel** that they can trust their parents, or need to have a sense of security.

Note. "(So that) the children **can** trust their parents" is unscorable.

c. parents **need to have** their children's trust or confidence.

2: Relationships—Basic Rights/Values

Keeping promises to one's children is **important** because:

a. this may bring the family closer together; for the sake of harmony or smoother relationships; (or) for the sake of (open) communication (between parents and children).

b. (otherwise) the parents will lose their children's respect.

3: Empathic Role-Taking—Societal Requirements

Keeping promises to one's children is **important** but:

parents have many responsibilities (and sometimes cannot keep a promise); (but) **priorities** (can) change (things).

Note. "Sometimes things come up," or "(but) they might have to pay a bill," is unscorable.

4: Empathic Role-Taking--Procedural Equity

Helping one's parents is **important** but:

you should consider the circumstances; or but each case is difference.

5: Normative Expectations--Societal Requirements

Helping one's parents is **important**:

a. (because) the parent's word should be law, or the parent is the head of the household.

Note. "(Because) the parent is the head" is unscorable.

b. (but) the camp or concert **should** have a higher priority.

6: Normative Expectations--Basic Rights/Values

Helping one's parents is **important** because:

children should respect their parents, or should help out of respect.

7: Normative Expectations--Responsibility

Helping one's parents is **important** because:

a. children must or should **learn** that they can't always do what they want, or that they **must** sacrifice sometimes; (because) **everyone in the family** or **each family member** should (be willing to) help out, or do their share; (or because) it is for the **whole** or **entire** family.

Note. "The children should help, too," "you can't always do what you want," or "it's for the family" is unscorable.

b. that **shows** the children are **responsible**; (or so that) the parents will realize how **responsible** the children are.

Keeping promises to one's children is **important** because:

c. your word is your bond.

Note. "A promise is a promise" is unscorable.

8: Normative Expectations--Consistent Practices

Keeping promises to one's children is **important** because:

Joe and Judy are old enough to be treated on an equal basis.

9: Prosocial Intentions--Character

Keeping promises to one's children is **important** because:

a. Joe or Judy is still young or developing, or his or her character is still forming; (because) the child looks up to the parent; (but) the parent should be a good guide, model, teacher, or influence; or should **set** a (good) example; (so that) the child will **learn** honesty, trust, or to keep or respect promises; (or so that) the child will be taught responsibility.

Note. "(Because) parents should practice what they preach" or "should be a good example" is unscorable. Also, "(because otherwise) the children will (one day grow up and) be dishonest, or will think it's all right to lie" is unscorable.

b. (because) the parent should be dependable or trustworthy.

c. (because otherwise) the child would become hypocritical; (or because otherwise) the parents would be teaching a double standard, or teaching that parents can lie but children can't.

10: Generalized Caring--Basic Rights/Values

Keeping promises to one's children is **important** because:

the parents should respect the child, or should treat the child as a person or human being; (or because) the child should have a voice in family affairs.

11: Intrapersonal Approval--Standards of Conscience

Helping one's parents is **important** because:

it helps the child's self-esteem or personal satisfaction.

a. (because) it means the children have learned from their parents' mistakes; (or because by doing so) the child may grow or mature.

b. (so that) the children will **learn to** be dependable, to sacrifice, or to share.

Form B

c. (because) **in this instance,** the parent is wiser than the child.

STAGE 4:

Systemic and Standard

1: Societal Requirements

Helping one's parents is **important** because:

a. the family **must** come before individual desires or recreational needs; (or because) a family **must** pull together.

Note. "(Because) the family comes first," "should come before anything else," or "should stick together" is unscorable.

b. the child **must** understand priorities, different levels of importance, or exceptional circumstances.

c. you have to have a head of the family, or someone has to be in charge.

d. the family is important for society.

2: Basic Rights/Values

Helping one's parents is **important** because:

a. that is what a family is all about, or children should **contribute** (to the family); for the sake of the **common** good, the whole of **the** family, or the family **unit**; (or) for the sake of family **unity**, solidarity, functioning, welfare, or survival.

Note. "(Because then) the family will be helped" is unscorable.

Keeping promises to one's children is **important** because:

b. promises are sacred.

c. Joe or Judy would be bowing to the wishes of a tyrant.

3: Responsibility (a = Orientation A)

Helping one's parents is **important**:

a. (because) the parent has the responsibility or authority, is the child's provider or guardian, or is legally entitled or in charge; (or because) the child is a minor or is still living at home.

b. (because) children have an obligation, or should feel or take responsibility (toward the needs of the family).

c. if it will help the parent to recognize an obligation to keep promises to the child (in the future).

Keeping promises to one's children is **important** because:

d. parents have an **obligation** or **responsibility** to keep their word or follow through on their **commitments**; (or because) that must be accepted as a part of parenthood.

Note. "Parents should keep their word" is unscorable.

4: Character

Keeping promises to one's children is **important**:

a. (because) children should be learning how to handle or to save money; (because) children should value or respect hard-earned money (and not get money free); (or in order) to instill a **sense of** responsibility.

b. (because) parents should provide a model or **integrity** or honor, or an example of **character**.

c. for the sake of the child's development of potential or development as an individual; or (in order) to encourage autonomy, independence, or self-sufficiency.

Note. "(Because) they'll be on their own soon" or "they'll need to know how to fend for themselves when they get older" is unscorable.

5: Consistent Practices

This aspect is not typically evidenced on this norm.

6: Procedural Equity (Orientation B)

Keeping promises to one's children is **important** because:

parents must earn or deserve their children's respect; (because) parents should not abuse their authority or misuse their power; for the sake of (keeping) respect; (or because otherwise) the parent is not worthy of the child's respect.

7: Standards of Conscience

Keeping promises to one's children is **important**:

a. for the sake of one's self-respect.

b. (so that) the child will have a sense of self-worth or personal value.

THE THEORY-DEFINING LEVEL:

Sociopolitical Philosophy

TP: Theoretical Principles

Helping one's parents is **important** because:

sometimes the common good requires that a contract be broken.

Keeping promises to one's children is **important** because:

all individuals, children no less than parents, have fundamental human rights.

11

Norm 7:

CONTRACT

The Contract norm section is perhaps the simplest in organization. Contract norm material is elicited on Questions 2 (keeping a promise to a friend) and 3 (keeping a promise to someone you hardly know). Since these evaluation questions elicit fairly general justificatory responses, there is little need to differentiate criterion justifications into Form A or Form B. There is also almost no need to differentiate criterion justifications by evaluative valence (important/not important), since most of the criterion justifications support an evaluation of keeping promises (whether to a friend or to a minimal acquaintance) as "important."

There is a certain elegance, then, to the format for structural presentations on Contract. This elegance enables us to clearly see reflection on promise-keeping progress from absolute justifications (Stage 1), to the instrumental orientation of Stage 2, to mutualistic considerations (Stage 3), and finally to justifications of promise-keeping in terms of basic standards, values, and societal requirements (Stage 4). A "Theoretical Principles" rating is given where fundamental rights are discussed in terms of a social contract reciprocity.

Many of the justifications for keeping promises focus on the consequences which would ensue if promises were not kept. The conceptualization of the "consequences," of course, changes qualitatively by stage. At Stage 1, the appeal is to predicted states or actions of the person to whom the promise is not kept: the person will not "be your friend," "will cry," or will "beat you up." By Stage 2, the consequences have generally become more conditional and calculative; the promise should be kept because "you could run into the same person again," and "you may want the person to like you." Also, "keeping a promise" at the lower levels is often understood as a matter of not tattling on a friend (e.g., if you don't keep a promise, the person "might tell on you"; Transition 1/2). By the third stage level, the "consequences" from breaking a promise have become emotionally interpenetrative: a friend "becomes a part of you," and the relationship could be destroyed by the broken promise; the other person's feelings would be hurt, and you would feel bad **inside.** Finally, the "consequences" at Stage 4 pertain to social or personal systems: to society's survival, to respecting and affirming the worth of others, and to one's self-respect.

The concern with consequences can be either feelings- or actions-oriented. At Stage 1, feelings are gross negative valences (sad, feel bad) which are necessarily predicted (**will** be sad, feel bad) unless overtly expressed (will **or might** cry). At Transition 1/2, the psychological valences are still undifferentiated but may be conditional (**might be** sad, **could** feel bad), as well as causal (could **make them** sad). At Stage 2 the emotion entails a retaliatory motivation (the other person "might get mad," or "won't like you"). At the 2/3 level, the emotional consequences specified are the other person's "disappointment" (either in not getting what they wanted, Stage 2; or in you as a person, Stage 3), and possible disinclination to trust you in the future. These justifications become more clearly empathic and mutualistic at Stage 3. Instead of "disappointment," the reference is to **hurt feelings;** instead of whether the person will "trust you" (trust as a verb), the Stage 3 appeal is to whether the person will **have** trust **in you** (an invested **state** of trust as a noun, or a condition of entrusted confidence). Also, the concern with retaliatory moods at Stage 2 entails a possible concern with social impression at Transition 2/3 ("bad reputation"), a concern which is clearly in focus at Stage 3 ("so that others will think of you as a good person").

Emotion references may also be self-directed, at higher levels entailing considerations of conscience. There is no reference to conscience per se at Stages 1 or 2, although there may be a Stage 2 suggestion that "you won't like yourself" if you break a promise. When conscience first comes in at Transition 2/3, it seems to be construed as a kind of external annoyance (your conscience would **bother** you, **keep hounding** you). By Stage 3, this nuisance connotation has dropped out (it would simply be "on your conscience"; or more positively, keeping a promise would "make you feel good **inside**"). Levels 3/4 and 4 entail justifications that more clearly refer to "internal" or autonomous self-judgments. The appeal at 3/4 is to "your **own** well-being," "your **personal** satisfaction," or "your **sense** of well-being" (a vague reference to one's "well-being" is unscorable). At Stage 4, self-judgments presuppose the maintenance of a consistent personal standard which makes possible an "integrity" which in turn generates a sense of "dignity," "honor," or "self-respect."

The concern with the consequences of breaking promises may also be action-oriented. At Stage 1, the "consequence" is punitive: whether you will get "punished" or "beat up." At Transition 1/2 the concern still has a punitive connotation but is more suggestive of an equal footing with the other person (you would "be in trouble **with** the friend"). The egalitarian assumption is fully clear at levels beyond 1/2. At Stage 2, the concern is mainly with advantages or disadvantages: whether the person will "keep a promise to you" if you keep the promise, or conversely with whether the person will "start a fight" if you don't. In the case of a stranger, keeping a promise may be rated **unimportant** because of the **lack** of advantages ("you will never see them again, so who cares?"). Levels 2, 2/3, and 3 are generally concerned with action consequences in terms of **reciprocity** of actions. At Stage 2, this reciprocity is manifested as a simple exchange, i.e., whether the person will "return the favor" or has done a favor for you. Instead of the future ("will") tense, Transition 2/3 uses the future subjunctive mood to imply a more hypothetical reciprocity: whether the other person **would** keep a promise to you, or whether you **would want** a promise to you broken. The reciprocity becomes explicitly hypothetical as a mutual ideal at Stage 3: you would **hope** the other person would keep a promise to you. The emphasis is also upon mutual expectations, not preferences: instead of "you would want. . .," the consideration may be that "you would **expect** the other person to keep the promise to you."

References to other **people** or friends rather than to the other person or "your friend" are more typical at levels beyond Stage 3. The concern with action consequences at 3/4 and 4 is in terms of functional necessities for interaction beyond that of a particular dyadic relationship. Transition 3/4 moves beyond a simple appeal to "the relationship" to a suggestion that **a** relationship is b**ased on** trust," or that **a** friend **has to be able** to depend on you"; the implication is that keeping promises serves as a required foundation for viable relationships. By Stage 4, the point is made that **"society** is based on trust," that "you wouldn't want to live in a society where you couldn't trust anyone," and that contract is indeed a "method of interaction" without which life is even "meaningless."

The "stranger" question allows a limited opportunity for distinguishing between A and B orientations. Encompassing the B orientation are affirmations of the importance of keeping a promise even to someone one scarcely knows on justice-oriented or ideological grounds. In contrast, Orientation A specifically supports a negation of the importance of keeping such promises. Stage 2 orientation B justifies this evaluation on the grounds that "strangers **need** promises kept, too," whereas Stage 2 Orientation A finds the notion of keeping a promise to a stranger nonsensical ("it doesn't matter, so why do it? That would be stupid"). Stage 3 Orientation B argues that promises, no matter to whom, are "precious"; Stage 3 Orientation A, on the other hand, devalues such promises since the minimal acquaintance would **"mean** nothing to you, there would be no relationship." Counterbalancing orientations at Stage 4 are difficult to identify, mainly because of the rarity of negative evaluations on the question at that stage.

Certain other discriminations by level in the Contract norm should also be discussed. One concerns the successive ways in which the consequences of breaking a promise for one's friends or friendship are construed. At Stage 1, "friend" is a label which can impulsively disappear with as much facility as it can be applied; hence there is the prediction that the other person "won't be" your friend any longer. There may also be a simple assertion that "it's your friend," which is stated as if it were a self-sufficient justification. Transition 1/2 extends beyond this labeling to entail an implicit suggestion of needs and disadvantages: the other person "might be your **best** friend." At Stage 2 the thought is explicitly expressed that your friend could in effect be a relatively scarce and hence rather valuable commodity: this "might be your **only** friend," you "may need" the person, or "friends are hard to find." The concern at Transition 2/3 that you could "lose a friend" raises the hint of a more intrinsic concern with the **friendship** involved. This possibility is explicitly expressed in Stage 3's direct appeal to "the relationship" as a value at stake. Again, higher levels address broader functional concepts. Promise-keeping as a generalized p**ractice** generates desired values ("if everyone kept their word there would be more understanding"; Transition 3/4) and even characterizes the desired ideal of **society. ("You wouldn't want to live in a society where** you couldn't trust anyone"; Stage 4).

Other discriminative questions concern relations between the Transitional 3/4 level and Stage 4. Stage 4 is concerned with promise-keeping as a "commitment" and "sign of character." Note that similar-sounding but not strictly synonymous phrases may be at the 3/4 level (or unscorable). Examples are suggestions that "your word is your bond," or that promise-keeping **"develops** character" or "shows **good** character." The implicit person conception here may still pertain to the normative expectations of a prosocial personality, rather than to the consistent standards of an individual with character or integrity (hence the transitional rating).

THE MONTAGES

Stage 1 (Unilateral and Simplistic)

Keeping a promise is **important** because: "You should always keep your promise (3). It's your friend (2), and if you don't keep your promise he won't be your friend. Besides, you shouldn't be a tattletale or tell a lie. If you don't keep the promise, the other person **will** be sad or feel bad; and he might cry (4), or beat you up (5)." But it is **not important**: "If the other person didn't do what his parents told him (1). And if it's a stranger, it's not important because you should never talk to strangers (3). They might ask you to do something bad (4)."

Transition 1/2

Keeping a promise is **important** because: "You should like your friend (1), and this friend might be your **best** friend. If you don't keep your promise, it will **make them** sad or they **may** feel bad (2). Also, they might tell on you (3)."

Stage 2 (Exchanging and Instrumental)

Keeping a promise is **important** because: "Your friend has probably helped you and may return the favor if you help him (1). Besides, children should keep their promises just like everyone else (2). You may like your friend (4) and may need him to help you someday (6). If you don't keep the promise, your friend won't like you, and you won't even like yourself (6)." But it is **not important** because: "If you hardly know them, then you can do what you want (3) because it won't matter anyway. They'll probably forget (6)."

Transition 2/3

Keeping a promise is **important** because: "You **would want** your friends to keep a promise to you (1). They are counting on you. They trust you, and you shouldn't let them down (3), especially if you like them **a lot** (2). After all, it's good to have someone you can trust, and you want to **gain** friends, not **lose** them (4). You would get a bad reputation, and your conscience would **bother** you (5)." But it is **not important** because: "You don't **even** know the person, and he is not important **to you** (4)."

Stage 3 (Mutual and Prosocial)

Keeping a promise is **important** because: "Your friend **has** faith in you. If it's a stranger, you may start a good relationship by showing trust. Then **you know** you have someone you can trust. Besides, you **would expect** them to keep a promise to you (1). The other person would feel hurt if you broke a promise (2), although a **true** friend would understand (1). In general, though, keeping a promise is what friends are for (3). It's selfish to break a promise, and you make a bad impression (4). You just don't feel good **inside** (6)."

Transition 3/4

Keeping a promise is **important** because: "Friendships are **based on** trust and honesty, and that's how friendships **develop.** It's important for **people** to be able to depend on you (1). That way there would be better communication or harmony in the world (2). After all, your word is your bond, and you should develop good character or virtue, in order to keep others' respect (5) and for the sake of your sense of well-being (6). But of course, it does depend on the circumstances (3)."

Stage 4 (Systemic and Standard)

Keeping a promise is important because: "Society is based on trust, and promises should be kept for the sake of order (1). Honesty is a standard everyone can accept, and you wouldn't want to live in a society where you couldn't trust anyone (2). After all, promises have intrinsic value. A promise is a commitment (3), and whether you keep it reflects the kind of person you are (4). You should keep a promise for the sake of self-respect (7)."

Theoretical Principles (TP)

Keeping a promise is important because: "That way you show that you respect the other person's claims and rights as equally important to your own."

STAGE 1:

Unilateral and Simplistic

1: Unilateral Authority

Keeping a promise is not important:

if the other person didn't do what his parents told him (to do).

2: Status

Keeping a promise is important because:

it's your friend.

3: Rules

Keeping a promise is:

a. (important because) you should always keep or follow your promise; (or because) everyone should keep their promises.

Note. Similar-sounding but qualified justifications, e.g., "you should always keep promises or else don't make them," are not scorable.

b. (important because) you should be nice to strangers; (or not important because) you should never talk to strangers.

4: Labels

Keeping a promise is important because:

a. you shouldn't be a tattletale; (because otherwise) you'd be lying, it's a lie, or it is bad or wrong: (or not important because) the other person could be bad, may have done something wrong, or may ask you to do something bad.

b. (otherwise) they won't be your friend, or the person would never be your friend (again).

c. (otherwise) they **will** be sad, **will** feel bad, or might cry.

5: Punitive Consequences

Keeping a promise is **important** because otherwise:

you get punished, or the other person might beat you up.

TRANSITION 1/2

1: Rules--Preferences

Keeping a promise is **important** because:

you should like your friend.

2: Labels--Advantages

Keeping a promise is:

a. (**important** because) he might be your **best** friend, (or otherwise) might not be your friend any more.

b. (**important** because otherwise) the person **may** feel bad, or you will **make** the other person sad or unhappy.

3: Punitive Consequences--Advantages

Keeping a promise is **important** because otherwise:

a. you would be in trouble (with the friend).

b. the person will tell **on** you or might tattle to others.

STAGE 2:

Exchanging and Instrumental

1: Exchanges

Keeping a promise is **important**:

a. (because) your friend (may have) helped you; (or **not important** because) the person (you hardly know) has done nothing for you.

b. (so that) the friend will return the favor; (or because otherwise) they may do the same thing to you.

2: Equalities (b = Orientation B)

Keeping a promise is **important** because:

a. children should keep their promises just like everyone else.

b. strangers **need** promises kept, **too.**

3: Freedoms

Keeping a promise is **not important** because:

(if you hardly know them then) you can do what you want.

4: Preferences

Keeping a promise is **important:**

a. if you want to, or because you (may) like your friend; if you **want** to have this friend; (or **not important** because if you hardly know them then) who cares?

b. (because) that person may not want anyone to know.

5: Needs

Keeping a promise is **important** because:

a. you **need** a friend, or this might be your **only** friend; because you may **need** the person (to do something for you someday); (or because otherwise) you won't have any friends.

b. (good) friends are hard to find.

c. friends **need** promises kept, or they may **need** what you promised them.

6: Advantages (g, h = Orientation B)

Keeping a promise is:

a. (**important** so that) the friend will keep a promise to you; if (you know) they won't tell on you; (because) you could run into the same person again; (or because otherwise) they may start a fight.

b. (**important** as that) the friend will like you or do you a favor; (or because otherwise) the person might get mad.

c. (**important** because otherwise) the person may not be able to do something.

d. (**important** because otherwise) you won't like yourself.

e. (**important** because otherwise) you might not like each other any more.

f. (**not important** because) you don't know what you're getting into, or they may cheat you.

g. (**not important** because) it won't matter, or the other person will never know or might forget anyway.

h. (**not important** because) then why do it (if you hardly know the person)?; (or because) that would be stupid (for someone you hardly know to ask you to keep a promise).

TRANSITION 2/3

1: Exchanges--Relationships

Keeping a promise is **important** because:

a. they **would** keep a promise to you; you **wouldn't want** someone to break a promise to you; or I **wouldn't want** it done to me.

b. the other person trusted you (enough to tell you something).

2: Preferences--Prosocial Intentions

Keeping a promise is **important** because:

you may like the person **a lot.**

3: Needs--Empathic Role-Taking

Keeping a promise is **important** because:

a. that person depends on or is counting on you; (because) you shouldn't let the other person down, or disappoint her; (because otherwise) their plans would be ruined.

Note. Distinguish this possibly empathic concern with not "ruining" someone's plans from a more pragmatic sentiment against frustrating someone else's opportunities (the other person "won't be able to do something"; Stage 2, Aspect 6). Also, "(because otherwise) you're not dependable" is unscorable.

b. they may need it (kept) **badly.**

c. (but) if it could **get** someone hurt, you should tell; (or unless) breaking the promise helps the other person.

4: Advantages--Relationships

Keeping a promise is:

a. (**important** because) that person could **become** your friend; if it is a **good** friend; (because then) you may **become** friends (with the stranger); (so that) you will keep your friends or make new friends, (because otherwise) you could **lose** a friend; (or because otherwise) they won't want you **for** a friend, or you (and the other person) won't be **friends.**

Note. (Important because otherwise) they may not want to be your friend" or "if you can't keep a promise, then you're not a friend" is unscorable.

b. (**important** because) you may need **help** (someday).

c. (**important** because) that person trusts you (to keep the promise) or will trust you (again); (or because otherwise) others won't believe you, you won't trust each other, or you could never trust anyone.

Note. "They are trusting you" is unscorable.

d. (**important** because) it is good or nice to have someone you can trust.

e. (**important** so that) you will get a good reputation, or so that the word will get around that you keep your promises; (or because otherwise) they may start rumors (about you).

f. (**not important** because) you don't **even** know the person; (or because) they are not important or special **to you.**

Note. "They are not important" is unscorable.
Also, "You don't know the person" is unscorable.

5: Advantages—Interpersonal Approval

Keeping a promise is **important** because otherwise:

your conscience would **bother** you or keep **hounding** you.

STAGE 3:

Mutual and Prosocial

1: Relationships (f = Orientation A)

Keeping a promise is:

a. (**important** because) a friendship should be sincere, or friends **should** trust **each other;** (in order) to start a good relationship or to have someone you can **relate to;** for the sake of the relationship, trust, or faith; (in order) to **gain** (their) trust; (so that) there won't be hard feelings; (or because otherwise) the friendship may be hurt, you won't feel as close, or you would lose trust (in each other).

Note. "**(Important** in order) to be faithful" is unscorable.

b. (**important** because) it **shows** others **that** you trust them, care, or have faith in them; (or because) the friend **has** trust or faith in you, or has confided in you.

c. (**important** so that) they will want to get to know you better; (or because) it would be a chance to get to know that person better.

d. (**important** in order) **to know** you have someone you can trust or confide in.

e. (**important** because) a friend becomes a part of you, or **means** a lot (to you); (or because) friendships are an important part of your life.

f. (**important** because) the friend **would expect** the same from you; friends **would want you to treat them the way you want them to treat you;** (or because) you **would expect** your friend to keep a promise to you.

g. (**important** but) a (true) friend would understand or wouldn't mind (if you had to break the promise).

h. (**not important** because) a stranger would **mean** nothing to you; (or because) there would be no relationship.

2: Empathic Role-Taking

Keeping a promise is **important**:

a. (because otherwise) the person could **feel** let down or hurt, or feels unimportant or taken for granted.

b. (because otherwise) you could have emotional problems or could become depressed.

c. if you can keep the promise without hurting someone; (or unless) the other person is using that promise to hurt someone.

Note. On Contract, "hurting someone" is rated Stage 3 because it almost always has a "feelings" connotation (cf. Transition 2/3 rating on some other norms).

3: Normative Expectations

Keeping a promise is **important** because:

that's what friends are for.

4: Prosocial Intentions

Keeping a promise is **important**:

a. (because) you think less of people who break promises.

b. (in order) to make or leave a good impression; (so that) others will **think of you as** a good person, or will know what you're really like; (or because otherwise) you'd worry about what people thought of you, or people would get a bad image or opinion.

c. (because otherwise) it is selfish or cruel, or shows you don't care about the other person.

Note. Non-interpersonal judgments, e.g., "breaking a promise is terrible," are not scorable.

d. (but) you shouldn't make a promise just to get rid of or take advantage of a person.

5: Generalized Caring (Orientation B)

Keeping a promise is **important** because:

promises are precious.

6: Intrapersonal Approval

Keeping a promise is **important** because:

it makes you feel good **inside** (or because otherwise) you would feel rotten or guilty.

Note. "It makes you feel good" is unscorable.

TRANSITION 3/4

1: Relationships--Societal Requirements

Keeping a promise is **important** because:

a. **relationships** are **based** or **built** on trust, honesty, or reliability; (because) **friendship** is **made up** of promises; (in order) to **establish** or **develop** trust, honesty, or openness, or to **build** or **make stronger** dependable relationships; (because) truth, faith, or honesty is important for any friendship or interaction; (or because otherwise) relationships cannot function.

Note. "(Because) trust is important in life" is unscorable.

b. people need to or have to depend on **each other;** (or because) people count on you **to keep your word;** (or because) **people** should be **able to** (have) trust (in) you.

Note. "They are trusting you" is unscorable.

c. there is a **bond** of trust or confidence (even if you aren't close).

2: Relationships--Basic Rights/Values

Keeping a promise is **important** because:

a. if everyone kept their word, there would be more openness, better communication or understanding, or greater harmony.

b. people should be respected, or for the sake of (showing) respect (for others).

3: Relationships--Procedural Equity

Keeping a promise is **important** but:

it **depends** on the **circumstances.**

Note. "It depends on the promise" or "it depends on the kind of friend" is unscorable.

4: Empathic Role-Taking--Societal Requirements

Keeping a promise is **important** but:

priorities (can) change (the conditions of the promise).

Note. "Sometimes you can't keep the promise" is unscorable.

5: Prosocial Intentions--Character

Keeping a promise is **important:**

a. (because) your word should be reliable; (in order) to show **good** character, faithfulness, virtue, or that you are respectable or honest; (in order) to **earn** trust; (because otherwise) it shows unreliability; (or because otherwise) you'll lose (others') respect.

Note. "(Because otherwise) you're not dependable" is unscorable.

b. (because) your word is you, or your word should be your bond; (because) you should be true to yourself, honest with yourself, or as good as your word; (or because otherwise) your word means nothing.

Note. "(Because) you gave your word," "you shouldn't say it if you don't mean it," "you should try to keep your word," or "a promise is a promise" is unscorable.

c. (because) it **develops** your character or trustworthiness; (because you should keep even unimportant promises) just to stay in practice; (or because) if you don't keep a promise to a stranger, then you won't be able to keep a promise to someone close to you, either.

d. (but) that **depends on** one's **morals.**

Note. This Transition 3/4 criterion justification is Type R, relativism of personal values.

6: Intrapersonal Approval--Conscience

Keeping a promise is **important:**

a. for the sake of your **own** well-being, your **sense of** well-being, or **personal** satisfaction.

Note. Unqualified references to "well-being" or "satisfaction" are unscorable.
b. (because) then you (know you) can trust yourself.

STAGE 4:

Systemic and Standard

1: Societal Requirements

Keeping a promise is **important** because:

society is based on trust or promises; for the sake of order, society, or survival; (because) trust is essential to the economy or government; (because) it is a method for interaction, dealings, or functioning; (or because otherwise) life is meaningless.

Note. On Contract, "order" is rated Stage 4 since it almost always has a societal connotation (cf. Transition 3/4 rating on the other norms).

2: Basic Rights/Values

Keeping a promise is **important** because:

a. you wouldn't want to live in a society where you couldn't trust anyone.

b. honesty is a standard everyone can accept.

c. **everyone** has the **right** to have a promise (to them) kept.

d. it affirms the worth of the other person.

e. promises are **sacred,** or have **intrinsic** value.

3: Responsibility

Keeping a promise is **important** because:

it is a commitment, responsibility, obligation, pact, contract, matter of honor, pledge, or statement of faith.

4: Character

Keeping a promise is **important:**

it reflects or is a sign of character, integrity, or the kind of person you are; (because) it shows self-respect; (or because otherwise) it shows a lack of responsibility or maturity.

5: Consistent Practices

Keeping a promise is **important** because:

if people break their promises **whenever** they wish, there would be chaos.

6: Procedural Equity

This aspect is not typically evidenced on this norm.

7: Standards of Conscience

Keeping a promise is **important:**

for the sake of self-respect, self-esteem, or of one's integrity, dignity, honor, or consistency.

THE THEORY-DEFINING LEVEL:

Sociopolitical Philosophy

TP: Theoretical Principles

Keeping a promise is **important:**

(in order) to show that you respect the other person's claims or rights as equally important to your own; (or because) it is the essence of the social contract.

12

Norm 8:

PROPERTY

The main thematic evolution discernible on the Property norm is the concept of the right to property. At Stage 2, the reference is simple and concrete (Joe or Judy "worked for, earned, or saved" the money). Transition 2/3 imparts a possible empathic concern (e.g., Joe earned the money **all by himself,"** or "worked **hard").** Stage 3 is marked by a direct reference to the child's sacrifice, deservingness, and feeling of pride. A closely related development proceeds from an assertion of preference ("wanted to go"; Stage 2), to a sympathetically elaborated preference (e.g., "wanted to go **badly";** Transition 2/3), to a Stage 3 relationship-based suggestion that taking the money would be "cruel" or "heartbreaking." Transition 3/4 asserts a discretionary entitlement allowable to the child as long as the money is managed reasonably. At Stage 4, the entitlement is seen in terms of the abstract right to a fair return on effort invested.

The importance of letting children keep money they've earned is also justified on the basis of role-taking appeals. Whereas Stage 2 reciprocity is concrete ("the children don't take their parents' things, so the parents shouldn't take their children's"), Transition 2/3 role-taking is more hypothetical ("the parents **wouldn't** like it if their money were taken"). Hypothetical role-taking is clearly expressed in terms of a socioemotional mutuality at Stage 3 ("How would the parents feel if. . .?"). At Stage 4, role-taking balances rights with responsibilities; thus it is pointed out that parents "shouldn't abuse their authority" and that the parent who does so "is not worthy of the child's respect."

There is also a concern with the consequences--to the child, the relationship, or the society--which would ensue from taking the money. The concern at the lowest levels is with negative affective states of an undifferentiated nature, either predicted ("will be sad;" Stage 1) or anticipated ("could **make** them sad," **"might** feel bad"; Transition 1/2). By Stage 2, the emotion implies a disadvantageous reciprocation ("will get mad," might not "like" the parents any more). The Transition 2/3 sentiment (the child "won't trust" the parent) hints at the relationship-based concerns of Stage 3 (there would be a "loss of trust" or harm to "the relationship"). Beyond Stage 3 the concern is with a possible "breakdown of communication" (implying a functional concern; Transition 3/4), and finally with the importance of property rights as the "basis of society" (Stage 4).

Letting the children keep money they've earned is occasionally evaluated as **not important.** At the lowest levels, the justifications seem to be based on a possible unilateral conception of authority at Transition 1/2 ("the parents can take the money back"), explicitly qualified by an asumption of need at Stage 2 ("the parents can take the money back **if they need to").** At higher levels, the appeal may be to prosocial intentions (the children should be "unselfish" if there is an emergency, Stage 3); to empathic role-taking (the parents "are having hard times," Stage 3) to the need to **learn** sacrifice or develop character (e.g., "it would show the children that they can't always have everything they want"; Transition 3/4); or to the parents' positional entitlements or jurisdiction (the child is "still under the parent's authority"; Stage 4).

Certain responses on the property norm are clssifiable as either Orientation A or Orientation B. Generally, Orientation A supports the unimportance of letting children keep earned money by appeals to the normative givens of the situation; whereas Orientation B supports the importance of letting children keep earned money by coordinating the situational givens with the injustice of taking away **earned** money. The situational givens appealed to in Orientation A may be the parents' prerogatives (in terms of needs at Stage 2: "the parents can take the money back **if they need to";** and in terms of positional entitlements at Stage 4: "the child is still under the parent's authority"). Stage 3 Orientation A usually focuses on the expected role of the good child ("children are **supposed to** honor their parents"). In contrast, Orientation B addresses but objects to parental authority in light of the injustice of the parents' misconduct. Stage 2 Orientation B sees the unfairness in terms of a concrete reversal: "the children don't take their parents' things, so the parents shouldn't take their children's." Stage 3 Orientation B points out that "children are people, too" and that there will not be much "trust" or "faith" in such a relationship, and asks how the parents would feel if the children acted that way to them. Stage 4 Orientation B specifically criticizes the parent's "abuse" of his or her "authority."

THE MONTAGES

Stage 1 (Unilateral and Simplistic)

Letting one's children keep earned money is **important** because: "The children **will** be unhappy if money is taken away from them (4)." But it is **not important:** "If the child didn't obey (1), because you should always obey your parents (3)."

Transition 1/2

Letting one's children keep earned money is **important** because: "The money belongs to the child (2). Taking the money can **make** the child unhappy, and the next time the child would lie to the parents (3)." But it is **not important** because: "The parents can take back the money (1)."

Stage 2 (Exchanging and Instrumental)

Letting one's children keep earned money is **important** because: "The parents keep their money, so the children should be able to keep theirs (2). Besides, the child worked for it (3), wanted to go (4), and needs the money (5). Furthermore, the children won't like the parents any more if the money is taken (6)." But it is **not important:** "If the parents buy you things (1), and if they **want** the money back, they can take it back (4).

Transition 2/3

Letting one's children keep earned money is **important** because: "The parents wouldn't like it if the tables were turned (1). Also, the child **went out** and worked **hard** (2) and would be let down because she wanted to go **badly** (3) and **really** needs the money (4). If the money is taken, the child won't trust the parents any more (5)." But it is **not important** because: "The child owes the parent **so** much anyway (1)."

Stage 3 (Mutual and Prosocial)

Letting one's children keep earned money is **important** because: "How would the parents feel if the tables were turned? If the parents take the money, there would be a **loss of** trust and faith in the parents (1). After all, the children worked **so** hard, and it would break their hearts for the parents to take the money (2). If the children don't get the rewards they deserve, they may just get lazy (3). Although the child should want to give if it's an emergency (4), their property should not be taken because children are people, too (5), and they should not be taken advantage of." But it is **not important** because: "The children should **think of** the help they have gotten from their parents (1), who may be having hard times (2)."

Transition 3/4

Letting one's children keep earned money is **important** because: "Otherwise there could be a breakdown in communication (1), and the child may no longer respect the parents. After all, children should have the right to decide how to spend their money (3), since they have the same right to property that everyone else has (6). Of course, the child must use the money reasonably, and the parents can give advice (4), but earning the money showed the child **is responsible.** Earning money helps the child **learn** not to be lazy (5). Besides, the parents should be **setting** a good example for their children (9). Of course, it does depend on the circumstances (2) and whether the child is willing to give consent (3)." But it is **not important** because: "The money may be needed for **necessities** (7), and the child may **choose** to **lend** the money (8)."

Stage 4 (Systemic and Standard)

Letting one's children keep earned money is **important** because: "Society is based on property rights, and respect for property is **important** for order (1). If the parent doesn't respect the child as an individual and does not grant his or her right to ownership (2), then such a parent isn't worthy of the child's respect (6). The child worked toward a goal and should be taught the value of money as well as helped to develop responsibility and self-sufficiency (4). The parents should not abuse their authority (6) because earning money gives a sense of self-worth and self-confidence (7)." But it is **not important** because: "Children should sometimes accept a responsibility to sacrifice for the sake of the family (3)."

Theoretical Principles (TP)

Letting one's children keep earned money is **important** because: "The child has a **moral right** as an **individual** to keep the money."

STAGE 1:

Absolute and Simplistic

1: Unilateral Authority

Letting one's children keep earned money is **not important** because:

maybe the child (whose money is taken) didn't obey.

2: Status

This aspect is not typically evidenced on this norm.

3: Rules

Letting one's children keep earned money is **not important** because:

you should (always) obey your parents.

Note. Any elaborated version of this justification, e.g., "you should help **in any way you can,**" is unscorable.

4: Labels

Letting one's children keep earned money is **important** because otherwise:

a. the child **will** be sad or unhappy, **will** feel bad, or may cry.

b. the parents are stealing.

5: Punitive Consequences

This aspect is not typically evidenced on this norm.

TRANSITION 1/2

1: Unilateral Authority--Advantages

Letting one's children keep earned money is **not important** because:

the parents can take the money back.

2: Labels--Freedoms

Letting one's children keep earned money is **important** because otherwise:

the money is theirs or not their parents'; (or because) it belongs to the children or the children own it.

3: Labels--Advantages

Letting one's children keep earned money is **important** because otherwise:

a. it would **make** the children sad or unhappy; (or because otherwise) the child **may** feel bad.

b. the children may lie or say they don't have the money.

STAGE 2:

Exchanging and Instrumental

1: Exchanges

Letting one's children keep earned money is:

a. (**important** because) the children don't take their parents' things (so the parents shouldn't take the children's).

b. (**not important** because) the parents buy the children things, or do things for the children.

2: Equalities

Letting one's children keep earned money is **important** because:

the parents keep their money (so the children should be able to keep theirs).

3: Freedoms

Letting one's children keep earned money is **important** because:

Joe or Judy worked for earned, or saved the money; (because) they earned it for themselves (not their parents); (because) they can do whatever they want with the money; (or because) why should the parents tell the child what to do (with the child's money)?

Note. Contingent propositions, e.g., "if you have earned something, it's yours," are unscorable, unless elaborated (e.g., "if you have worked **so hard** for something, it **should be** yours"; Stage 3 Aspect 2a). Also, unelaborated references to rights, e.g., "they have a right to it," are unscorable.

4: Preferences

Letting one's children keep earned money is **important:**

a. (unless) the parents **want** the money back.

Form A

b. (because) Joe wants to go to camp, or doesn't want to give up the money.

Form B

c. (because) Judy wanted to go to the concert, or didn't want to give up the money.

5: Needs

Letting one's children keep earned money is **important** because:

the children need the money; (or **not important** because) the parents can take the money back **if they need to.**

6: Advantages

Letting one's children keep earned money is **important:**

<u>a.</u> (so that) the children can have fun.

<u>b.</u> (because otherwise) the children will be mad or may not like the parents, or may steal the money back (anyway).

<u>Note.</u> "They might fight" is unscorable.

TRANSITION 2/3

1: Exchanges--Relationships

Letting one's children keep earned money is:

<u>a.</u> (**important** because) the parents **wouldn't** like it if the money were taken away from them (so they shouldn't take their children's money).

<u>b.</u> (**not important** because) the parents help the children; (or because) the child owes the parents **so** much anyway.

2: Freedoms--Empathic Role-Taking

Letting one's children keep earned money is **important** because:

Joe worked h**ard, went out and** earned it, earned the money (all by) **himself,** or **was willing to** work (for the money).

3: Preferences--Empathic Role-Taking

Letting one's children keep earned money is **important** because:

Judy wanted to go b**adly** or **very much;** (because) she **expected** to keep the money; (because) money you've earned (yourself) is **special;** (or because otherwise) the child will be disappointed or let down, or her plans would be ruined.

4: Needs--Empathic Role-Taking

Letting one's children keep earned money is **important** because:

the child **really** needs the money; (or **not important)** if the parent needs the money b**adly.**

5: Advantages--Relationships

Letting one's children keep earned money is **important** because otherwise:

the children won't rely on, trust, or count on their parents for help.

STAGE 3:

Mutual and Prosocial

1: Relationships (b, c = Orientation B)

Letting one's children keep earned money is:

a. (**important** because) the parent should (instead) be thankful (that the child worked so hard).

b. (**important** because) how would the parents feel (if the children took their money)?

c. (**important** because otherwise) the child could **lose** faith (in the parent), or there would be a **loss of** trust.

d. (**not important** because) the children should **think of** the help they have gotten from their parents.

2: Empathic Role-Taking

Letting one's children keep earned money is **important**:

a. (because) the children sacrifice or worked **so hard.**

b. (because) children have pride or feel good (inside when they have earned money); (because) children cherish money they've earned, or the things children have earned **mean** a lot (to them); (because taking the money) is cruel or heartbreaking; (or because otherwise) the child would become insecure or untrusting.

c. unless the parents are having hard times.

3: Normative Expectations

Letting one's children keep earned money is:

a. (**important** because) the children used their talent or ability, or deserve the things they earn; (or because) the money is their reward (for working hard).

Note. "They should be able to keep it" is unscorable.

b. (**important** because otherwise) they may not want to work or earn money any more, or may just get lazy or take from others.

c. (**not important** because) children are **supposed to** honor or respect their parents.

4: Prosocial Intentions

Letting one's children keep earned money is **important** but:

a. the child should want to give if the money is for an emergency; (but) children should be **willing to** help their parents; (but sometimes) the child should be unselfish (enough to give) or should not (even) think of the money; (or unless) the parents want the money for something unselfish.

b. it may be for the child's own good (not to let the child spend the money the way he wants).

5: Generalized Caring

Letting one's children keep earned money is **important** because:

children are people, too.

6: Intrapersonal Approval

This aspect is not typically evidenced on this norm.

TRANSITION 3/4

1: Relationships--Basic Rights/Values

Letting one's children keep earned money is **important** because otherwise:

there could be a breakdown in communication.

2: Empathic Role-Taking--Procedural Equity

Letting one's children keep earned money is **important** but:

it depends on the situation or circumstances.

3: Normative Expectations--Basic Rights/Values

Letting one's children keep earned money is **important** because:

a. parents should respect their children.

b. children have the **right to decide** how to spend their money, or **should** be **allowed** to **manage** the money; (because) **it's** her **decision** to do what she wants with the money; (or unless) the money was taken without the child's consent; (or **not important** because) it would **show** the children that they can't always have everything they want.

Note. "The child has a right to his money," "the parents should let the children spend the money on what they want," or "(but) the child might decide to just give them the money" is unscorable.

c. (**important** because otherwise) the child may no longer respect his parents; (or **important** but) the child should trust the parents' judgment.

4: Normative Expectations--Responsibility

Letting one's children keep earned money is **important** but:

the children must use the money reasonably or constructively; (but) the parents can give advice or supervise (how the children use the money); (or unless) the money is being spent on something wrong or inappropriate.

Note. "The parents should help the child set up a savings account" is unscorable.

5: Normative Expectations—Character

Letting one's children keep earned money is **important** because:

<u>a.</u> earning the money showed the child **is responsible.**

<u>b.</u> it is **important** for character development or to help them mature; (because) the child should **learn** to work hard or not be lazy; (or because) it **teaches** responsibility, or then they learn to be responsible.

Form B

<u>c.</u> helping to buy her school clothes is learning responsibility.

6: Normative Expectations—Procedural Equity

Letting one's children keep earned money is **important** because:

the parents shouldn't steal from anyone, including their children; (or because) the children have the same rights to (their) property (that everyone else has).

7: Prosocial Intentions—Societal Requirements

Letting one's children keep earned money is **important** unless:

the money is needed for **necessities,** survival, or **higher priorities.**

Note. "It is needed for food for the family" is unscorable.

8: Prosocial Intentions—Basic Rights/Values

Letting one's children keep earned money is **important** but:

the child may **choose** to **lend** the money (to the parents).

Note. "But maybe the child will give them the money anyway" is unscorable.

9: Prosocial Intentions—Character

Letting one's children keep earned money is **important** because:

the parents should **set** a (good) example (for the children); (or because) that **shows** how to act with money.

Note. "Parents should be a good example" is unscorable.

STAGE 4:

Systemic and Standard

1: Societal Requirements

Letting one's children keep earned money is **important** because:

the right of ownership or respect for property is **important** for order; (or because) society is based on property rights.

2: Basic Rights/Values

Letting one's children keep earned money is **important** because:

a. Joe or Judy has a right to a fair return for his or her effort, or has a right to ownership.

b. the child should be respected as an individual.

3: Responsibility

Letting one's children keep earned money is:

a. (**important** because) children should have (a sense of) responsibility.

b. (**not important** because) children who live at home are still under their parents' authority.

c. (**not important** because) children should (sometimes) **accept** a **responsibility** (to sacrifice for the sake of the family).

4: Character

Letting one's children keep earned money is **important** because:

a. Joe or Judy worked toward or achieved a goal, or accepted a responsibility.

b. children **should** be given a **sense of** responsibility, or **should** learn or be taught the value of work, money, achieving a goal, or ownership; (or because) children **should** be helped to **develop** a sense of **accomplishment**, or **should learn** to be self-sufficient.

Note. "Then in the future they will know how to handle money" is unscorable. Also, "then they can accomplish something or make it on their own" is unscorable.

5: Consistent Practices

This aspect is not typically evidenced on this norm.

6: Procedural Equity

Letting one's children keep earned money is **important** because:

the parents should not abuse their authority or misuse their power, or should be worthy of their children's respect.

7: Standards of Conscience

Letting one's children keep earned money is **important** because:

earning money gives a sense of self-worth or self-confidence.

THE THEORY-DEFINING LEVEL:

TP: Theoretical Principles

Letting one's children keep earned money is **important** because:

the child has a **moral right** as an **individual** to keep the money.

REFERENCE NOTES

1. Kohlberg, L., Hewer, A., & Levine, C. **A response to critics.** Manuscript in preparation, Harvard University, 1981.

2. Gibbs, J. C., Widaman, K. F., & Colby, A. **The measurement of sociomoral reflection.** Paper presented at the meeting of the American Psychological Association, Montreal, September 1980.

3. Gibbs, J. C., Widaman, K. F., Colby, A., & Fenton, E. **Construct validation of the Sociomoral Reflection Measure.** Paper presented at the meeting of the Society for Research in Child Development, Boston, April 1981.

4. Berkowitz, M. W. **Concurrent validity of the Sociomoral Reflection Measure.** Unpublished manuscript, Marquette University, 1980.

5. Kernan, M., & Gibbs, J. C. **The development of reflective sociomoral thought: A two-year longitudinal study.** Manuscript in preparation, Birmingham Southern College, 1981.

6. Gibbs, J. C., & Burkhart, J. E. **Sex differences in the expression of reflective sociomoral thought.** Manuscript in preparation, State University, 1982.

7. Arnold, K. D., Ahlborn, H. H., & Gibbs, J. C. **Sociomoral reflection in delinquents: An intervention study.** Paper presented at the Conference on Adolescents and Their Families, Columbus, Ohio, April 1981.

8. Fuller, R. L., Gibbs, J. C., Clark, P. M., & Goodrick, T. S. **Relations between locus of control, field independence, and substage orientations of sociomoral cognition.** Manuscript in preparation, Ohio State University, 1981.

9. Kohlberg, L., & Shulik, R. **Moral development in the adult years.** Unpublished manuscript, Harvard University, 1981.

REFERENCES

American Psychological Association. **Standards for educational and psychological tests** (Rev. ed.). Washington, D.C.: American Psychological Association, Inc., 1974.

Bachrach, R., Huesman, L. R., & Peterson, R. A. Relation between locus of control and development of moral judgment. **Child Development,** 1977, **48,** 1340-1352.

Blasi, A. Bridging moral cognition and moral action: A critical review of the literature. **Psychological Bulletin,** 1980, **88,** 1-45.

Bloom, A. H. Two dimensions of moral reasoning: Social principledness and social humanism in cross-cultural perspective. **Journal of Cross-Cultural Psychology,** 1977, **101,** 29-44.

Brandt, R. B. **Ethical theory: The problems of normative and critical ethics.** Englewood Cliffs, N.J.: Prentice-Hall, 1959.

Broughton, J. The cognitive-developmental approach to morality: A reply to Kurtines and Greif. **Journal of Moral Education,** 1978, **7,** 81-96.

Brown, R., & Herrnstein, R. J. **Psychology.** Boston: Little, Brown, 1975.

Colby, A. The evolution of a moral developmental theory. **New Directions for Child Development,** 1978, **2,** 89-104.

Colby, A., Kohlberg, L., Candee, D., Gibbs, J. C., Hewer, A., Kaufman, K., Power, C., & Speicher-Dubin, B. **Assessing moral judgment: A manual.** New York: Cambridge University Press, in press.

Colby, A., Kohlberg, L., Gibbs, J. C., & Lieberman, M. A longitudinal study of moral judgment. **Monographs of the Society for Research in Child Development,** in press.

Connolly, J., & McCarrey, M. The relationship between levels of moral judgment maturity and locus of control. **Canadian Journal of Behavioral Science,** 1978, **10,** 162-175.

Cowan, P. A. **Piaget with feeling: Cognitive, social, and emotional dimensions.** New York: Holt, Rinehart & Winston, 1978.

Damon, W. **The social world of the child.** San Francisco: Jossey-Bass, 1977.

Davison, M. L., & Robbins, S. The reliability and validity of objective indices of moral development. **Applied Psychological Measurement,** 1978, **2,** 391-403.

DeVries, R. Relationships among Piagetian, psychometric, and achievement measures. **Child Development,** 1974, **45,** 746-756.

Dewey, J., & Tufts, J. H. **Ethics.** New York: Holt, 1908.

Edwards, C. P. Societal complexity and moral development: A Kenyan study. **Ethos,** 1975, **3,** 505-527.

Elkind, D. C. Piagetian and psychometric conceptions of intelligence. **Harvard Educational Review,** 1969, **39,** 319-337.

Enright, R. D., Franklin, C. C., & Manheim, L. A. Children's distributive justice reasoning: A standardized and objective scale. **Developmental Psychology,** 1980, **16,** 193-202.

Feffer, M. H., & Suchotliff, L. Decentering implications of social interaction. **Journal of Personality and Social Psychology,** 1966, **4,** 415-422.

Flavell, J. H., Botkin, P., Fry, C., Wright, J., & Jarvis, P. **The development of role-taking and communication skills in children.** New York: John Wiley, 1968.

Fowler, J. **Stages of faith: The psychology of human development and the quest for meaning.** New York: Holt, Rinehart & Winston, 1981.

Froming, W. J., & McColgan, E. B. Comparing the Defining Issues Test and the Moral Dilemma Interview. **Developmental Psychology,** 1979, **15,** 658-659.

Furth, H. G. Piaget, I.Q., and the nature-nurture controversy. **Human Development,** 1973, **16,** 61-73.

Gibbs, J. C. Kohlberg's stages of moral judgment: A constructive critique. **Harvard Educational Review,** 1977, **47,** 43-61.

Gibbs, J. C. Kohlberg's moral stage theory: A Piagetian revision. **Human Development,** 1979, **22,** 89-112. (a)

Gibbs, J. C. The meaning of ecologically oriented inquiry in contemporary psychology. **American Psychologist,** 1979, **34,** 127-140. (b)

Gibbs, J. C. Psychology and epistemology: Reply to Rosenberg. **American Psychologist,** 1980, **35,** 672-673.

Gibbs, J. C., Widaman, K. F., & Colby, A. Construction and validation of a simplified, group-administerable equivalent to the Moral Judgment Interview. **Child Development,** in press.

Greenspan, S. Social intelligence in the retarded. In N. R. Ellis (Ed.), Handbook of mental deficiency, psychological theory, and research. Hillsdale, N. J.: Lawrence Erlbaum Associates, 1979.

Guilford, J. P. The nature of human intelligence. New York: McGraw-Hill, 1967.

Haan, N., Smith, M. B., & Black, J. Moral reasoning of young adults: Political-social behavior, family background, and personality correlates. Journal of Personality and Social Psychology, 1968, 90, 183-201.

Hartshorne, H., May, M. A., et al. Testing the knowledge of right and wrong. New York: Religious Education Association, 1927.

Hogan, R. A dimension of moral judgment. Journal of Consulting and Clinical Psychology, 1970, 35, 205-212.

Keating, D. P. A search for social intelligence. Journal of Educational Psychology, 1978, 70, 218-223.

Kohlberg, L. The development of children's orientations toward a moral order. I: Sequence in the development of human thought. Vita Humana, 1963, 6, 11-33.

Kohlberg, L. Stage and sequence: The cognitive-developmental approach to socialization. In D. A. Goslin (Ed.), Handbook of socialization theory and research. Skokie, Ill.: Rand McNally, 1969.

Kohlberg, L. The claim to moral adequacy of a highest stage of moral judgment. Journal of Philosophy, 1973, 70, 630-646. (a)

Kohlberg, L. Continuities in childhood and adult moral development revisited. In P. B. Baltes & L. R. Goulet (Eds.), Lifespan developmental psychology (2nd ed.). New York: Academic Press, 1973. (b)

Kohlberg, L. Moral stages and moralization: The cognitive-developmental approach. In T. Lickona (Ed.), Moral development and behavior: Theory, research, and social issues. New York: Holt, Rinehart & Winston, 1976.

Kohlberg, L. Foreword. In J. R. Rest, Development in judging moral issues. Minneapolis: University of Minnesota Press, 1979.

Kohlberg, L. The meaning and measurement of moral development: Heinz Werner Lecture Series, Vol. 13, 1979. Worcester, Mass.: Clark University Press, 1981.

Kohlberg, L., & Kramer, R. Continuities and discontinuities in childhood and adult moral development. Human Development, 1969, 12, 93-120.

Kuhn, T. S. The structure of scientific revolutions. Chicago: University of Chicago Press, 1962.

Kurtines, W., & Greif, E. G. The development of moral thought: Review and evaluation of Kohlberg's approach. Psychological Bulletin, 1974, 81, 453-470.

Loevinger, J., & Wessler, R. **Measuring ego development** (2 vols.). San Francisco: Jossey-Bass, 1970.

Maitland, K. A., & Goldman, J. R. Moral judgment as a function of peer group interaction. **Journal of Personality and Social Psychology,** 1974, **30,** 699-704.

Maqsud, M. Locus of control and stages of moral reasoning. **Psychological Reports,** 1980, **46,** 1243-1248.

Osipow, S. H., & Walsh, W. B. Social intelligence and the selection of counselors. **Journal of Counseling Psychology,** 1973, **20,** 366-369.

O'Sullivan, M., & Guilford, J. P. Six factors of behavioral cognition: Understanding other people. **Journal of Educational Measurement,** 1975, **12,** 255-271.

Page, R., & Bode, J. Comparison of measures of moral reasoning and development of a new objective measure. **Educational and Psychological Measurement,** 1980, **40,** 317-329.

Perry, W. G. **Forms of intellectual and ethical development in the college years: A scheme.** New York: Holt, Rinehart & Winston, 1968.

Piaget, J. **The moral judgment of the child.** New York: Free Press, 1965. (Originally published, 1932.)

Piaget, J. **Biology and knowledge: An essay on the relations between organic regulations and cognitive processes.** Chicago: University of Chicago Press, 1971. (Originally published, 1967.)

Pittel, S. M., & Mendelsohn, G. A. Measurement of moral values: A review and critique. **Psychological Bulletin,** 1966, **66,** 22-35.

Rest, J. R. Longitudinal study of the Defining Issues Test: A strategy for analyzing developmental change. **Developmental Psychology,** 1975, **11, 738-748.**

Rest, J. R. **Development in judging moral issues.** Minneapolis: University of Minnesota Press, 1979.

Rest, J. R., Cooper, D., Coder, R., Masanz, J., & Anderson, D. Judging the important issues in moral dilemmas--an objective test of development. **Developmental Psychology,** 1974, **10,** 491-501.

Rotter, J. B. Generalized expectancies for internal versus external control of reinforcement. **Psychological Monographs,** 1966, **80,** (Whole No. 609).

Selman, R. L. Social-cognitive understanding: A guide to educational and clinical practice. In T. Lickona (Ed.), **Moral development and behavior: Theory, research, and social issues.** New York: Holt, Rinehart & Winston, 1976.

Selman, R. L. **The growth of interpersonal understanding: Developmental and clinical analyses.** New York: Academic Press, 1980.

Stephens, W., McLaughlin, J., Miller, C., & Glass, G. Factorial structure of selected psycho-educational measures and Piagetian reasoning assessments. **Developmental Psychology,** 1972, **6,** 343-348.

Thorndike, R. L. Intelligence and its use. **Harper's Magazine,** 1920, **140,** 227-235.

Tuddenham, R. D. Theoretical regularities and individual idiosyncrasies. In D. R. Green, M. P. Ford, & G. B. Flamer (Eds.), **Measurement and Piaget.** New York: McGraw-Hill, 1971.

Turiel, E. Conflict and transition in adult moral development. **Child Development,** 1974, **45,** 14-29.

Walker, R. E., & Foley, J. M. Social intelligence: Its history and measurement. **Psychological Reports,** 1973, **33,** 839-864.

Wechsler, D. **The measurement and appraisal of adult intelligence** (4th ed.). Baltimore: Williams & Wilkins, 1958.

Weinstein, E. A. The development of interpersonal competence. In D. A. Goslin (Ed.), **Handbook of socialization theory and research.** Skokie, Ill.: Rand McNally, 1969.

Weisz, J. R. Transcontextual validity in developmental research. **Child Development,** 1978, **49,** 1-12.

Welsh, R. S. Severe parental punishment and delinquency: A developmental theory. **Journal of Clinical Child Psychology,** 1976, **5,** 17-21.

Witkin, H. A. **Cognitive styles in personal and cultural adaptation: Heinz Werner Lecture Series, Vol. 11, 1977.** Worcester, Mass.: Clark University Press, 1978.

Wohlwill, J. **The study of behavioral development.** New York: Academic Press, 1973.

Appendix A

THE

SOCIAL REFLECTION

QUESTIONNAIRE

(Forms A and B)

AND

SRM RATING FORM

SOCIAL REFLECTION QUESTIONNAIRE

Instructions

In this booklet are two social problems with questions for you to answer. We are asking the question not just to find out your opinions about what should be done in the problems, but also to understand **why** you have those opinions. Please answer all the questions, especially the "why" questions. Feel free to use the backs of the pages to finish writing your answers if you need more space.

Name: _____

Age: _____

Sex: (circle one): male/female

Date: _____

PROBLEM ONE

In Europe, a woman was near death from a special kind of cancer. There was one drug that the doctors thought might save her. It was a form of radium that a druggist in the same town had recently discovered. The drug was expensive to make, but the druggist wanted people to pay ten times what the drug cost him to make.

The sick woman's husband, Heinz, went to everyone he knew to borrow the money, but he could only get together about half of what the druggist wanted. Heinz told the druggist that his wife was dying and asked him to sell it cheaper or to let him pay later. But the druggist said, "No. I discovered the drug, and I'm going to make money from it." So the only way Heinz could get the drug would be to break into the druggist's store and steal the drug.

Heinz has a problem. He should help his wife and save her life. But, on the other hand, the only way he could get the drug she needs would be to break the law by stealing the drug.

What should Heinz do?

should steal/should not steal/can't decide (circle one)

Why?

_____

_____

_____

Let's change things about the problem and see if you still have the opinion you circled above (should steal, should not steal, or can't decide). Also, we want to find out about the things you think are important in this and other problems, especially **why** you think those things are important. Please try to help us understand your thinking by WRITING AS MUCH AS YOU CAN TO EXPLAIN YOUR OPINIONS--EVEN IF YOU HAVE TO WRITE OUT YOUR EXPLANATIONS MORE THAN ONCE. Don't just write "same as before." If you can explain better or use different words to show what you mean, that helps us even more. Please answer all the questions below, especially the "why" questions.

1.   What if Heinz's wife asks him to steal the drug for her? Should Heinz:

steal/should not steal/can't decide (circle one)?

1a.   How important is it for a husband to do what his wife asks, to save her by stealing, even when he isn't sure whether that's the best thing to do?

very important/important/not important (circle one)

1b. WHY is that very important/important/not important (whichever one you circled)?

_____

_____

_____

_____

2. What if Heinz doesn't love his wife? Should Heinz:

        steal/not steal/can't decide (circle one)?

2a. How important is it for a husband to steal to save his wife, even if he doesn't love her?

        very important/important/not important (circle one)

2b. WHY is that very important/important/not important (whichever one you circled)?

_____

_____

_____

_____

3. What if the person dying isn't Heinz's wife but instead is a friend (and the friend can get no one else to help)? Should Heinz:

        steal/not steal/can't decide (circle one)?

3a. How important is it to do everything you can, even break the law, to save the life of a friend?

        very important/important/not important (circle one)

3b. WHY is that very important/important/not important (whichever one you circled)?

_____

_____

_____

_____

4a. What about for a stranger? How important is it to do everything you can, even break the law, to save the life of a stranger?

very important/important/not important (circle one)

4b. WHY is that very important/important/not important (whichever one you circled)?

_____

_____

_____

_____

5.   What if the druggist just wants Heinz to pay what the drug cost to make, and Heinz can't even pay that? Should Heinz:

steal/not steal/can't decide (circle one)?

5a. How important is it for people not to take things that belong to other people?

very important/important/not important (circle one)

5b. WHY is that very important/important/not important (whichever one you circled)?

_____

_____

_____

_____

6a. How important is it for people to obey the law?

very important/important/not important (circle one)

6b. WHY is that very important/important/not important (whichever one you circled)?

_____

_____

_____

_____

7.   What if Heinz does steal the drug? His wife does get better, but in the meantime, the police take Heinz and bring him to court. Should the judge:

    jail Heinz/let Heinz go free/can't decide (circle one)?

7a.   How important is it for judges to go easy on people like Heinz?

    very important/important/not important (circle one)

7b.   WHY is that very important/important/not important (whichever one you circled)?

_____

_____

_____

_____

8.   What if Heinz tells the judge that he only did what his conscience told him to do? Should the judge:

    jail Heinz/let Heinz go free/can't decide (circle one)?

8a.   How important is it for judges to go easy on lawbreakers who have acted out of conscience?

    very important/important/not important (circle one)

8b.   WHY is that very important/important/not important (whichever one you circled)?

_____

_____

_____

_____

9.   What if Heinz's wife never had cancer? What if she was only a little sick, and Heinz stole the drug to help her get well a little sooner? Should the judge:

    jail Heinz/let Heinz go free/can't decide (circle one)?

9a.   How important is it for judges to send people who break the law to jail?

    very important/important/not important (circle one)

9b.   WHY is that very important/important/not important (whichever one you circled)?

_____

_____

_____

_____

PROBLEM TWO

Joe is a fourteen-year-old boy who wanted to go to camp very much. His father promised him he could go if he saved up the money for it himself. So Joe worked hard at his paper route and saved up the $40 it cost to go to camp and a little more besides. But just before camp was going to start, his father changed his mind. Some of his father's friends decided to go on a special fishing trip, and Joe's father was short of the money it would cost. So he told Joe to give him the money Joe had saved from the paper route. Joe doesn't want to give up going to camp, so he thinks of refusing to give his father the money.

Joe has a problem. Joe's father promised Joe he could go to camp if he earned and saved up the money. But, on the other hand, the only way Joe could go would be by disobeying and not helping his father.

What should Joe do?

should refuse/should not refuse/can't decide (circle one)

Why?

_____

_____

_____

Let's change things about the problem and see if you still have the opinion you circled above (should refuse, should not refuse, can't decide). Also, we want to find out about the things you think are important in this and other problems, and especially **why** you think those things are important. Please try to help us understand your thinking by WRITING AS MUCH AS YOU CAN TO EXPLAIN YOUR OPINIONS--EVEN IF YOU HAVE TO WRITE OUT YOUR EXPLANATIONS MORE THAN ONCE. Don't just write "same as before." If you can explain better or use different words to show what you mean, that's even better. Please answer all the questions below, especially the "why" questions.

1.   What if Joe hadn't earned the money? What if the father had simply given the money to Joe and promised Joe could use it to go to camp--but now the father wants the money back for the fishing trip? Should Joe:

refuse/not refuse/can't decide (circle one)?

1a.   How important is it for parents to keep their promises about letting their children keep money--even when their children never earned the money?

very important/important/not important (circle one)

1b.   WHY is that very important/important/not important (whichever one you circled)?

_____

_____

_____

_____

2a.   What about keeping a promise to a friend? How important is it to keep a promise, if you can, to a friend?

         very important/important/not important (circle one)

2b.   WHY is that very important/important/not important (whichever one you circled)?

_____

_____

_____

_____

3a.   What about to anyone? How important is it to keep a promise, if you can, even to someone you hardly know?

         very important/important/not important (circle one)

3b.   WHY is that very important/important/not important (whichever one you circled)?

_____

_____

_____

_____

4.   What if Joe's father hadn't **told** Joe to **give** him the money but had just **asked** Joe if he would **lend** the money? Should Joe:

         refuse/not refuse/can't decide (circle one)?

4a.   How important is it for children to help their parents, even when their parents have broken a promise?

         very important/important/not important (circle one)

4b.   WHY is that very important/important/not important (whichever one you circled)?

_____

_____

_____

_____

5.   What if Joe did earn the money, but Joe's father did not promise that Joe could keep the money?

Should Joe:

        refuse/not refuse/can't decide (circle one)?

5a.   How important is it for parents to let their children keep earned money --even when the children were not promised that they could keep the money?

        very important/important/not important (circle one)

5b.   WHY is that very important/important/not important (whichever one you circled)?

_____

_____

_____

_____

6.   What if the father needs the money not to go on a fishing trip but instead to pay for food for the family? Should Joe:

        refuse/not refuse/can't decide (circle one)?

6a.   How important is it for children to help their parents--even when it means that the children won't get to do something they want to do?

        very important/important/not important (circle one)

6b.   WHY is that very important/important/not important (whichever one you circled)?

_____

_____

_____

SOCIAL REFLECTION QUESTIONNAIRE

Instructions

In this booklet are two social problems with questions for you to answer. We are asking the question not just to find out your opinions about what should be done in the problems, but also to understand **why** you have those opinions. Please answer all the questions, especially the "why" questions. Feel free to use the backs of the pages to finish writing your answers if you need more space.

Name: _____

Age: _____

Sex: (circle one): male/female

Date: _____

Form B   (code #: _____)

PROBLEM ONE

Mrs. Jefferson had no more than four months to live because of a very bad cancer. She was in terrible pain, and she was so weak that an extra amount of a special painkiller would make her die quickly and with no pain. She was sometimes delirious and almost crazy with pain. During the times when she was calm, she would ask the doctor to give her enough of the painkiller to kill her. She said she couldn't stand the pain, and she was going to die in a few months anyway. But the doctor said no, so Mrs. Jefferson started asking her husband to do it. The only way Mr. Jefferson could get enough painkiller to kill her would be to steal several bottles of the special drug from the doctor's bag the next time the doctor comes.

Mr. Jefferson has a problem. His wife has asked him to help her by killing her, since she is in terrible pain and is going to die in a few months anyway. But, on the other hand, the only way he could do this would be to break the law by stealing the special drug.

What should Mr. Jefferson do?

should steal/should not steal/can't decide (circle one)

Why?

_____

_____

_____

Let's change things about the problem and see if you still have the opinion you circled above (should steal, should not steal, can't decide). Also, we want to find out about the things you think are important in this and other problems, especially **why** you think those things are important. Please try to help up understand your thinking by WRITING AS MUCH AS YOU CAN TO EXPLAIN YOUR OPINIONS--EVEN IF YOU HAVE TO WRITE OUT YOUR EXPLANATIONS MORE THAN ONCE. Don't just write "same as before." If you can explain better or use different words to show what you mean, that helps us even more. Please answer all the questions below, especially the "why" questions.

1.   What if Mr. Jefferson's wife pleads with him to steal the special painkiller? Should Mr. Jefferson:

steal/not steal/can't decide (circle one)?

1a.   How important is it for a husband to do what his wife asks, even when he isn't sure whether that's the best thing to do?

very important/important/not important (circle one)

1b.   WHY is that very important/important/not important (whichever one you circled)?

_____

_____

_____

_____

2.   What if Mr. Jefferson doesn't love his wife? Should Mr. Jefferson:

           steal/not steal/can't decide (circle one)?

2a.   How important is it for a husband to steal to help his wife end her pain, even if he doesn't love her?

2b.   WHY is that very important/important/not important (whichever one you circled)?

_____

_____

_____

_____

3.   What if the person dying is not Mr. Jefferson's wife but instead is a friend (and the friend can get no one else to help)? Should Mr. Jefferson:

           steal/not steal/can't decide (circle one)?

3a.   How important is it to do everything you can, even break the law, to help a friend die sooner to escape terrible pain?

           very important/important/not important (circle one)

3b.   WHY is that very important/important/not important (whichever one you circled)?

_____

_____

_____

_____

4.   What if the woman isn't dying? What if she is not sick but instead is unable to walk--a cripple--and wants to die? Should Mr. Jefferson:

           steal/not steal/can't decide (circle one)?

4a.   How important is it for people to live even when they don't want to?

very important/important/not important (circle one)

4b.   WHY is that very important/important/not important (whichever one you circled)?

_____

_____

_____

_____

5.   What if Mr. Jefferson isn't sure what he should do but thinks of the fact that the only way he could get the special painkiller would be by stealing it? Should Mr. Jefferson:

steal/not steal/can't decide (circle one)?

5a.   How important is it for people not to take things that belong to other people?

very important/important/not important (circle one)

5b.   WHY is that very important/important/not important (whichever one you circled)?

_____

_____

_____

_____

6a.   How important is it for people to obey the law?

very important/important/not important (circle one)

6b.   WHY is that very important/important/not important (whichever one you circled)?

_____

_____

_____

_____

7.   What if Mr. Jefferson does steal the drug? His wife does die quickly and without pain, but soon after that the police take Mr. Jefferson and bring him to court. Should the judge:

    jail Mr. Jefferson/let Mr. Jefferson go free/can't decide (circle one)?

7a. How important is it for judges to go easy on people like Mr. Jefferson?

        very important/important/not important (circle one)

7b. WHY is that very important/important/not important (whichever one you circled)?

_____

_____

_____

_____

8.   What if Mr. Jefferson tells the judge that he only did what his conscience told him to do? Should the judge:

    jail Mr. Jefferson/let Mr. Jefferson go free/can't decide (circle one)?

8a. How important is it for judges to go easy on lawbreakers who have acted out of conscience?

        very important/important/not important (circle one)

8b. WHY is that very important/important/not important (whichever one you circled)?

_____

_____

_____

_____

9.   What if Mrs. Jefferson never had cancer? What if she was only a little sick, and Mr. Jefferson stole the special drug to help her get well a little sooner? Should the judge:

    jail Mr. Jefferson/let Mr. Jefferson go free/can't decide (circle one)?

9a. How important is it for judges to send people who break the law to jail?

        very important/important/not important (circle one)

9b.   WHY is that very important/important/not important (whichever one you circled)?

_____

_____

_____

_____

PROBLEM TWO

Judy is a twelve-year-old girl. Her mother promised her that she could go to a special rock concert coming to their town if she saved up from baby-sitting and lunch money so she would have enough money to buy a ticket to the concert. She managed to save up the five dollars the ticket cost plus another four dollars. But then her mother changed her mind and told Judy that she had to spend the money on new clothes for school. Judy was disappointed and decided to go to the concert anyway. She bought a ticket and told her mother that she had only been able to save four dollars. That Saturday she went to the performance and told her mother that she was spending the day with a friend. A week passed without her mother finding out. Then Judy told her older sister, Louise, that she had gone to the performance and had lied to their mother about it. Louise wonders whether to tell their mother what Judy did.

Louise has a problem. Louise knows that Judy doesn't want to be told on, and their mother did promise Judy she could go to the rock concert if she earned and saved up the money. But, on the other hand, their mother would want to know about Judy's lying and disobeying.

What should Louise do?

        should tell/should keep quiet/can't decide (circle one)

Why?

_____

_____

_____

    Let's change things about the problem and see if you still have the opinion you circled above (should tell, should keep quiet, or can't decide). Also, we want to find out about the things you think are important in this and other problems, especially **why** you think those things are important. Please try to help us understand your thinking by WRITING AS MUCH AS YOU CAN TO EXPLAIN YOUR OPINIONS--EVEN IF YOU HAVE TO WRITE OUT YOUR EXPLANATIONS MORE THAN ONCE. Don't just write "same as before." If you can explain better or use different words to show what you mean, that helps us even more. Please answer all the questions below, especially the "why" questions.

1.   What if Judy hadn't earned the money? What if the mother had simply given the money to Judy and promised Judy she could use it to go to the concert-- but now the mother wants the money back to help with buying Judy her school clothes? Should Louise:

        tell/keep quiet/can't decide (circle one)?

1a.   How important is it for parents to keep their promises about letting their children keep money, even when the children never earned the money?

       very important/important/not important (circle one)

1b.   WHY is that very important/important/not important (whichever one you circled)?

_____

_____

_____

_____

2a.   Louise thinks about the fact that her sister is her friend. How important is it to keep a promise, if you can, to a friend?

       very important/important/not important (circle one)

2b.   WHY is that very important/important/not important (whichever one you circled)?

_____

_____

_____

_____

3a.   What about to anyone? How important is it to keep a promise, if you can, even to someone you hardly know?

       very important/important/not important (circle one)

3b.   WHY is that very important/important/not important (whichever one you circled)?

_____

_____

_____

_____

4.   What if Judy has earned a lot of money--so much money that she could have gone to the rock concert and still given her mother enough money to help pay for new school clothes? Should Louise:

tell/keep quiet/can't decide (circle one)?

4a.   How important is it for children to help their parents, even when their parents have broken a promise to them?

very important/important/not important (circle one)

4b.   WHY is that very important/important/not important (whichever one you circled)?

_____

_____

_____

_____

5.   What if Judy did earn the money, but their mother did not promise that Judy could spend the money she earned the way she wants? Should Louise:

tell/keep quiet/can't decide (circle one)?

5a.   How important is it for parents to let their children keep earned money --even when the children were not promised that they could spend the money the way they wish?

very important/important/not important (circle one)

5b.   WHY is that very important/important/not important (whichever one you circled)?

_____

_____

_____

_____

6. What if the mother needs the money to pay for food for the family? Should Louise:

tell/keep quiet/can't decide (circle one)?

6a.   How important is it for children to do everything they can to help their parents--even when it means that the children won't get to do something they want to do?

very important/important/not important (circle one)

6b.   WHY is that very important/important/not important (whichever one you circled)?

_____

_____

_____

_____

PROTOCOL STAGE RATING

CODE #: _____

FORM: A/B (circle one)

RATER: _____

DATE: _____

MODAL: _____

SRMS: _____

GLOBAL: _____

Prob-lem	Norm (question)	Question Referent	Aspect Citation	Level	Comments (e.g., Orientation A or B)
One	1: Affil. (1b, 2b, 3b)				
	2: Life (4b)				
	3: LwPrp. (5b, 6b)				
	4: Legal Justice (7b, 9b)				
	5: Con-science (8b)				
	6: Fam. Affil. (1b, 4b, 6b)				
Two	7: Contract (2b, 3b)				
	8: Property (5b)				

Stage: Weightings

Computational Space

1: _____

2: _____

3: _____

4: _____

Total: _____

TR: _____ A: _____

TP: _____ B: _____

Appendix B

NORM EXERCISES

AND

ANNOTATED

SCORING KEYS

NORM 1:

Affiliation (Marriage and Friendship)

1. Helping one's spouse (even if he doesn't love her) is not important because: if he doesn't love his wife why should he save her even if its his
wife. (Form A)

2. Helping one's spouse is not important because: it is not important because he might not want her to die and if he lover he wouldn't want her
to die. (Form B)

3. Helping one's friend is important: if you may steal for a good reason but
it is a leagil. (Form B)

4. Helping one's wife is not important because: some people don't do what
other people ask them to do. People don't no what to do about it. (Form
B)

5. Helping one's friend is not important because: trying to get a friend to
do something for you by stealing something is not really a friend. (Form
A)

6. Helping one's wife even when he doesn't love her is not important because: if he doesn't love her he could easily rid her by stealing the
drug. If charges a pressed, they would be dropped because she pleaded for
drugs. (Form B)

7. Helping one's wife is not important because: I don't believe in making
someone do something they don't want too and if it goes against Mr.
Jeffersons values then his wife should try to understand. (Form B)

8. Helping one's wife is very important because: if he cares about her a lot
he sould save here live or he will be hurt for the rest of his life.
(Form A)

9. Helping one's friend is important because: he might loss a best friend if
he don't and he might loss his life stealing it. (Form A)

10. Helping one's wife is very important because: A husband's love for his
wife should be greater than any other force on earth. Stealing the drug
was fulfilling that bond of love. The ultimate of sacrificing his freedom, pride or possibly chancing jail is his duty as a man and even more
as her husband. (Form A)

11. Helping one's wife is important because: I would say it is important because a husband and wife should be able to depend on one another. I don't
think this should be done in every case (example would be wife wanting
husband to steal simply for greed). (Form B)

12. Helping one's friend is important because: it is important to help them
get rid of pain but it is'nt right braek the law or steal. (Form B)

13. Helping one's friend is important because: It still is important to do as
much as you can to help a fellow human being. (Form A)

14. Helping one's wife even if he doesn't love her is **important** because: **if he didn't love her it wouldn't be as important as stealing if he loved her. (Form A)**

15. Helping one's wife is **not important** because: **the issue is a saving of a human life, not the particular relationship described in the story—at least in my opinion. Of course it is easier to feel an obligation because of the relationship, but I feel it is just a matter of degree. For instance, I feel the same way about people in Cambodia, but I am not moved to action. (Form A).**

16. Helping one's wife even if he doesn't love her is **not important** because: **one should never steal, no matter what the circumstances, even if he doesn't love her. (Form A).**

17. Helping one's wife is **important** because: **he could do it for his wife and get in trouble or not get in trouble. (Form B)**

18. Helping one's wife is **not important** because: **That isn't the issue. It's whether a person has a right to die without suffering or whether it's a person's responsibility to preserve life. (Form B)**

19. Helping one's wife even if he doesn't love her is **not important** because: **if he doesn't love her than why risk getting caught stealing a drug that your unimportant wife needs. (Form A)**

20. Helping one's friend is **not important** because: **I don't think it's important for anyone to brake the law their are always other ways not breaking the law. (Form B)**

21. Helping one's wife even if he doesn't love her is **very important** because: **I think it is very important. Even if he doesn't love her he can't just stand around and let her die when there's something he could do that might save her. (Form A)**

22. Helping one's friend is **important** because: **it depends on how close you are to that friend. People need help, and sometimes you will be the only one they can depend on. You must come through and help them to the best of your abilities. (Form A)**

23. Helping one's wife is **very important** because: **a person's life is more important than someone getting punished for a crime. If there is even a slight chance at saving a life it should be taken. If the druggist valued his own life at all he would give Heinz the drug because he has no right to say who lives or dies. (Form A)**

24. Helping one's friend is **important** because: **like above, the Golden Rule comes into play. Man's law is not good sometimes as in this case and it would be moral to steal. (Form B)**

25. Helping one's friend is **very important** because: **if he had a friend who had this disease and that friend was only one who could help. He would want that friend to save the other person's life. (Form A)**

26.   Helping one's friend is **not important** because: he would be breaking the law, get blamed for something his wife wanted him to do, and go to jail. (Form B)

27.   Helping one's friend is **important** because: It is important to be true to a friend, but one must also be true to oneself and therefore one should not take the risk in breaking the law. (Form B)

28.   Helping one's wife is **very important** because: I think if Heinz wouldn't do it to save his own wifes life that he must not love her very much. (Form A)

29.   Helping one's wife even if he doesn't love her is **important** because: it is important because his sense of duty should oblige him to do so. Maybe he doesn't love her anymore, but when he married her, he has accepted to be her friend. And friends should help one another when the asking is justified. (Form B)

30.   Helping one's wife is **important** because: He should not steal. Because he could go into jail by stealing. (Form B)

NORM 2:

Life

1.   Saving the life of a stranger is **not important** because: not important because it is a stranger and you do not no how bad he or her we need it. Anywhae he could go to prison. (Form A)

2.   Saving the life of a stranger is **important** because: It would be cruel to not help someone who is dying. (Form A)

3.   Living even when you don't want to is **important** because: you were not put on this earth to try and kill yourself, you should enjoy being alive and love it. (Form B)

4.   Living even when you don't want to is **important** because: well if I where her I would want to live not die. Dieing is a problem in the family it upsets everybody. (Form B)

5.   Saving the life of a stranger is **not important** because: I would not steal for a stranger because I don't think I should have to go to jail for a stranger that I have no compassion for. (Form A)

6.   Saving the life of a stranger is **not important** because: this stranger you don't kow what he could do. (Form A)

7.   Saving the life of a stranger is **important** because: you should save a stranger from dying but why should he steal. (Form A)

8.   Saving the life of a stranger is **important** because: a life is sacred and as people who should be concerned with everyone's welfare. Laws are made by people and can be changed. There are times when the law should be broken. It would be up to the person to decide whether or not he is willing to risk his neck for a stranger which he has no feeling for. (Form A)

9. Living even when you don't want to is **very important** because: **you can have some of the greatest times when you are handicapped!** (Form B)

10. Living even when you don't want to is **very important** because: **people heive lives to and they have to go on even if they don't like it.** (Form B)

11. Living even when you don't want to is **important** because: **whether the person is crippled or whole he/she still has an impact on the lives of those around him—it can be for good or not. But, whatever the influence, people should live out their lives and experience the whole thing. No one should quit.** (Form B)

12. Saving a stranger's life is **not important** because: **if he stold some medicen that stranger can tell the police.** (Form A)

13. Living even when you don't want to is **very important** because: **most of the time they need someone. They realy want to live but need more adention.** (Form B)

14. Living even when you don't want to is **very important** because: **it is very important to think and learn and love and thank God you is liveing to by someboddy.** (Form B)

15. Living even when you don't want to is **very important** because: **all that woman is doing is feeling sorry for herself and thats one thing I cant stand is self pity. She has to try to adjust and make a new life for herself it may be hard but if she has any kind of courage she can and will do it.** (Form B)

16. Saving a stranger's life is not **important** because: **I don't think that a stranger could be that important to you, that you would want to save his life. It could, however, affect the number of friends you make in the future.** (Form A)

17. Living even when you don't want to is **very important** because: **life is a precious gift from God and we don't have the right to refuse him.** (Form B)

18. Saving a stranger's life is **important** because: **It still doesn't matter. This person should still be able to live. After all, he's not a stranger to everyone. Someone knows and loves him.** (Form A)

19. Saving a stranger's life is not **important** because: **Later on when you're done and out that stranger won't remember you. He'll just spit on you.** (Form A)

20. Saving a stranger's life is very **important** because: **again, the mans obligation does not end because it is not his wife or friend. The fact that the one in need is a human being places him in the seat of responsibility. The fact that he has a power to choose gives him the obligation.** (Form A)

21. Saving a stranger's life is not **important** because: **I wouldn't break the law for a stranger because if you did it for a wife or a friend they**

would probably do it for you to but I wouldn't get myself into trouble for someone I don't even know. (Form A)

22. Saving a stranger's life is **important** because: **a selfish human should not be allowed to hold strings on someone's life. (Form A)**

23. Saving a stranger's life is **not important** because: **there's no obligation because there's no bond between the bond. At least, not enough to provoke breaking the law. (Form A)**

24. Saving a stranger's life is **not important** because: **if he means nothing to you, you could consider stealing, although trying your hardest for another means of saving his life without jeopardizing yours. (Form A)**

25. Saving a stranger's life is **important** because: **saving a persons life is the most important thing I can think of. (Form A)**

26. Living even when you don't want to is **very important** because: **other people want her to live. 1 against more than one. (Form B)**

27. Living even when you don't want to is **very important** because: **if he/she wants to die and you refuse he/she may want to commit suicide. (Form B)**

28. Saving a stranger's life is **important** because: **you wouldn't want to put you're life on the line to save someone you don't even know, but you can help as much as you can. (Form A)**

29. Living even when you don't want to is **very important** because: **the best example of usefullness of a supposedly useless life is Helen Keller—another is Charley Boswell. (Form B)**

30. Living even when you don't want to is **very important** because: **God didn't give people a body to abuse. (Form B)**

NORM 3:

Law and Property

1. Not stealing is **very important** because: **if you had something special and someone stold it. It wouldn't be there for you to have something special. (Form B)**

2. Not stealing is **very important** because: **The reason why is because it doesn't belong to you, and they might have worked hard for whatever it is. (Form A)**

3. Not stealing is **very important** because: **it is not yours and kids could be put in a detention home and men and women could be put in jail. (Form A)**

4. Not stealing is **very important** because: **some people would not take things from any body, and they do not want anybody taking things from them. (Form A)**

5. Not stealing is **important** because: **they have worked for it and it is there's no matter how selfish. But in this case there is an exception. (Form A)**

6. Obeying the law is **very important** because: **if everyone didn't obey the law a lot of people would be hurt and it would not be safe in to many places. (Form B)**

7. Obeying the law is **very important** because: **I'm talking about God's law and not Man's. Because man's law is only in play for a short time, considering the aspect of eternity. To follow man's law, though, it is better to do it if it complies with the certain situation you're in. (Form B)**

8. Obeying the law is **very important** because: **you could go to jail or get electrocuted in the electret chair. (Form B)**

9. Not stealing is **very important** because: **It could be very dangerous to take something like the pain killer because it could harm you instead of helping you die. (Form B)**

10. Obeying the law is **very important** because: **Laws were set up to make life better for everyone, even if they are not well accepted. If he stole, he would be infringing upon the rights of the druggist.**

11. Not stealing is **very important** because: **its very important because if everyone took what wasn't theres the world would be worse than it is today. (Form A)**

12. Not stealing is **very important** because: **he should think about his life and future so he would not get involved with he's wife's death. (Form B)**

13. Obeying the law is **very important** because: **if we didn't have law country would be something else. (Form B)**

14. Not stealing is **very important** because: **because you will be steal other people things. (Form B)**

15. Not stealing is **very important** because: **they bought them and the maybe need them like kid home work from ther teacher just like if you rob a bank the banker will git in trouble from the people. (Form A)**

16. Obeying the law is **very important** because: **If no one obeyed the law we would have mass chaos. (Form B)**

17. Not stealing is **not important** because: **the question of whether or not to steal for ethical reasons is redundant. The moral difference between humanity and ethics ranks highly. (Form B)**

18. Not stealing is **very important** because: **if everyone went around stealing I think the world would always be at war. I think by stealing is the lowest anyone could get. I don't consider the above example stealing. (Form B)**

19. Not stealing is **very important** because: **taking things from others is really mean. Like if Heinz took that drug it would not be right because this is like the druggist pride & joy because he found something that can safe lives. (Form A)**

20. Obeying the law is **very important** because: **the laws keep our society in**

order. If people would obey the laws our society would have fewer problems (thefts, fires, murders, accidents, etc. (Form A)

21. Not stealing is important because: some rules and regulations should
exist in society so that everyone is aware of the boundaries. (Form B)

22. Obeying the law is very important because: if nobody obeyed the law life
would be unhappy. People wouldn't be able to earn money to buy things
from other countries. People would be murdered if they got in a small ar-
guement. (Form B)

23. Not stealing is not important because: it is never important to steal for
any reason. (Form A)

24. Obeying the law is very important because: if no one obeyed the law, then
the world would be overthrown with crime. (Form A)

25. Obeying the law is important because: you have to abide by the law. People can't run around breaking the law just because they feel like it.
(Form A)

26. Obeying the law is very important because: you break the law you have to
pay the price like sentenced in jail for the west of your life. (Form A)

27. Not stealing is very important because: if no one obeyed the law then
there would be no way to predict behavior in society. In every situation,
your actions are dictated by the actions of those around you—if their
actions don't fit a pattern to which you can relate, than your response
also fits no pattern & society is chaos. (Form B)

28. Obeying the law is very important because: I think it is very important
oboying the law because you don't no what could happen to you. (Form A)

29. Obeying the law is very important because: it is very important to obey
the law, for the reason of preserving some sort of harmony and to prevent
chaos and to protect the rights of others. (Form A)

30. Not stealing is important because: stealing does not alter ownership.
Having something in one's possession does not mean it is owned. And without proper ownership, one has no legitimate rights to use. (Form B)

NORM 4:

Legal Justice

1. Going easy on people like Heinz is very important (cf. Sending lawbreakers to jail is not important) because: the man is helping his wife
and because he loves his wife and can't aford to pay the money. (Form A)

2. Going easy on people like Heinz is important (cf. Sending lawbreakers to
jail is not important) because: the man saved a life. It is better to
steal than to let someone die. The judge should fine Heinz, put him on
probation, and warn him never to break the law again, but to ask the
authority's help. (Form A)

3. Sending lawbreakers to jail is very important because: if easy on one

person then he'd have to be easy on every one and nobody would bet in jail. (Form B)

4. Going easy on people like Mr. Jefferson is **very important** (cf. Sending lawbreakers to jail is **not important**) because: **because Mrs. Jefferson told Mr. Jefferson to steel the drugs. (Form B)**

5. Sending lawbreakers to jail is **very important** because: **he shouldn't send Heinz to jail, he should send the doctor, because the doctor said that she was ding when she wasn't, he was trying to make money. (Form A)**

6. Sending lawbreakers to jail is **very important** because: **the law must be enforced, even if it is incorrect. One cannot let a person go free because one "feels sorry" for him. If one would do this, then he/she would be opening the floodgates for many more to break the same law. (Form B)**

7. Going easy on people like Heinz is **important** (cf. Sending lawbreakers to jail is **not important**) because: **he would already be being punished for 2 things. Already his wife died plus now he has to stay in jail. (Form A)**

8. Sending lawbreakers to jail is **very important** because: **thats what laws are for and if people break them they should be punished to try and prevent other people from doing the same thing. (Form B)**

9. Going easy on people like Heinz is **very important** (cf. Sending lawbreakers to jail is **not important**) because: **Heinz bid not no if his wife would get better. (Form A)**

10. Sending lawbreakers to jail is **very important** because: **It is very important for judges to send people to jail who do wrong. If everyone who broke the law, was set free, no one would obey laws. (Form B)**

11. Going easy on people like Heinz is **not important** (cf. Sending lawbreakers to jail is **important**) because: **I don't think it is important at all he commited a crime and he should pay just like everyone else does. (Form A)**

12. Going easy on people like Heinz is **important** (cf. Sending lawbreakers to jail is **not important**) because: **the judge has a hard decision to make but for Heinz's own benefit & the benefit of society he has to deal with the situation as it is & a crime was committed whatever the reasons behind it. (Form A)**

13. Sending lawbreakers to jail is **very important** because: **it will lern people a lesen. (Form A)**

14. Sending lawbreakers to jail is **important** because: **now we can consider the justness of good and bad laws. In this Christian perspective we render unto Ceaser that which is Ceaser's and unto God that which is God's. If a law is unjust according to Christian principal (and God's law always outweighs Ceaser's) we should be willing to suffer the consequences if we break the civil law we feel to be unjust, such as "separate but equal facilities." However, we must be willing to go to jail for breaking the civil law. (Form B)**

15. Going easy on people like Heinz is **very important** (cf. Sending law-

breakers to jail is **not important**) because: **extenuating circumstances should always be considered in dealing with human situations. No two people or situations are alike and no set rules apply to all situations equally. (Form A)**

16. Sending lawbreakers to jail is **important** because: **it really depends on the facts of the different cases. (Form A)**

17. Going easy on people like Heinz is **very important** (cf. Sending lawbreakers to jail is **not important**) because: **it is his fault and he sould take the punishment and go to jell. (Form A)**

18. Sending lawbreakers to jail is **important** because: **breaking the law is very bad he should to to jail for a couple of months to see how it feels. (Form B)**

19. Sending lawbreakers to jail is **very important** because: **if the law is broke and someone got hurt and you are the someone you wouldn't want him to go free and hurt someone else.**

20. Going easy on people like Heinz is **important** (cf. Sending lawbreakers to jail is **not important**) because: **you have to understand the facts and what went on and feelings. (Form A)**

21. Going easy on people like Heinz is **not important** (cf. Sending lawbreakers to jail is **important**) because: **what he did was wrong and he should put him in jail because other people would just get out of evreything. (Form A)**

22. Going easy on people like Mr. Jefferson is **not important** (cf. Sending lawbreakers to jail is **important**) because: **we don't know if Mr. Jefferson feelings towards his wife were to help her or get rid of her. This is very contriversial. (Form B)**

23. Going easy on people like Heinz is **not important** (cf. Sending lawbreakers to jail is **important**) because: **they have to learn. (Form A)**

24. Sending lawbreakers to jail is **very important** because: **consistency builds security and trust in people's minds. If the laws start varying to fit different situations people don't have as much respect for laws and therefore violate them. (Form A)**

25. Going easy on people like Heinz is **not important** (cf. Sending lawbreakers to jail is **important**) because: **if one person started doing this then they would have everyone using this as an excuse to steal. I don't think maybe they should be extremely hard on him, but shouldn't let him free either. (Form A)**

26. Going easy on people like Mr. Jefferson is **not important** (cf. Sending lawbreakers to jail is **important**) because: **people would kill people and say she or he wanted me to kill them, and get away with it. (Form B)**

27. Going easy on people like Heinz is **important** (cf. Sending lawbreakers to jail is **not important**) because: **Heinz stole this drug in order to save a human being, but judges shoul not be to easy or hard criminals will get let of easy. (Form A)**

28. Going easy on people like Mr. Jefferson is **important** (cf. Sending law-breakers to jail is **not** **important** because: **certainly it is obvious that one who steals or kills because of pressure from one who is suffering cannot possibly be held on the same level as one who brutally murders someone. Mr. Jefferson will suffer the remainder of his life no matter which decision he makes and additional punishment whould not be justified. (Form B)**

29. Going easy on people like Mr. Jefferson is **important** (cf. Sending law-breakers to jail is **not** **important**) because: **he was doing one thing to help his wife and he was stealing. (Form B)**

30. Sending lawbreakers to jail is **important** because: **It is important that people who break the law for no reason of importance, like life—death, go to jail. This includes people who steal money and food. Although they are essential, everyone else earns their own food and money, so the criminal should, too. (Form B)**

NORM 5:

Conscience

1. Going easy on people who have acted out of conscience is **very important** because: **he is nice and cine. (Form B)**

2. Going easy on people who have acted out of conscience is **not important** because: **It was his moral obligation. (Form A)**

3. Going easy on people who have acted out of conscience is **not important** because: **some people have consciences that are not very moral, this should not influence a judge. What is fair and just should be the determining factor of the situation. The judge should not let him go free because of his conscience but because that would be the fair thing to do. (Form A)**

4. Going easy on people who have acted out of conscience is **important** because: **He can't control himself he do it because he love his wife. (Form B)**

5. Going easy on people who have acted out of conscience is **not important** because: **he could be telling a lie. (Form B)**

6. Going easy on people who acted out of conscience is **important** because: **maybe he thinks he was only thinking of conscience and not thinking of his wife the memery would be on him for the west of his life. (Form A)**

7. Going easy on people who acted out of conscience is **important** because: **people do all most everying that there conscience tells them to do. (Form A)**

8. Going easy on people who acted out of conscience is **important** because: **its important but how do you prove they did? It would depend on the case and what was a stake. (Form A)**

9. Going easy on people who acted out of conscience is **not important** because: **a guy could say he killed someone because his conscience says to. (Form A)**

10. Going easy on people who have acted out of conscience is not important because Jefferson did no harm, he thought, because of his conscience. Everyone has the right to his own conscience, but not break the law. (Form B)

11. Going easy on people who acted out of conscience is important because: Conscience is one of many things that all people have. sometimes your conscience can take over your life. (Form A)

12. Going easy on people who acted out of conscience is not important because: conscience is a mighty flimsy excuse. Suppose someone said his "conscience" told him to murder a man who was advocating civil rights for blacks. Each society must have norms, with some room for fluctuations. (Form B)

13. Going easy on people who acted out of conscience is not important because: what if you were like Jim Jones of Jonestown and your conscience told you to kill a thousand people then because of your conscience you've taken 1,000's of lives that might not want to be taken away. (Form B)

14. Going easy on people who acted out of conscience is very important because: he probly won't do it again. (Form A)

15. Going easy on people who acted out of conscience is important because: when people act out of their conscience they be trying to do the right think for the person who is in trouble. (Form B)

16. Going easy on people who acted out of conscience is very important because: laws have to be made so that there is a common consensus as to what is right and what is wrong. If judges "bend" the laws they lessen the degree of authority. (Form A)

17. Going easy on people who acted out of conscience is important because: I guess that if the man did it for her benefit and acting out of conscience mind that is important factor but he still broke the law. He should be punished. (Form B)

18. Going easy on people who acted out of conscience is important because: the judge should not play favorites to anyone. If he feels the only fair thing to do would be to jail him then he should. (Form B)

19. Going easy on people who acted out of conscience is very important because: they should go hard on Heinz. You do not do what other people tell you to do. (Form A)

20. Going easy on people who acted out of conscience is not important because: his envirement helped his conscience so if his conscience told him to steel he must not have had a good envirement. (Form B)

21. Going easy on people who acted out of conscience is not important because: they might trick they might act like they are paralize. (Form A)

22. Going easy on people who acted out of conscience is important because: It is important for judges to consider conscience, but they must also take into consideration the good of society. Many criminals feel that their consciense told them what to do, but their victims and society may have a different view. (Form A)

23. Going easy on people who acted out of conscience is **not important** because: **the judge has his responsibility to evaluate the situation and deel with it according to the law. (Form A)**

24. Going easy on people who acted out of conscience is **very important** because: **he did what Mrs. Jefferson told him to do. And Mrs. Jefferson wanted to kill her ownself. (Form B)**

25. Going easy on people who acted out of conscience is **important** because: **it should be taken into account, especially if it were humanitarian in concept. (Form B)**

26. Going easy on people who acted out of conscience is **not important** because: **he shouldn't pay attention to his conscience if their that bad. (Form B)**

27. Going easy on people who acted out of conscience is **not important** because: **a good judge would look at all circumstances, pressures, and motives. It is not possible to say flatly that he should go easy on people wo have acted out of conscience without knowing more facts. Hopefully the judge would give a good interpretation of the letter and intent of the law. (Form B)**

28. Going easy on people who acted out of conscience is **very important** because: **the reason why it is importan is that he should not of stold the drugs. (Form B)**

29. Going easy on people who acted out of conscience is **very important** because: **when deciding a case the judge should examine the motives behind the act. In this case the judge should realize the extremity of the situation and let Heinz go free. (Form A)**

30. Going easy on people who acted out of conscience is **important** because: **the judge should understand that he did it to save a life and should go a little easier on him. (Form A)**

NORM 6:

Family Affiliation

1. Helping one's parents is **important** because: **if the parnet can help the child, the child can help the parnet. (Form B)**

2. Helping one's parents is **important** because: **the parents are the bosses. (Form A)**

3. Helping one's parents is **very important** because: **it is better for a whole family to be happy and healthy instead of just one child. (Form A)**

4. Helping one's parents is **not important** because: **not that important when the parents broke there promise. (Form A)**

5. Helping one's parents is **very important** because: **the parents might end up doing it for them anyway. (Form B)**

6. Keeping promises to one's children is **very important** because: **it is important for anyone to keep his word. It is very important for parents to**

keep their word to their children. Their children will lose faith, trust, and respect for them if they lie or mistreat their children. (Form A)

7. Helping one's parents is **very important** because: **it is important for the parents to have a good relationship with their children. Both make mistakes ocassionally, but it shouldn't be a matter of revenge. (Form B)**

8. Helping one's parents is **very important** because: **the kid earned the money. (Form B)**

9. Keeping promises to one's children is **important** because: **it is not the end of you like you can do it some other time. (Form B)**

10. Helping one's parents is **very important** because: **To me a sacrifice for someone in your family is nothing—it is a sign of love. If gestures such as this one are made then the family will run more smoothly. (Form A)**

11. Helping one's parents is **important** because: **if their parents break a promise they will probably have a good reason, but if you don't help them and there is no excuse then your parents will be very hurt. (Form B)**

12. Helping one's parents is **very important** because: **your part of the family too! (Form A)**

13. Helping one's parents is **very important** because: **you should always give you parents help. No matter what. (Form A)**

14. Helping one's parents is **very important** because: **very important becous it is right to obey your parents. (Form A)**

15. Helping one's parents is **important** because: **children should help their parents, when possible, out of respect. However, parents need to respect their children. (Form B)**

16. Helping one's parents is **very important** because: **be nice and gentow to your parents. (Form B)**

17. Keeping promises to one's children is **very important** because: **It is a gift to go along with a promise. Parents, not only children to parents, have to respect what they say and not dishonor their kids. (Form A)**

18. Helping one's parents is **very important** because: **in a family situation you are all in it together. When needs arise they must be met by the resources of the entire family. (Form A)**

19. Keeping promises to one's children is **very important** because: **it's very important to stick to your promises and not break your promise. (Form B)**

20. Keeping promises to one's children is **very important** because: **they should not break a promise. (Form B)**

21. Helping one's parents is **very important** because: **your mother and father broght you up in the world and got you on your feet. (Form B)**

22. Helping one's parents is **very important** because: **they still are their parents and what they said might have been the best thing for them. (Form B)**

23. Helping one's parents is **important** because: **children should respect and help their parents whenever possible. (Form A)**

24. Helping one's parents is **very important** because: **if they had to brake a promise it would be there chose. (Form A)**

25. Helping one's parents is **very important** because: **their parents usually provide most of what is needed. I think just because you love them and they love you is reason enough. (Form A)**

26. Helping one's parents is **very important** because: **there parents need help them bad or they would not ask. (Form A)**

27. Keeping promises to one's children is **very important** because: **it is very important because Joe might have been waiting to go to camp for a long time. (Form A)**

28. Keeping promises to one's children is **important** because: **it is important that parents keep any promise whether has something to do with money or not. But the parents should also make their children learn responsibility by letting them earn money. (Form A)**

29. Keeping promises to one's children is **important** because: **children have to mind their parents and it is stupid to tell you child that they could go and then turn around and so no. (Form B)**

30. Helping one's parents is **very important** because: **if you love your mother and you want to do what she wants you to do then do it. (Form B)**

NORM 7:

Contract

1. Keeping a promise (to a friend) is **very important** because: **you should keep the promise because if you don't you might loose a friend. (Form A)**

2. Keeping a promise (to a friend) is **very important** because: **because your telling a lie to your friend. (Form B)**

3. Keeping a promise (to a friend) is **important** because: **because he's your best frind and you like him very much. (Form A)**

4. Keeping a promise (to a friend) is **very important** because: **it shows you have true friendship. (Form A)**

5. Keeping a promise (to a stranger) is **very important** because: **it is best to keep promises whenever possible, although loss of virtue is the price paid for a broken promise. (Form B)**

6. Keeping a promise (to a stranger) is **important** because: **because you don't know this person very hard you know that if you tell them they mite blabbered it all over town. (Form B)**

7. Keeping a promise (to a stranger) is **important** because: **if you promise something to someone you should keep that promise. (Form A)**

8. Keeping a promise (to a stranger) is **very important** because: **any person**

wants what he take seriously to be respect it hurts no one to return such respect. (Form B)

9. Keeping a promise (to a friend) is **very important** because: **It is extremely important to keep a promise to a friend. A friendship will develop out of trust. A person will loose faith in another if they can't rely on them. (Form A)**

10. Keeping a promise (to a stranger) is **very important** because: **of the many different stimuli and changing activities in the world today honesty is one virtue that everyone can relate to. If everyone would keep their word there would be more openness and the problems caused could be defined better and worked out much sooner and easier. (Form A)**

11. Keeping a promise (to a friend) is **important** because: **so your friend can trust you to keep a promise. (Form A)**

12. Keeping a promise (to a friend) is **very important** because: **the ability to have faith in another person is a very important basis for life. The stability will encourage children to model themselves in a positive manner and therefore create positive mental attitudes. (Form B)**

13. Keeping a promise (to a stranger) is **important** because: **that would help you to gain more friends and people would think of you as a good person. (Form A).**

14. Keeping a promise (to a stranger) is **very important** because: **her might bet you up. (Form A)**

15. Keeping a promise (to a stranger) is **very important** because: **the person to whom you gave your word is not that important. It is the promise itself that should have value. (Form B)**

16. Keeping a promise (to a friend) is **very important** because: **a friend is hoping you don't tell something and you do you are almost hearting a friends heart. (Form B)**

17. Keeping a promise (to a stranger) is **very important** because: **but if they do something wrong you should tell. (Form B)**

18. Keeping a promise (to a stranger) is **not important** because: **they might forget that they had not know. (Form A)**

19. Keeping a promise (to a stranger) is **very important** because: **honesty is important. Dishonesty helps no situation or relationship. (Form A)**

20. Keeping a promise (to a stranger) is **important** because: **It's also fairly important to always keep promises, even to people you don't know because you should try to stay consistant in your beliefs. (Form A)**

21. Keepng a promise (to a stranger) is **very important** because: **they would start out thinking of you as a liar and tell their friends too. (Form B)**

22. Keeping a promise (to a friend) is **very important** because: **if one goes to the extent of committing himself in a promise, then it must be kept if at all possible. (Form A)**

23. Keeping a promise (to a stranger) is **not important** because: **if it is a stranger you shouldn't even talk to them. (Form B)**

24. Keeping a promise (to a stranger) is **very important** because: **if you think you can't keep a promise, don't make it. (Form A)**

25. Keeping a promise (to a stranger) is **not important** because: **if they don't give me nothing i don't give them nothing that's the way i fell. (Form A)**

26. Keeping a promise (to a stranger) is **very important** because: **a promise shouldn't be broken or else you'll be sad. (Form B)**

27. Keeping a promise (to a friend) is **very important** because: **its important to be able to place your trusts in others but if someone told me something that they were doing I wouldn't tell because it's none of my business to tell on them. (Form B)**

28. Keeping a promise (to a friend) is **important** because: **Joe might not never have any friends in his life. (Form A)**

29. Keeping a promise (to a friend) is **important** because: **it's important to keep a promise to a friend, also to anybody else one knows, not necessarily friends only, because our words reflect the kind of a person we are. (Form B)**

30. Keeping a promise (to a friend) is **important** because: **one should never ask another to "promise" anything. But teenagers use this as security for secrets and friendships. As an adult, I don't promise or ask for promises. I have outgrown this stage, but I can remember when promises were important! (Form B)**

NORM 8:

Property

1. Letting one's children keep earned money is **very important** because: **if you worked and worked for the money you shouldn't let them take it. If they ask for $2 you could give them something like that. (Form A)**

2. Letting one's children keep earned money is **important** because: **motivation to be self sufficient would decrease if rewards of labor were taken away. (Form A)**

3. Letting one's children keep earned money is **very important** because: **they should not take it ask for it. And mabey he would give him the money. (Form A)**

4. Letting one's children keep earned money is **very important** because: **the parents can't take away money from their friends or relatives, why should they be able to take away money from their children which doesn't belong to the parents. (Form A)**

5. Letting one's children keep earned money is **important** because: **if the parints did not promes and what the money back they should be able to take it back. (Form A)**

6. Letting one's children keep earned money is **important** because: **if the parents take the money then the child will get mad at their parents and it might end up in an argument or fight. (Form B)**

7. Letting one's children keep earned money is **very important** because: **parents should be trying to teach their children that if they earn money the right way (thru jobs, etc.) then it's theirs to do with it what they want. (Form A)**

8. Letting one's children keep earned money is **important** because: **it's the children's money and they can do what the want to with with it. (Form B)**

9. Letting one's children keep earned money is **not important** because: **I believe that, with the children's consent, it would be OK to take children's money. Under dire economic circumstances, it would be all right for the parents to expect the children to help out with expenses. (Form B)**

10. Letting one's children keep earned money is **important** because: **you are steal your child money. (Form B)**

11. Letting one's children keep earned money is **important** because: **a child needs to learn responsibility, one way of doing this is by letting the child earn. But if the parents take the money away, it will do the child no good. (Form A)**

12. Letting one's children keep earned money is **important** because: **my views are for children, I want my kids to have things they want, but it would be nice for me to see them give the money back to help their parents out. (Form A)**

13. Letting one's children keep earned money is **important** because: **thir children will liy to thim. (Form A)**

14. Letting one's children keep earned money is **very important** because: **the child begins to lose faith in the parent. The child finds no one to turn to in the future and their could be a communication breakdown. (Form A)**

15. Letting one's children keep earned money is **important** because: **You owe your parents so much money, you would work a million years and not be able to pay it all back. (Form B)**

16. Letting one's children keep earned money is **important** because: **gives the child a sense of achievement and teaches them to spend it effectively. (Form B)**

17. Letting one's children keep earned money is **very important** because: **The child feels proud of himself that he can earn money and do something constructive with it. (Form A)**

18. Letting one's children keep earned money is **very important** because: **when they grow up they know if they make money its theirs to keep. (Form A)**

19. Letting one's children keep earned money is **very important** because: **very important because if you had spent all day long making the money and then came home and found that your mother was going to take it. (Form B)**

20. Letting one's children keep earned money is **important** because: **although it is good to let a child keep what they earn, as long as you tell them that they might not be able to keep it, it would be fair to take it. Parents spend a lot of time and money on a child and it is concievably possible with todays pries that they may need it to continue to function. (Form A)**

21. Letting one's children keep earned money is **important** because: **it is the children money for them to sped. (Form B)**

22. Letting one's children keep earned money is **important** because: **it is up to Judy to negotiate how she spends the money with her mother. The communication alone would be good for the relationship. (Form B)**

23. Letting one's children keep earned money is **important** because: **that what that child has worked hard for--and the money is there reward. (Form B)**

24. Letting one's children keep earned money is **important** because: **the money was made by Judy and she should be able to spend it anyway she wishes. Her mother should only help Judy in the decision of how to spend the money. (Form B)**

25. Letting one's children keep earned money is **important** because: **they should be able to take it or give it. (Form A)**

26. Letting one's children keep earned money is **very important** because: **parents are always telling you to have responsibility and money is just one thing along the field of responsibility. (Form B)**

27. Letting one's children keep earned money is **very important** because: **kids must learn to earn on their own. Parents have their own money. (Form A)**

28. Letting one's children keep earned money is **important** because: **they shouldn't Becaus Joe work hard to earn the money a wanted to go camping very much. (Form A)**

29. Letting one's children keep earned money is **not important** because: **it is important that the child develops good spending habits and above all have a sense of responsibility toward his family. The child should realize that his parents have helped him and he should be willing to help in return. (Form B)**

30. Letting one's children keep earned money is **important** because: **the children earned the money through their own toil and/or labor. (Form A)**

ANNOTATED SCORING KEYS

Scoring Key for Norm 1: Affiliation

Practice Item: Aspect Citation; Stage or Transitional Level

1:	6(d); 2		5:	1(e); 3
	2(a); 1		6:	6(d); 2
2:	4(e); 2			4(c); 2
	5(a); 2/3		7:	3;2
3:	5(c); 2/3			7(a); 3/4
4:	unsc.			1(e); 3

8:	4(d); 3		21:	8(b); 2/3
9:	4(a); 2/3		22:	1(c); 3
10:	3(a); 3			6(c); 2/3
	5(a); 3/4		23:	5(d); 3
	6(b); 2			4(b); 3/4
	3(a); 4		24:	1(d); 3
11:	1(a); 3/4			1(c); 4
	2(a); 3/4			2(a); 3/4
12:	4(i); 2		25:	1(a); 2/3
	4(c); 1		26:	4(a); 1/2
13:	6(b); 3/4			4(c); 2
14:	unsc.			5; 1
15:	3(a); 4		27:	1(c); 3
16:	2(a); 3/4			7; 3/4
17:	4(a); 1/2			6(b); 2
18:	4(d); 3/4		28:	5(b); 2/3
	2(g); 3		29:	3(a); 4
	3(a); 4			5(a); 3/4
19:	6(b,d); 2			1(b); 2/3
20:	unsc.		30:	4(a); 1/2

Annotations:

1. Since "if he doesn't love her" in the response is merely a repetition from the question, it is not considered scorable per se.

4. This seems to be merely a comment, and hence is not scorable.

5. A transposition is helpful here. The response can be transposed into, "A real friend wouldn't ask you to help by stealing."

6. An inference is required in matching "he could easily [get] rid [of] her" to "(then) he could marry someone else" in the criterion justification as well as "she pleaded . . ." to "she wanted . . ." in the latter criterion justification.

7. This response would entail only Stage 2 and Stage 3 ratings if the subject had not brought up the question of whether the act "goes against Mr. Jefferson's values."

8. Use of the prescriptive "should" (in the context of: "if he loves her he **should** want to help her") makes the response Stage 3 rather than Transition 2/3 (Aspect 5a). "Hurt" is clinically Stage 3, but since it is consistent with more than three adjacent stage levels (it could even be Stage 1), it is not scorable.

9. Reference to **losing** a friend ("he might loss[sic] a best friend") makes Transition 2/3 the best fit. Without this feature, the reference to "best friend" (underscore added) would make Transition 1/2 Aspect 1 the best fit. Also, if the response had entailed a reference to the difficulty of **replacing** lost friends, the rating would be Stage 2 Aspect 5(d).

10. Regarding the first part of the response, "a husband's love for his wife should be greater than any other force on earth" is matched to "a husband should love his wife" in the Stage 3 CJ. Regarding the latter part, the size of the unit is unclear, a fact which offers alternative scoring strategies. The strategy used in the key assumes the smallest possible units: "chancing jail" is rated separately from "duty as a man and . . . as her husband." This is the simpler approach. A more difficult--but clinically more valid--approach is to consider the last sentence in its entirety. Since the point is confusing, a transposition helps, e.g., "the ultimate sacrifice of jail is part of his duty as a human being and as a husband." The transposition helps make clear that the two ideas,

"chancing jail" and "duty" are integral to a broader thought. So transposed, the response is a marginal fit to Stage 4 Aspect 3(a). Note that regardless of which strategy you use, the rating that would be assigned for the norm is Stage 4.

11. One must infer the "depends on" element in the second sentence of the response.

12. Stage 2 is relatively the best fit because of the pragmatic element ("got rid of the pain"), but the fit is poor because the preferential element ("want to") is absent and must be assumed.

14. This response merely puts into sentence form the evaluation already provided that stealing the drug "even if he doesn't love her" is important.

15. A transposition helps, e.g., "Heinz has an obligation to save a human life, apart from the feelings of the particular relationship." The key is "obligation." The respondent's distinction between feelings and obligations is not directly scorable, although it supports an assumption that the thinking is beyond Stage 3.

17. Although the connotation of contingency implies Stage 2, the direct reference to getting into trouble makes Transition 1/2 the better fit.

18. "Without suffering" can be matched to "end her suffering," Stage 3, if a molecular strategy is used (see discussion in Question 10).

19. "Unimportant" is not sufficiently discriminative to be scorable.

20. This response entails merely a bare valuation and a practical suggestion ("their [sic] are always other ways"). See "Types of Unscorable Response," Chapter 4.

21. The action-oriented **"can't just stand around** and let her die" (underscore added) is slightly closer to Transition 2/3 Aspect 8(b), "he shouldn't **just** let her die," than it is to the empathic feelings-oriented Stage 3 Aspect 4(f), "shouldn't (just) watch her suffer."

22. Note that Transition 3/4 Aspect 2(b) is not as good a fit because it requires a reference to the **level** of friendship. Also, "sometimes you will be the only one they can depend on" does not entail the reciprocal idea ("depend on **one another")** required for a match to Transition 3/4 Aspect 1.

24. "Higher law" or "God's law" must be inferred in the response.

25. The role-reversal is made clearer with a transposition, e.g., "If Heinz were the friend, Heinz would want to be helped." "Would **want"** makes Transition 2/3 a better fit than Stage 3, which requires "would **expect"** or "would **hope."**

26. Stage 2 Aspect 2(b) seems also implied here, but the reference to "blamed" makes Transition 1/2 a better fit.

28. The connotation of disapproval may imply Stage 3, but Transition 2/3 provides the better fit.

Scoring Key For Norm 2: Life

Practice Item: Aspect Citation; Stage or Transition Level

1:	5(a); 2/3		8:	2(a); 4
	1(a); 1/2			5(b); 3/4
2:	4(a); 3			2(f); 4
3:	2(b); 2/3			6(a); 3/4
	4(a); 3			1(c); 3
4:	4(c); 2		9:	6(e); 2
	4; 2/3		10:	4(b); 3/4
5:	4(a); 3		11:	2(b,g); 4
6:	5(b); 1			4(b); 3/4
7:	6(d); 2		12:	1(b); 1/2

13:	2(c); 2/3	21:	1(a); 2/3
	5(a); 2/3		1(a); 1/2
14:	1(c); 2/3		6(a); 2/3
15:	4(c); 3	22:	2(b); 3/4
	4(b); 3/4	23:	1; 3/4
16:	6(a); 2/3	24:	1(c); 3
17:	5(a); 3	25:	unsc.
	1(d); 3	26:	4(d); 2
18:	3(a); 2/3	27:	unsc.
19:	6(b); 2	28:	6(a); 2/3
20:	3(b); 4	29:	2(g,b); 4
	2(b); 3	30:	2(b); 2/3

Annotations

1. An inverse from **"not important"** is necessary for the match. Transition 2/3 is a closer fit than Stage 2 Aspect 5(a) because of the adverbial emphasis ("how bad") in the response.
2. An inverse as well as an inference is required in matching "it would be **cruel** to not help someone who is dying" in the response to "it is the **human** thing to do."
4. This response is scorable because, although it is close to a disclosure, its hypothetical status does suggest an orientation to the dilemma.
5. This response is also very close to a disclosure but does have hypothetical and prescriptive content that relates to the dilemmma action. The match also requires an inverse.
6. An inference is required in matching "you don't know what he could do [to you]" to "the stranger could grab . . . kill you" in the criterion justification.
7. The first part of the response is simply a prescriptive evaluation ("you should save a stranger from dying"), although if it had read, "You should **always** save a stranger," it would have been inversely scorable to Stage 1, Aspect 3(b). "Why should he steal?" is a Stage 2 match because of its interrogative form.
8. This response is quite packed with at least marginally scorable justifications. An inference and a completion are required for matching to Transition 3/4 Aspect 5(b) the response: "as people [we] should be concerned with everyone's welfare." This match is not close; nor is the match to Transition 3/4 Aspect 6(a). "Risk his neck" is interpreted as "risk his life" and hence is not scorable at Stage 2.
9. An inference is required in matching "you can have some of the greatest times" in the response to "you can have fun" in the criterion justification.
10. The obligatory or "character" quality of "have to go on," although minimal, makes the Transition 3/4 criterion justification a better fit than the simpler Stage 2 Aspect 4(c), "should want to live."
11. The suggestion that the "impact . . . can be good" permits a marginally acceptable fit to the Stage 4 criterion justification. Also, "quit" is inferentially close to "cop-out" in the Transition 3/4 criterion justification.
13. An inference is required in matching "they need someone" or "more adention [sic]" to Transition 2/3.
15. The Stage 3 match for "feeling sorry for herself" is scorable only if one adopts a molecular scoring strategy. Scoring at Stage 3 is unnecessary if a more global or molar strategy is used.

16. In addition to matching "I don't think that a stranger could be that im-
     portant **to you**" (underscore added), one can match, with inference, "it
     could . . . affect the number of friends you make in the future" to "the
     stranger could become a friend" in the criterion justification.
17. Note that the latter part of the sentence, "We have no right to **refuse
     him** (underscore added), is interpersonally oriented and missing the ju-
     risdictional or decision-oriented quality evident in Transition 3/4
     Aspect 2(c).
18. If the second part of the response had read, "this person, **like anyone
     else,** should still be able to live," it would have been matchable to
     Stage 2 Aspect 2(a). The last sentence provides the match to Transition
     2/3.
19. An inverse is required for the match.
20. The fragment "one in need" is matched to Stage 3 by the molecular scoring
     only.
21. The implication is that the stranger probably would **not** do it for you.
     The response is also close, however, to Stage 2 Aspect 1, since the "if
     you did it" in the response can be interpreted as raising a temporal
     question of concrete advantage. The response, "I wouldn't get myself into
     trouble," is scorable because of its hypothetical form, although it is
     close to being a disclosure.
23. Correct to: "no bond between the two."
24. The scorable feature of the response is "means nothing **to you** (underscore
     added)."
27. This is unscorable because it is nonsensical.
30. Transition 2/3 provides relatively the best match, although the fit is
     poor.

Scoring Key For Norm 3: Law and Property

Practice Item: Aspect Citation; Stage or Transitional Level

1:	2(a); 3		15:	3; 2
2:	1(a); 1/2			5(a); 2
	2; 2/3			4; 1/2
3:	1(a); 1/2		16:	3(b); 3
	5(a); 1		17:	unsc.
4:	1; 2/3		18:	5(a); 3/4
5:	3; 2			4(b); 3
	1(a); 1/2		19:	2(a); 3
	4(e); 3		20:	1(a); 4
	4(b); 3/4		21:	5(a); 3/4
6:	5; 2/3			8; 3/4
	6(a); 2/3		22:	1(b); 3
7:	3(c); 4			6(f); 2
	4(b); 3/4		23:	unsc.
8:	4; 1/2		24:	6(b); 2/3
	5(a); 1		25:	8; 3/4
9:	6(g); 2		26:	1(c); 2
10:	1; 3/4		27:	1(a); 4
	2(c); 4		28:	4; 1/2
11:	6(b); 2/3		29:	5(b); 3/4
12:	6(a); 2			3(b); 3
13:	unsc.			2(c); 4
14:	4(b); 1		30:	2(c); 4

Annotations

1. This match requires inference.
3. The physicalistic phrase "put in" makes the latter part of the response Stage 1.
4. Although it is not clear whether the thought is Transition 2/3 or Stage 2 Aspect 1, the higher level is assigned in accordance with Rule 3 (see Chapter 4).
5. Note the qualification, "no matter how **selfish**" (underscore added) is scorable (Stage 3).
7. Transition 3/4 is also scored if one is using the molecular strategy.
9. A transverse from a "you" to a "her" referent is required.
11. This is not a close fit, but the response is somewhere in the Stage 2-- Stage 3 range and Transition 2/3 is the intermediate level (Rule 3, Chapter 4). "Worse" can be somewhat related to "bad shape" in the criterion justification.
12. The orientation here seems to be to pragmatic advantages ("he should think about his future"), although if the allusion to "involvement" had been elaborated it might have been scorable at Stage 3.
13. "Something else" is non-discriminative across more than three levels (see Rule 1, Chapter 4).
14. "You will be steal [sic]" is matched to "that's stealing" in the criterion justification.
15. An inference is required in matching "they bought them" to "earned" in Aspect 3 of Stage 2. Also, a transverse is required in matching "the **banker** will git [sic] "in trouble" (underscore added) to "(so that) **you** won't get in trouble" (underscore added) in the criterion justification.
17. The intended thought of this respondent seems impossible to fathom. The response must be classified as "word salad" (see Unscorability section, Chapter 4).
18. Some inference is required in matching "the lowest anyone could get" to "despicable" in the Stage 3 criterion justification.
19. Some inferential work is required in matching "this is like the druggist [sic] pride & joy" to "it might **mean** a lot to them" in the criterion justification.
20. Note that if the respondent had written "to keep order in society" instead of "to keep society in order," the rating would be Transition 3/4 Aspect 5(a) rather than Stage 4.
21. Some inference is required in matching "so that everyone is aware of the boundaries" to "because otherwise people . . . will lose sight of right and wrong" in the criterion justification.
22. Although "life would be unhappy" is close to Transition 3/4 Aspect 1, it is an exact fit to Stage 3.
23. The qualifier "for any reason" makes this response pseudo-Stage 1 and hence unscorable.
28. The physical connotation of "what could happen to you" renders Transition 1/2 a better fit than Stage 2 Aspect 6(c). A broad reference to possible disadvantage, e.g., "you don't know what your're getting into," would have been scorable as Stage 2.
29. Some inferential work is required.

Scoring Key For Norm 4: Legal Justice

Practice Item: Aspect Citation; Stage or Transitional Level

1: 3(a); 2/3
    5(d); 2

2: 5; 3
3: 2; 2/3

```
        6(a); 2              18:  4(a); 1
  4:  1(b); 1                     2; 1/2
  5:  4(d); 3              19:  5(b); 2/3
  6:  1(c); 4              20:  2(a); 3
        5(b); 4            21:  4(a); 1
        5(a); 4                  6(a); 2
  7:  5(c); 2              22:  4(a); 3
  8:  2(a); 3/4            23:  2; 1/2
  9:  6(d); 2          24:  5(a); 4
 10:  6(a); 2                  6(a); 3/4
 11:  2; 2/3              25:  3(c); 3
 12:  2(a); 4            26:  5(c); 3/4
        5(b); 4                6(a); 2
 13:  2; 1/2             27:  5; 3
 14:  7; 4                    3(b); 3
        4(a); 3/4        28:  1(a); 3/4
        3(b); 4              4(c); 3
 15:  6(a); 4                6; 3
 16:  1(a); 3/4          29:  4(a); 1
 17:  4(c); 2            30:  10; 3/4
```

Annotations

5. An inference is required in matching "was trying to make money" to "was greedy" in the CJ.

6. A considerable inference is required in matching "must be enforced even if it's incorrect" in response to "must be enforced even if a **particular law** is incorrect" in the CJ. "Particular" is not specified in the response, making this rating marginally appropriate only. Also, a slight inference is required in matching "feels sorry" to "emotions" in the second CJ. Finally, an inference is required in matching "floodgates" to "precedent" in the last CJ cited.

7. An inference is required in matching the response to "the husband doesn't need any more hassles" in the CJ.

8. Note that the latter part of the response is an evaluative opinion rather than a justification and therefore is unscorable.

9. An inference is required.

10. An inference is required in matching "no one would obey laws" to "everyone would be doing it" in the CJ. Also, the reference to people "who **do wrong**" (underscore added) is not sufficient for a Stage 1 rating (although a response such as "people who do wrong are bad" would be scorable as Stage 1 Aspect 4).

12. "For the benefit of society" in the response is matched to "(in order) to help society" in the CJ. Also, an inference is required in matching "he **has to** deal with the situation as it is a crime was committed whatever the reasons behind it" (underscore added)" to Aspect 5(b).

14. **"Should be willing to suffer the consequences"** (boldface added) is Transition 3/4, whereas **"must** be willing to go to jail" (boldface added) is Stage 4.

15. Stage 4 is a closer match than is Transition 3/4 Aspect 1(a) because the response is quite elaborated, as is the Stage 4 CJ cited. Specifically, "no two . . . situations are alike" in the response is matched to "each case is different" in the CJ.

17. The match requires an inverse from "it's his fault" to "it wasn't his fault" in the CJ.

18. A slight inference is required in matching "breaking the law is very bad"

to "he did something bad" in the CJ. Also, a considerable inference is required for matching the "to see how it feels" idea to the retributive "teach him a lesson" part of the Transition 1/2 CJ.

19. An inference is required in matching "hurt someone" to "wasn't hurting anyone" in the CJ.
20. An inference is required.
21. "Get out of everything" in the response seems slightly closer to "get off easy" in the Stage 2 CJ than to the more equity-oriented "would have to be let free" idea of Transition 2/3 Aspect 2.
22. The reference in the response to Mr. Jefferson's "feelings . . . to help her" renders—with inference—the Stage 3 match more appropriate than a match to Stage 2. With a transverse (from "Heinz" to "the judge"), the response is also matchable to Stage 3 Aspect 2(a).
26. Considerable inference is required.
28. The appeal to differential judgment ("cannot be on the same level") according to circumstance makes Transition 3/4 a better fit than Stage 3 Aspect 3(a).
29. The first part of the response is unscorable. "Was stealing" in the latter part is matched to "stole the drug, took something that wasn't his" in the CJ.
30. An inverse inference is required in matching the first response idea to "(not important because) this was a life or death situation" in the CJ. Also, the last sentence is unscorable because it is consistent with more than three adjacent levels (Rule 2).

Scoring Key For Norm 5: Conscience

Practice Item: Aspect Citation; Stage or Transitional Level

			6(b); 3/4
1:	4(a); 1	17:	4(a); 3
2:	7,3(b); 4	18:	4(c); 3/4
3:	4(f); 3	19:	3; 2
	4(b); 3/4	20:	4(b); 1
4:	3; 2	21:	6(a); 2
	2(b); 2/3	22:	2(a); 4
5:	6(a); 2		8(a); 3/4
6:	6; 3		2(a); 4
7:	--; 1/2	23:	3(a); 4
8:	1; 3/4		1; 3/4
9:	5(a); 3/4	24:	1(a); 1
10:	3(a); 3/4		4(e); 2
11:	3; 2	25:	2(a); 4
12:	3(a); 3	26:	5; 2/3
	5(a); 3/4	27:	1; 3/4
	5(a); 4		6(a); 4
13:	5(a); 3/4	28:	3(b); 1
14:	1(a); 1/2	29:	1; 3/4
15:	3(a); 2/3		2(a); 3
16:	5(a); 4	30:	2(a); 3

Annotations

2. Not a close fit to either CJ. An inverse is required in matching to 3(b).
3. A transverse (from "self" to "conscience" in the criterion justification) as well as an inverse is required in matching "can't control himself" in the response to "you can control your conscience" in criterion justification.

6. Although the first part of the response is garbled, the latter part is scorable.

7. This response (which is close to being unscorable) could be interpreted just as readily in terms of either Stage 1 or Stage 2 (see opening discussion in Chapter 9). Since the two stages entail three adjacent levels (1, 1/2, 2), Rule 2 (see Chapter 4) applies: the intermediate level (Transition 1/2) is assigned.

10. The first sentence in the response is not matchable to Transition 3/4 Aspect 8(a) since the response refers to the question of "harm" rather than right or wrong. Also, the second sentence is matched, with inference, to "although he was morally right, he was still legally wrong."

11. "Your conscience can take over your life" is matched to "your conscience is powerful" in the criterion justification.

12. Regarding the latter part of the response, an inference is required in matching "society must have norms" to "you must have a common standard" in the criterion justification. The reference to "fluctuations" is too cryptic for a match to Stage 4 Aspect 6(b).

13. An inference is required.

14. An inverse inference is required.

15. Transition 3/4 Aspect 8(a) is **not** an appropriate match because he **thought** or **felt** is missing from the response.

17. "Conscience . . . is important . . . but he still broke the law" is not sufficiently specific for a match to Transition 3/4 Aspect 3(a).

20. An inference is required. Making the match is especially difficult because "not important" was inappropriately specified by the subject.

22. For the Transition 3/4 match, "right" must be inferred in the response.

28. The response should be scored despite the inconsistency between the evaluation and the justification.

29. "The judge should realize" is matched, with inference, to "should have a heart" in the criterion justification. (In molar scoring, one would not score this fragment.)

30. The "save a life" reference in the response is unscorable.

Scoring Key For Norm 6: Family Affiliation

Practice Item: Aspect Citation; Stage or Transitional Level

1:	1(b); 2	15:	6; 3/4
2:	2; 1		10; 3/4
3:	4; 2/3	16:	4(a); 1
4:	2; 2	17:	6; 4
5:	6(a), 2	18:	1(a); 4
6:	1(f); 3	19:	unsc.
	2(b); 3/4	20:	3(c); 1
7:	1(d); 3	21:	1(a); 2/3
	2(a); 3	22:	4(b); 3
8:	3(b); 2	23:	6; 3/4
9:	6(b); 2	24:	5(d,a); 2
10:	4(a); 3	25:	1(a); 2
	2; 4		4; 2/3
11:	6; 2/3	26:	5; 2/3
	2(c); 3	27:	3(b); 2/3
12:	3(b); 3	28:	9(a); 3/4
13:	unsc.	29:	3(a); 1
14:	4(d); 1	30:	4; 2/3
			4(a); 2

Annotations

2. An inference is required.
3. An inference is required.
4. The response is equally consistent with the inversion of Transition 1/2 Aspect 2, and with Stage 2 Aspect 2. Therefore, Rule 3 applies, and the upper adjacent level (Stage 2) is assigned.
5. An inference is required.
8. The match requires a transverse across norm questions (from "keeping promises to one's children" to "helping one's parents").
10. The justification that "the family will **run** more smoothly" (underscore added) makes Stage 4 (see "family functioning" in the criterion justification) a better fit than that provided by the more general Transition 3/4 "harmony."
13. A pseudo Stage 1 still results from the "no matter what," even though that fragment was placed as a separate sentence by the subject.
14. An inverse inference is required.
17. "Parents, not only children to parents, have to respect what they say and not dishonor their kids" can be fit to either "parents must deserve their children's respect" (Stage 4) or "parents should respect the child" (Transition 3/4). The higher of the two adjacent levels is assigned in accordance with Rule 3. Earlier in the response, the meaning of the reference to "gift" is too unclear to be scorable.
18. An inference is required.
20. This response is scorable since "never" in the criterion justification is not underlined.
21. An inference is required.
22. Note that "they **still** are their parents" (underscore added) is not a fit to Stage 1 because of the qualification ("still").
24. The element of need must be inferred from "had to."
25. "Parents provide what is needed" is matched to "give the children" in the Stage 2 criterion justification.
27. An inference is required.
30. "If . . . you want to do what she wants you to do" is matched to "if the child **wants** to help them" in the criterion justification.

Scoring Key For Norm 7: Contract

Practice Item: Aspect Citation; Stage or Transitional Level

1:	4(a); 2/3	13:	4(a); 2/3
2:	4(a); 1		4(b); 3
3:	2(a); 1/2	14:	5; 1
	2; 2/3	15:	2(e); 4
4:	1(a); 3	16:	3(a); 2/3
5:	5(a); 3/4		2(a); 3
6:	3(b); 1/2	17:	4(a); 1
7:	unsc.	18:	6(g); 2
8:	2(b); 3/4	19:	1(a); 3/4
9:	1(a); 3/4	20:	7; 4
	1(b,a); 3	21:	4(b); 3
10:	2(b); 4		4(e); 2/3
	5(a); 3/4	22:	3; 4
	2(a); 3/4	23:	3(b); 1
11:	4(c); 2/3	24:	unsc.
12:	1; 4	25:	1(a); 2
	5(c); 3/4	26:	4(c); 1

| 27: | 1(b); 3/4 | | 29: | 4; 4 |
| 28: | 5(a); 2 | | 30. | unsc. |

Annotations

4. An inference is required in matching "it shows you have true friendship" to "a friendship should be sincere" in CJ.
5. An inference is required.
7. Bare valuation. Note, however, that "you should keep your promises" without the qualifying phrase **"if** you promise something to someone" would be scorable as Stage 1.
8. A plausible transposition would be: "any person wants what he says to be taken seriously and respected; it hurts no one to provide such respect." Once transposed, the response becomes more clearly scorable.
9. An inference is required in matching "a friendship will develop out of trust" to the Transition 3/4 CJ.
10. "Honesty" is one virtue that everyone can relate to" is matched to "honesty is a standard that everyone can accept." "Virtue" is also scored by molecular scoring.
11. An inference is required.
12. "The ability to have faith in another person is a very important part of life" is matched either to "relationships are based on trust" (Transition 3/4) or to "society is based on trust." By Rule 3, the upper adjacent level is assigned for the response rating. Also, an inference is required for matching the second sentence in the response (cf. Family Affiliation Transition 3/4 Aspect 9a).
15. An inference is required in matching "it is the promise itself that should have value" to "promises . . . have intrinsic value" in the CJ.
16. An inference is required in matching "friend" is hoping you don't tell something" to the Transition 2/3 CJ.
17. An inference is required.
18. The latter part of the response obscures the meaning slightly but not enough to render the response unscorable.
19. "Dishonesty helps no . . . relationship" is matched, with some inference, to "honesty is important for any friendship or interaction."
20. **"Consistant [sic] in your beliefs"** (boldface added) makes Stage 4 ("for the sake of . . . consistency") a closer fit than Transition 3/4 Aspect 5(a) or 5(b).
21. "Thinking of you as a liar" suggests a concern with making a bad impression (cf. **"Think of you** as a good person").
26. Matching "you'll be sad" to "they will be sad" in the CJ requires a transverse (from "you" to "they").
27. A transverse inference is required in matching "its [sic] important to be able to place your trust [sic] in others" to "people should be **able to** have trust in you" in the CJ.
28. The concern in the response with Joe's **need** for friends must be inferred.

Scoring Key For Norm 8: Property

Practice Item: Aspect Citation; Stage or Transitional Level

			7:	4(b); 4
1:	2; 2/3		8:	2; 1/2
2:	4(b); 4			3; 2
3:	unsc.		9:	3(b); 3/4
4:	6; 3/4			7; 3/4
5:	4(a); 2		10:	4(b); 1
6:	6(b); 2		11:	5(b); 3/4

12: unsc.
13: 3(b); 1/2
14: 1(c); 3
    5; 2/3
    1; 3/4
15: 1(b); 2/3
16: 4(b); 4
17: 2(b); 3
    4; 3/4
18: unsc.
19: 2; 2/3
20: 1(b); 2
    5; 2
    7; 3/4

21: 2; 1/2
22: 3(b); 3/4
    1; 3/4
23: 2; 2/3
    3(a); 3
24: 4, 3(b); 3/4
25: 1; 1/2
26: 3(a); 4
27: 4(b); 4
28: 2; 2/3
    3; 2/3
29: 4(b); 4
    1(d); 3
30: 2; 2/3

Annotations

1. An inference is required in matching "worked **and worked**" (underscore added) to "worked hard" in the CJ.

4. An inference is required.

7. Considerable inference is required in matching to "taught . . . ownership" and "self-sufficient" in the CJ. The response is also consistent with Transition 3/4 Aspect 5(b), but the upper adjacent level is assigned (Rule 3).

9. An inference is required in matching "with the children's consent" to "children have the right to decide." Relatively closest fit. Also, "dire economic circumstances" matches the cited Stage 3 aspect equally as well as it does Transition 3/4. The upper adjacent level is assigned in accordance with Rule 3.

12. This sounds "Stage 3'ish," but it is unscorable because it is a disclosure ("I want my kids to have the things they want").

14. A considerable inference is required in matching "turn to" to "count on for help."

18. The response is not close enough to Stage 4 (or any other level) to be scorable. The response cannot be scored Stage 2 or Transition 1/2 since it is elaborated (see Note).

20. An inference is required for the first Transition 3/4 match. Also, an inference is required in matching "they need it **to continue to function** (underscore added)" to "survival" in the CJ. "Need" is separately scored by the molecular strategy.

22. Inference and inverse required in matching "the communication itself would be good for the relationship" to the CJ.

24. The latter sentence in the response can be rated as Transition 3/4, even though the citation spans two CJs and aspects.

25. Inference required. The response is scorable even though it is a non sequitur in relation to the evaluation.

27. **"learn** to earn **on their own"** (underscore added) in the response is matched to "learn to be self-sufficient" in the CJ. The response idea may also be viewed as consistent with Transition 3/4 Aspect 5(b); nonetheless, the higher adjacent level if assigned (Rule 3).

29. The reference to developing "good spending habits" is aso consistent with Transition 3/4 Aspect 5(b). Regarding the Stage 3 fit, "should realize" in the response is matched to "should think of" in CJ.

30. "Their own toil or labor" in the response is matched to "earned the money (all by) himself" in the CJ. Stage 3 Aspect 3(a) does not offer quite as close a match.

Appendix C

PROTOCOL EXERCISES

AND

ANNOTATED

SCORING KEYS

PROTOCOL 1: FORM A

Problem 1

1. Helping one's spouse is **very important** because: **saving someones life is more important than committing a crime because he loves her.**

2. Helping one's spouse (even if he doesn't love her) is **important**: **if he didnt love her it wouldn't be as important as stealing if he loved her.**

3. Helping one's friend is **very important** because: **his friend can't get help anywhere else and Heinz is his friend so he should help.**

4. Helping a stranger is **important**: **it all depends on how badly the stranger is hurt or how bad the stranger aches and who he is.**

5. Not stealing is **very important** because: **if it wasn't everyone would go around taking everyone elses things**

6. Obeying the law is **very important** because: **people would stealing, killing speeding and more people would go to jail.**

7. Going easy on people like Heinz is **important** (cf. sending lawbreakers to jail is not important): **the drugist was selling the drug at a very unreasonable price and he just wanted to save his wife.**

8. Going easy on people who acted out of conscience is **important**: **maybe he didn't want to steal the drug but his conscience told him to.**

9. Sending lawbreakers to jail is **very important** because: **the same people would be out on the street commiting a crime again.**

Problem 2

1. Keeping promises to one's children is **very important** because: **parents should never break promises to their children even if they promise 3 or 4 times.**

2. Keeping a promise to a friend is **important** because: **really nobody should ever break a promise.**

3. Keeping a promise to a stranger is **important**: **if you promise something to someone you should keep that promise.**

4. Helping one's parents is **important**: **if children have something their parents need they should help them out.**

5. Letting one's children keep earned money is not **important**: **if they earned the money they should be able to keep it.**

6. Helping one's parents is **very important** because: **they need to help thier parents they should because it needs to be done.**

PROTOCOL 2: FORM A

Problem 1

1. Helping one's spouse is **important** because: a **person should should try to save someone's life even if he had to steel as long as he paid when he could.**

2. Helping one's spouse (even if he doesn't love her) is **important** because: **even if he dosn't love her she is still a human being but maybe it doesn't matter as much to save her then.**

3. Helping one's friend is **important** because: **this person has as much right to life as his wife and Heinze should try to save him.**

4. Helping a stranger is not **important**: **for me I wouldn't if I didn't know the person. But I think someone close to him should try.**

5. Not stealing is **important** because: **people have a right to keep what belongs to them but if they have a drug that could keep someone from dieying they should share it.**

6. Obeying the law is **very important**: **the Law was made to protect people and their property. If everyone broke the law a lot of inocent people would be hurt.**

7. Going easy on people like Heinz is **important** (cf. sending lawbreakers to jail is not important): **Heinz shouldn't go scott-free, but should be fined, the judge has to consider that it saved a live and Heinz did it as a last choise.**

8. Going easy on people who acted out of conscience is not **important**: **what his conscience tells him shouldn't matter it's what he does. people could tell a judge that their conscience told them to do it & be released.**

9. Sending lawbreakers to jail is **important** because: **if they don't get punished they will think they can get away with everything.**

Problem 2

1. Keeping promises to one's children is **important**: **it is important to keep promises because if you break yours in the future children will think they can break theirs.**

2. Keeping a promise to a friend is **important** because: **it establishes trust and you may lose friends if you keep breaking promises.**

3. Keeping a promise to a stranger is **important** because: **you want people to trust you and then they might like you more and you would have a better reputation.**

4. Helping one's parents is not **important**: **if the parent has promised some-**

thing they should keep to it and unless it is something very important there is no reason why they should.

5. Letting one's children keep earned money is important: if the children are the ones to spend it how they chose (with some guidence).

6. Helping one's parents is important in this case yes because if there is no food the whole fmaily would be hungry.

PROTOCOL 3: FORM B

Problem 1

1. Helping one's spouse is not important: giving in to the wishes of a loved one is not always the way to show love & concern.

2. Helping one's spouse (even if he doesn't lover her) is important: to his own peace of mind.

3. Helping one's friend is not important: it is not our place to decide when a dying person's life should end.

4. Living even when you don't want to is important: many persons who have thought their lives were hopeless because of a handicap have gone on to very productive lives with help and concern of others.

5. Not stealing is important: we musn't covet or take others belongs, we should treat others with the respect that we want them to treat us with.

6. Obeying the law is important: a society, a home or a life must have order if it is to be fruitful.

7. Going easy on people like Mr. Jefferson is not important (cf. Sending lawbreakers to jail is important): the law must be upheld if we are to have a society without complete disorder.

8. Going easy on people who acted out of conscience is not important: many people break the law and feel that their conscience is clear, they have distorted thinking of right an wrong.

9. Sending lawbreakers to jail is very important: people become less conscious of right & wrong if those who break the law are not punished.

Problem 2

1. Keeping promises to one's children is important: a parent's credability is at stake when promises arent kept.

2. Keeping a promise to a friend is important: a friend is a person you can depend on, a person who can't keep a promise is not dependable.

3. Keeping a promise to a stranger is important: your integrity as a responsible person is at stake.

4. Helping one's parents is important: children should be obedient and helpful to their parents as long as the parents are not breaking the laws. As

long as the parent is giving the care and providing the needs of the child the children should show them respect.

5. Letting one's children keep earned money is **very** important: would take away the desire of the child to be industrious and motivated.

6. Helping one's parents is **important**: as long as the parents explain the problem and are honest I think the child would feel priviledged to help.

PROTOCOL 4: FORM B

Problem 1

1. Helping one's spouse is **very** important: if he loved his wife and didn't want to see her die in pain I think he should help get it over with so that he won't suffer seing her die in pain.

2. Helping one's spouse (even if he doesn't love her) is **very** important: if he does't love his wife. The faster he gets it over with the better.

3. Helping one's friend is **important**: it is important because if everyone else turned her down you are put into the situation to do it. If he is a good friend he will help her from the pain.

4. Living even when you don't want to is **very** important because: he/she has relitives, friends, cousins, etc. that wants her to live.

5. Not stealing is **very** important because: whatever he is stealing might be very important in the life of another person.

6. Obeying the law is **very** important because: if you break the law you get put down on record, and many other people find out about it and turn agains you.

7.   Going easy on people like Mr. Jefferson is **important** (cf. Sending law-breakers to jail is not important) because: Mr. Jeffeson is helping his wife die. Many other people would suffer along with Mrs. Jefferson.

8. Going easy on people who acted out of conscience is **important** because: she did tell him to do it. Mr. Jefferson was doing only what he was told, even though he wanted to help his wife.

9. Sending lawbreakers to jail is **very** important because: if they send them to jail they probly won't make the same mistake about breaking the law again.

Problem 2

1. Keeping promises to one's children is **not** important: if the parents take the money now, when the child gets it again he/she will think twice before spending it.

2. Keeping a promise to a friend is **very** important: it is important because your friend will respect you more. Also if her friend would help Louise, then Louise should help her friend.

3. Keeping a promise to a stranger is **very important** because: **that person will like you more and you will eventually become friends.**

4. Helping one's parents is **very important** because: **they have done many other things bringing you up in life. I think Judy should still help her parents.**

5. Letting one's children keep earned money is **important** because: **if the parents take the money then the child will get mad at their parents and it might end up in an argument or fight.**

6. Helping one's parents is **very important** because: **if it is to help the family and she doesn't give them the money, the parents might go out an steal.**

PROTOCOL 5: FORM A

Problem 1

1. Helping one's spouse is **very important** because: **if very Bad problem.**

2. Helping one's spouse (even if he doesn't love her) is **not important** because: **it is not right to steal.**

3. Helping one's friend is **not important** because: **is breaking the law.**

4. Helping a stranger is **not important** because: **it is very bad.**

5. Not stealing is **very important** because: **would not be nice to.**

6. Obeying the law is **very important**: **don't know—sorry.**

7. Going easy on people like Heinz is **very important** (cf. Sending law-breakers to jail is not important): **I want him to go to jail.**

8. Going easy on people who acted out of conscience is **very important**: **I should not steal.**

9. Sending lawbreakers to jail is **very important**:——————

Problem 2

1. Keeping promises to one's children is **very important**: **it is in Important.**

2. Keeping a promise to a friend is **very important**: **it is in Important.**

3. Keeping a promise to a stranger is ——————:——————

4. Helping one's parents is **very important**: **you should not tale a lie.**

5. Letting one's children keep earned money is **very important**: **you should obey.**

6. Helping one's parents is **very important**:——————

PROTOCOL 6: FORM B

Problem 1

1. Helping one's spouse is not important: if he is unsure the action his wife is asking is the best thing, he would be foolish to do it because of many of the consequences that can follow. I believe in devotion to your husband or wife, but your own conscience must also be considered.

2. Helping one's spouse (even if he doesn't love her) is not important: his devotion for his wife must still be present, but, again, if he is unsure himself if it is a right or wrong thing to do, it is not good to steal the pain killer.

3. Helping one's friend is not important: I think it is morally wrong to try to kill someone to help them escape pain.

4. Living even when you don't want to is very important: if they want to die, they are rejecting what God has giving them. Many times we would like to take the easy way out instead of making the best of what we have. Just because we haven't accepted a certain situation is not a valid reason to end our life.

5. Not stealing is important: it is important for people to respect the rights of others, and taking things that don't belong to them can impinge on these rights. There are certain cases that can be justified for this type of action, but not the one presented here.

6. Obeying the law is important: if there was no law, then there would be no order. Law is needed. There are cases where obeying the law could come second in importance to something else, but the law should be highly regarded.

7. Going easy on people like Mr. Jefferson is not important (cf. Sending lawbreakers to jail is important): it is important for the judge to take all things into consideration but this judgment should be according to that.

8. Going easy on people who acted out of conscience is important: it is somewhat important for the judge to understand this aspect of the case, but not necessarily to go easy on him.

9. Sending lawbreakers to jail is important: it is important to uphold the law, especially in a society like ours. Without the order this provides, there would be a lot more crime. But, on the other hand, other factors must be taken into consideration. In this case, as in many others, there is not always a definitely right or wrong answer. Circumstances must be taken into consideration, but also the law must be upheld.

Problem 2

1. Keeping promises to one's children is important: if the parents keep their promises they will set values very important for the children. They will learn things of importance if they are given an example by their parents.

2. Keeping a promise to a friend is **important**: being loyal to a friend is **important**. You should regard their trust in you very highly because much is based on trust.

3. Keeping a promise to a stranger is **important**: it is **important** to keep the trust of someone even if you hardly know them. It would be a lot harder to do this if you didn't know then really close, but it is still **important**.

4. Helping one's parents is **important**: children should be willing to help their parents a lot, because they owe everything to their parents. They should talk to their parents to help them realize what they did was wrong.

5. Letting one's children keep earned money is **important**: the child should learn values and the action of a parent reflect very highly on the children. By earning the money the child has shown responsibility, and if this money is taken away, so will the meaning of earning the money.

6. Helping one's parents is **important**: it's hard for children to realize that other things come first besides them. They should want to help their parents because their parents are always willing to help them. This type of family tie is very **important**.

PROTOCOL 7: FORM A

Problem 1

1. Helping one's spouse is **very important** because: **he wants to save her life because he loves her.**

2. Helping one's spouse (even if he doesn't love her) is **very important** because: **event if he doesn't love he should save her life.**

3. Helping one's friend is **very important** because: **is the best thing in life and if you lose that it's almost like losing your mother.**

4. Helping a stranger is **important** because: **the stranger could be a bad person that steals and breaks the law and you could get into big trouble.**

5. Not stealing is **very important** because: **you could go to jail for a lot of years.**

6. Obeying the law is **very important** because: **if Heinz steals he could go to jail but if he doesn't his wife will die.**

7. Going easy on people like Heinz is **very important** (cf. Sending law-breakers to jail is not important) because: **only stole to save a life.**

8. Going easy on people who acted out of conscience is **very important** because: **he saved a life.**

9. Sending lawbreakers to jail is **very important** because: **if the law is broken for the wrong reason they should go to jail.**

Problem 2

1. Keeping promises to one's children is **very important** because: **if a promise is broken that could heart a kids heart.**

2. Keeping a promise to a friend is **important** because: **a friends is not important as a family relationship.**

3. Keeping a promise to a stranger is **not important** because: **that person could be very bad.**

4. Helping one's parents is **very important** because: **a parent is a person you should love.**

5. Letting one's children keep earned money is **very important:** **if you brake a childs hearts its like killing him.**

6. Helping one's parents is **very important** because: **you were help when you were little.**

PROTOCOL 8: FORM A

Problem 1

1. Helping one's spouse is **important** because: **you want to make your wife happy but, in the same respect you can't do everything she asked she would walk all over you.**

2. Helping one's spouse (even if he doesn't love her) is **very important** because: **he must have loved her at one time and she is a human being and you can't let the druggist be the decider that she dies.**

3. Helping one's friend is **very important** because: **a friend is someone you can tell your problems and are really close to and you can't just leave him hanging. And one man like to drugest shouldn't be the decider of someone life: Thats Gods Job!!!**

4. Helping a stranger is **important** because: **you have to be careful you are not sure about this person and you could give him this drug and have bad affects from it. Because you don't know his background.**

5. Not stealing is **important** because: **what is yours is yours but, that person if there is an ironic situation should comply with the needs of the particular person.**

6. Obeying the law is **very important** because: **if no one obeyed the laws why have them. And the laws are set up to help us not hurt us.**

7. Going easy on people like Heinz is **important** (cf. Sending lawbreakers to jail is not important) because: **the reason that he was doing it for was to save a life not take one. And the judge has to understand he loves his wife.**

8. Going easy on people who acted out of conscience is **not important** be-

cause: **there conscience could be warped or they could be crazy so the judge would have to decide the state of mind the convicted is.**

9. Sending lawbreakers to jail is not **important** because: **that is not always the answer but most of the time it is. The case would have to be listened to and then evaluated from there wether they should to to jail.**

Problem 2

1. Keeping promises to one's children is **very important** because: **parents are trying to teach morals and they should stick to there promises.**

2. Keeping a promise to a friend is **very important** because: **you want to be loyal to a friend or he is really not your friend.**

3. Keeping a promise to a stranger is **very important** because: **if your word is no good than what about you is good.**

4. Helping one's parents is **very important** because: **your parents make a lot of sacrifises for you and you should make them for them.**

5. Letting one's children keep earned money is **very important** because: **they worked for it and earned it by themselfves. And should be aloud to have that awarded to them.**

6. Helping one's parents is **very important**: **like I said your parents make alot of sacrifices for us we should want to make them for them.**

PROTOCOL 9: FORM A

Problem 1

1. Helping one's spouse is very **important**: **I think it is very important if you go to church you should not steal because it agins the law to steal.**

2. Helping one's spouse (even if he doesn't love her) is not **important**: **if he doesn't love here why should he save her.**

3. Helping one's friend is not **important**: **not important to stael it is agins the law you maybe get shot, hit wine you are runing or tack to the hosptle.**

4. Helping a stranger is not **important** because: **you are stealing agin.**

5. Not stealing is very **important**: **it is very important because it belongs to someone lise.**

6. Obeying the law is **very important**: **very important.**

7. Going easy on people like Heinz is **important** (cf. Sending lawbreakers to jail is not important): **if I was the judge I'd put them in jail.**

8. Going easy on people who acted out of conscience is **important**: **I can not decide.**

9. Sending lawbreakers to jail is **very important**: **I do not wont to said.**

Problem 2

1. Keeping promises to one's children is **very important**: I do not why people say they do have money and they have money.

2. Keeping a promise to a friend is **very important**: you should keep a promise.

3. Keeping a promise to a stranger is **very important**: he should keep a promise. He said that the boy can go to camp if he had the 45 dollars but a fishing trimp.

4. Helping one's parents is **can't decide**: a man who is mian.

5. Letting one's children keep earned money is **very important** because: he said can go to the camp.

6. Helping one's parents is **very important**: I wod not lend the money because He earned the money.

PROTOCOL 10: FORM A

Problem 1

1. Helping one's spouse is **important**: you should always listen to what your wife says and do what she says if it makes sense.

2. Helping one's spouse (even if he doesn't love her) is **not important**: if he doesnt love her why should be risk his own neck to steal the pills & kill her.

3. Helping one's friend is **important**: it is important to help your freinds as much as you possibly can.

4. Helping a stranger is **very important**: they can still lead productive lives when they learn to live being crippled.

5. Not stealing is **very important** because: people own things, if you want them you ask for them or buy them if you still can't get them tuff find someone else who has them.

6. Obeying the law is **very important**: if you had no laws the world would be total chaos. Stealing, killing, people would.

7. Going easy on people like Heinz is **important** (cf. Sending lawbreakers to jail is not important): they are still killing but it is to save someone he loves from pain.

8. Going easy on people who acted out of conscience is **important**: in cases like Mr. Jefferson he should go easy but revenge killings or other things of people who have acted out of conscience should be taken less easily.

9. Sending lawbreakers to jail is **very important**: anyone who breaks the law should be punished but people react to their feelings and the judge must make a hard decision.

Problem 2

1. Keeping promises to one's children is not important: if the children want the money bad enough they will earn it themselves.

2. Keeping a promise to a friend is important: it is important to keep your word to your freinds because a part of freindship is not lieing to each other.

3. Keeping a promise to a stranger is important: it is important to keep your word to anyone because they might make other plans.

4. Helping one's parents is very important: if you help your parents they will help you back. Either way the money is for her so she shouldn't complain.

5. Letting one's children keep earned money is very important: if I earn the money I think I should be able to keep it unless my parents need it very badly.

6. Helping one's parents is important: your parents help you throughout your life you should help them if you can.

PROTOCOL 11: FORM A

Problem 1

1. Helping one's spouse is very important because: she must want him to go to jail real quick or she dont love him very much.

2. Helping one's spouse (even if he doesn't love her) is not important: if you dont love her why should you go out and break the law.

3. Helping one's friend is not important: if your not going to break the law for wife why should you break the law for a friend.

4. Helping a stranger is not important: now if you don't even know this person and you are going to break the law for him and not your wife you would have to be crazy or sick in the head.

5. Not stealing is very important: well he would have to find a way to pay the man or he will just go to jail.

6. Obeying the law is very important because: with out the law we would have killers walking around on the streets and killing people.

7. Going easy on people like Heinz is not important (cf. Sending lawbreakers jail is important) because: he stole the drug. Say someone stole your car and they found it I suspose you would tell the judge to go easy on him no you would tell him to hang him.

8. Going easy on people who acted out of conscience is very important: well his conscience is going to put him in jail.

9. Sending lawbreakers to jail is very important because: we wouldn't be

able to walke down the street in peace or you might get mugged, or rapped.

Problem 2

1. Keeping promises to one's children is **very important:** why should people lie purpose cause if you tell one lie it leads up to another one.

2. Keeping a promise to a friend is **not important:** hes not in your life.

3. Keeping a promise to a stranger is **not important:** if you dont know them why should you

4. Helping one's parens is **very important** because: they had you they should have you doing something for them.

5. Letting one's children keep earned money is **not important** because: if they needed to eat he wouldnt be able to go nowere.

6. Helping one's parents is **very important** because: they could strave.

PROTOCOL 12: FORM B

Problem 1

1. Helping one's spouse is **very important** because: they have probably been through a lot together and shouldn't just give up when times get rough but to keep up love & friendship especially now when times so rough.

2. Helping one's spouse (even if he doesn't love her) is **important** because: he is her husband and I think that a death request is kinda important to feel cause it must be pretty important to the person dying or else they wouldn't have asked it.

3. Helping one's friend is **very important** because: when your friends or married that usually means you've been through a lot together & it's important to keep helping the person in desparate time in life.

4. Living even when you don't want to is **very important:** I think just because your going through rough time in life mean you should give up all hope & think you'll never be happy. Chances are you will be happy if you try.

5. Not stealing is **very important:** I think he should try to figure out some way by not stealing it first. You shouldn't take from other people. Cause they may want it or need it as much as you do.

6. Obeying the law is **very important** because: if nobody obeyed the law a lot of people would probably be dead, raped etc. cause a lot more people would go crazy if no law than if there was a law.

7. Going easy on people like Mr. Jefferson is **important** (cf. Sending law-breakers to jail is not important): even though Mr. Jefferson thought he was helping his wife a filling her last request, he shouldn't be put in jail. But then again he did steal & what if the judge let everyone get off easy where would we be then?

8. Going easy on people who acted out of conscience is **important**: Mr. Jefferson still knew the consequences and the judge can't let a robber go just because the robber was doing what conscience told him.

9. Sending lawbreakers to jail is **very important**: when Mr. Jefferson stole the drugist may have helped his wife but killed someone that really needed it bad. People should get punished so chances higher won't do again & know what did was wrong.

Problem 2

1. Keeping promises to one's children is **very important**: very important because when they grow up they need to know how to save money wisely to survive.

2. Keeping a promise to a friend is **very important**: that friend is needing your help, advice or etc. and to go back on that is like knowing you won't be friends anymore and excepting this. or if not that drastic have friend mad for a little while.

3. Keeping a promise to a stranger is **very important** because: you have told them you would do something, taken on the respondsibility and they are depending and trusting you. To go back on your word could put you in a bind.

4. Helping one's parents is **very important**: it was Judy's mony & her mother wasn't being fair when changes mind. But still you should respect what someone says & still trust them & not hold grudge just for 1 mistake.

5. Letting one's children keep earned money is **very important**: it not only lets the child have fun but they may have worked hard for the money & to hand it over to parents isn't fair. not unless parents were in poverty Then you should help them out.

6. Helping one's parents is **very important**: everyone has to sacrifice for everyone else at one time or another & everyone should help each other out when possible.

PROTOCOL 13: FORM A

Problem 1

1. Not stealing is **not important**: the important thing to do is save his wifes life whether or not she asks him to steal.

2. Helping one's wife even if he doesn't love her is **very important**: it is important to save any life, love should not enter the picture.

3. Helping one's friend is **very important**: it is very important to save any life. I couldn't stand by and watch a friend die just for a druggist to make a more than ample profit.

4. Helping a stranger is **very important**: its' important to save a life whether its' a strangers' or friends'.

5. Not stealing is **very important**: it is very important not to steal but I

would condone stealing under extenuating circumstances, such as to save a life. Society as we know it would collapse if everybody went around stealing.

6. Obeying the law is **very important** because: society needs laws to protect people. I feel it would be a greater crime to watch somebody (when the life could be saved) than to steal.

7. Going easy on people like Heinz is **very important** (Sending lawbreakers to jail is not important) because: society should provide services to save lifes. A situation like this should not arise, measures should be taken to prevent it occuring. The Judge could make Heinz pay the cost of the drug (not the price the druggist asked).

8. Going easy on people like Heinz is **important** (Sending lawbreakers to jail is not important): in Heinz's case it was the only moral thing to do. In general it depends on the crime & circumstances.

9. Going easy on people like Heinz is **important** (Sending lawbreakers to jail is not important): if the individual jailed is a menace to society then he should be jailed. I don't think Heinz was a menace to society. If jail acts as a deterrant its' useful, or if jail can rehabilitate once again its' useful.

Problem 2

1. Keeping promises to one's children is **very important**: so they learn to trust people.

2. Keeping promises to a friend is **very important** because: friends should trust each other. A breach of promise destroys trust & who wants to live in a society where you can't trust anybody (George Orwells "1984").

3. Keeping promises to a stranger is **important**: idealy its' very important, however I would take a promise from someone I didn't know with a pinch of salt.

4. Keeping promises to one's children is **important**: its' important to help people, maybe one can help them keep their promise.

5. Letting children keep their own money is **important**: if a child earns the money then that child has the right to decide what its' spent on.

6. Helping one's parents is **important**: in this situation Joe should put his family's well being first. He can go to camp next year but his family needs food now.

ANNOTATED SCORING KEYS

Scoring Key For Protocol 1

Question Referent: Aspect Citation; Stage or Transitional Level

Problem One	Problem Two
Affiliation	**Family Affiliation**
1: 5(d); 3	1: 3(c); 1
5(a); 2/3	4,6: 5(a); 2

2:   unsc.   Contract
3:   2(a); 1   2:   3(a); 1
Life   3:   unsc.
4:   5(a); 2/3   **Property**
Law   5:   unsc.
5,6: 6(f); 2
6:   6(e); 2   **Protocol Stage Rating**
Legal Justice   Modal: 2
7:   --; 2/3   SRMS: 214
     3(a); 2/3   Global: 2
9:   6(c); 2
Conscience
8:   3; 2
     1(a); 1

Annotations

Problem One

1. A slight inference is required in matching "saving someone's [sic] life is more important than committing a crime" to "saving a life is more important than **obeying** the law" in CJ.

7. Since "the druggist was selling the drug at a very unreasonable price" is consistent with either Stage 2 Aspect 5(d) or Stage 3 Aspect 4(d), the intermediate level (Trnsition 2/3) is assigned in accordance with Rule 2.

8. There are two approaches--either one acceptable--to the assessment of this response. The more holistic approach is to infer match between the whole response "maybe he didn't want to steal the drug but his conscience told him to" and "his conscience was forcing him to do it, he couldn't help it" in the Stage 2 CJ. The more differentiated approach is to match (using an inverse) "maybe he didn't want to" to "he **wanted** to help his wife," Stage 2 Aspect 4(b), and then match "his conscience told him to" to Stage 1 Aspect 1(a). Either way, the stage for the norm is Stage 2.

9. A slight inference is required in matching "because the same person would be out on the street committing a crime again" to "(so that) they won't **go out** and steal again" in CJ.

Problem Two

2. The "really" is presumably added merely for emphasis. A substantive elaboration would have rendered the response unscorable at Stage 1.

8. See note under the Stage 2 Aspect 3 CJ. The response seems too close to the example of a "contingent proposition" to be scorable.

Scoring Key For Protocol 2

Question Referent: Aspect Citation; Stage or Transitional Level

Problem One   Problem Two
Affiliation   **Family Affiliation**
1:   unsc.   1:   unsc.
2:   5(a); 3   4:   unsc.
3:   4(a); 3/4   6:   4; 3/4
Life   7(a); 3/4
4:   1(c); 3

Law
5: 9(d); 3/4
    6(b); 3/4
6: 6(a); 2/3
Legal Justice
7: 4(b); 2/3
9: 6(a); 2
Conscience
8: unsc.

Contract
2: 1(a); 3/4
    4(a); 2/3
3: 4(c); 2/3
    6(b); 2
    4(e); 2/3
Property
5: 4; 3/4

Protocol Stage Rating
Modal: 3
SRMS: 329
Global: 3(4)

Annotations

Problem One

3. A slight inference is required in matching "this person has as much right to life as his wife" in response to the CJ ("everyone has the right to live").
4. An inverse is required in matching "someone close to him should try" to "you would not be close to a stranger."
5. "People have a right to keep what belongs to them" is not Transition 3/4 Aspect 6(c) because the concept of respect (or the violation of respect for rights) is not evident in the response.
6. The specification of protection against harm in the response makes Transition 2/3 a more appropriate rating than Transition 3/4 Aspect 6(b).
7. A considerable inference is required in matching "did it as a last choise [sic]" to "desperate" in the CJ.
8. The response is unscorable because it is nondiscriminative across more than three levels (2, 3, 3/4; inclusive of 2/3).
9. The match is to "will figure they can get off easy" in the CJ.

Problem Two

1. See Note associated with Transition 3/4 Aspect 9(a).
4. The qualifier "important' is insufficiently discriminative to permit a stage rating.
6. Note "in this case" in the response.
8. Note "with some guidence" [sic] in the response.

Scoring Kay For Protocol 3

Question Referent: Aspect Citation; Stage or Transitional Level
Problem One
Affiliation
1: 4(a); 3
    4(c); 3
2: 6; 3
3: 4(e,c); 3/4
Life
4: 2(g); 4
Law
5: 4(b); 3
    6(c); 3/4

Problem Two
Family Affiliation
1: unsc.
4: 6; 4
6: unsc.
Contract
2: unsc.
3: 4; 4
Property
5: 3(b); 3

6:    1(a), 2(b); 4
Legal Justice
7:    1(c); 4
      5(a); 4
9:    4(b); 3/4
Conscience
8:    5(a); 4

Protocol Stage Rating
Modal: 4
SRMS: 381
Global: 4

Annotations

Problem One

1. An inverse is required in matching the response, "giving in to the wishes of a loved one is **not** always the way to show love & concern" (underscore added), to Stage 3 Aspect 4(c), "to **show** that he loves her."
5. The response is equally consistent with Stage 3 Aspect 1(a) and Transition 3/4, so the upper adjacent level is assigned in accordance with Rule 3.
7. A slight inference is required in matching "if we are to have a society without complete disorder" in response to "(in order) to keep society in order" in CJ.
8. A considerable inference is required in matching "feel that their conscience is clear . . . they have distorted" to "whenever they feel **justified**" in the CJ. The response is not Transition 3/4 Aspect 8(a) because the subjective appeal is criticized.
9. A slight inference is required.

Problem Two

1. The response (particularly "credability [sic]" is unscorable because it is nondiscriminative across more than three levels.
4. Considerable inference is required.
5. The response is slightly closer to Stage 3 than to Transition 3/4 Aspect 5(b) or the Stage 4 Aspect 4(b), both of which stress an element of teaching or learning.

Scoring Key For Protocol 4

Question Referent: Aspect Citation; Stage or Transitional Level

Problem One
Affiliation
1:    5(a); 2/3
      2(a,i); 3
2:    --; 2/3
3:    7(b); 2/3
Life
4:    4(d); 2
Law
5:    2(a); 3
6:    6(a); 2
      4; 1/2
Legal Justice
7:    2(b); 3
9:    4(b); 3

Problem Two
Family Affiliation
1:    unsc.
4:    1(a); 2
      1(a); 2/3
6:    6(d); 2
Contract
2:    5(a); 3/4
      1; 2/3
3:    6(b); 2
      3(a); 2/3
Property
5:    6(b); 2

Conscience

8:    1(a); 1
      3; 2
      4(b); 2

Protocol Stage Rating

Modal: 3
SRMS: 263
Global: 3(2)

Annotations

Problem One

2. Since "the faster he gets it over with the better" in response could have either a Stage 2 Aspect 6(e) or a Stage 3 Aspect 2(g) significance, the intermediate level (Transition 2/3) is assigned in accordance with Rule 2.
5. A considerable guess and inverse inference is required in matching the response to "it might **mean** a lot to them" in the CJ.
6. An inference is required in matching "turn agains [sic] you" to "get you" in the Transition 1/2 CJ.
7. A transverse is required in matching "other people would suffer" in the response to "her suffering" in the CJ.
8. Note the transverse (from wife referent in response to "conscience" in CJ) involved in the match to Stage 2 Aspect 3.
9. Inference required.

Problem Two

2. "Your friend will respect you" is matched by inversing to: "(otherwise) you will lose others' respect" in the CJ. Regarding the second response, Transition 2/3 is an upper adjacent rating since the response seems also interpretable in terms of Stage 2 Aspect 1(a).
4. "Bring you up in life" is matched to "have brought them up" in the Transition 2/3 CJ.

Scoring Key For Protocol 5

Question Referent: Aspect Citation; Stage or Transitional Level

Problem One
Affiliation
1:    unsc.
2,3: 3; 1
Life
4:    4(a); 1
Law
5:    4; 1
6:    unsc.
Legal Justice
7:    unsc.
9:    unsc.
Conscience
8:    3(b); 1

Problem Two
Family Affiliation
1:    unsc.
4:    3(b); 1
6:    unsc.
Contract
2,3: unsc.
Property
5:    3; 1

Protocol Stage Rating
Modal: 1
SRMS: 100
Global: 1

Annotations

Problem One

4. One must infer that "it" in the response refers to stealing.

8.   Despite the "I" referent, the response is scorable (with a transverse to
     "you") since it is prescriptive.

Scoring Key For Protocol 6

Question Referent: Aspect Citation; Stage or Transitional Level

Problem One

Affiliation
1:   6(b); 2
     7; 3/4
2,3: unsc.
Life
4:   1(d); 3
     5(b); 3/4
Law
5:   2(c); 4
5,6: 4(b); 3/4
6:   5(a); 3/4
     4(b); 3/4
     9(a); 3/4
Legal Justice
7:   2(a); 3
9:   4(c), 2(b); 3/4
     2(c,a); 3/4
     6(a); 4
Conscience
8b: 2(a); 3

Problem Two

Family Affiliation
1:   9(a); 3/4
4:   1(a); 2
     1(e); 3
6:   7(a); 3/4
     1(a); 3
     2(a); 3/4
Contract
2:   2(b); 3/4
     1(b); 3
     1; 4
3:   1(a); 3
Property
5:   4(b); 4
     5(a); 3/4

Protocol Stage Rating
Modal: 4
SRMS: 369
Global: 4(3)

Annotations

Problem One

1.   An inference is required in matching "he would be foolish to do it be-
     cause of many of the consequences that can follow" in response to "he
     doesn't know what he is getting into" in CJ.
2.   The response is nondiscriminative across more than three levels (Transi-
     tion 2/3, Stage 3, and Stage 4). Stage 4 is a possibility since the ad-
     verb "must" (in "his devotion for his wife must still be present") can be
     interpreted as entailing an obligatory implication.
4.   An inference is required in matching "they are rejecting what God has
     giving [sic] them" in response to the CJ. Also, an inference is required
     in matching "taking the easy way out" to "cop-out."
5.   Transition 3/4 Aspect 6(c) is not as close as Stage 4 Aspect 2(c).
6.   An inference is required in matching "highly regarded" to "respected" in
     the latter transition 3/4 CJ.
7.   An inference is required.
8.   Note that the reference to "this aspect of **the** case" (underscore added)
     is not sufficient for a match to Transition 3/4 Aspect 1 (**"depends on** the
     case").
9.   "Circumstances **must** be taken into consideration" (underscore added) is
     matched to "the judge must recognize special circumstances" in CJ.

Problem Two

2.   "Much is based on trust" is consistent with either **"relationships** are
     based on trust," Transition 3/4 Aspect 1, or **"society** is based on trust,"

Stage 4 Aspect 1. Stage 3 is not appropriate because of the differentia-
tion of functional levels implied by "based on." The upper adjacent
level, Stage 4, is assigned in accordance with Rule 3. Other ratings are
by the molecular strategy, and include an inference ("regard . . . very
highly" to "respect" in the Transition 3/4 CJ).

4.   An inference as well as a transverse are required in matching the second
      sentence to the Stage 3 CJ.
5.   The Stage 4 rating is an upper adjacent rating, since the concern with
      learning values (the referent for "values" must be inferred) is also
      consistent with Transition 3/4 Aspect 5(b). Also, an inference is
      required in matching "by earning the money, the child has shown responsi-
      bility" to the transition 3/4 CJ.
6.   An inference is required in matching "it's hard for children to **realize**
      that other things come first besides them" to "children should **learn** that
      they can't always do what they want" in the CJ.

Scoring Key For Protocol 7

Question Referent: Aspect Citation; Stage or Transitional Level

Problem One   Problem Two
Affiliation   **Family Affiliation**
1:    4(e); 2   1:   2(d); 3
      5(a); 2/3   4:   4(a); 3
2:    unsc.   6:   1(a); 2/3
3:    4(a); 2/3   **Contract**
Life   2:   1(a); 3
4:    5(b); 1   3:   4(a); 1
      1(a); 1/2   **Property**
Law   5:   2(b); 3
5,6: 4; 1/2
6:    3(b); 1/2
Legal Justice   **Protocol Stage Rating**
7:    3(a); 2/3   Modal: 3
9:    5(a); 2/3   SRMS: 243
Conscience   Global: 2(3)
8:    unsc.

Annotations

Problem One

3.   A completion (inferring "friend") is necessary for the match.
4.   The Stage 1 rating is more appropriate than that suggested by Stage 2 As-
      pect 6(c) ("could be a **crook**"), which imparts a con man connotation
      (faking, tricking you) not necessarily inferrable in the simpler Stage 1
      reference to "bad person."
7.   **"Only**" stole to save a life" (underscore added) in the response is
      matched to **"just** wanted to save her" in the CJ. A completion (inferring
      "he") is necessary.

Problem Two

2.   The response is still scorable at Stage 3 even though it seems to imply
      an inverse relation to the CJ and uses transverse content ("family rela-
      tionship").

4.   A transposition of "a parent is a person you should love" to "you should love your parent" makes clearer the match to "children **should** love their parents" in the CJ.

Scoring Key For Protocol 8

Question Referent: Aspect Citation; Stage or Transitional Level

Problem One
Affiliation
1:     4(a); 2
2:     4(e); 3
       5(a); 3
2,3: 4(b); 3/4
3:     1(a); 3
       8(b); 2/3
Life
4:     unsc.
Law
5:     1(a); 1/2
       5(a); 2
6:     6(b); 3/4
Legal Justice
7:     2(a); 3
       3(a); 2/3
9:     1(a); 3/4
Conscience
8:     4(e); 3
       1; 3/4

Problem Two
Family Affiliation
1:     9(a); 3/4
4,6: 1(a); 3
Contract
2:     1(a); 3
3:     5(b); 3/4
Property
5:     3; 2/3
       3(a); 3

Protocal Stage Rating
Modal: 3
SRMS: 343
Global: 3(4)

Annotations

Problem One

1.   A slight inference is required in matching "you want to make your wife happy" to "he wants to help her" in CJ.
4.   See note under Stage 2 Aspect 6(d). Also, "bad affects [sic]" is ambiguous.
5.   A transverse (from "yours" to "theirs") is required for the match to Transition 1/2.
6.   "If no one obeyed the laws, why have them" is nondiscriminative. Also, an inference is required in matching "the laws were **set up** to help us" (underscore added) to "laws are **made** for the **people**" in the CJ.
8.   A considerable inference is required in matching "the judge would have to decide the state of mind the convicted is [sic]" to "the judge **should evaluate** the situation" in the CJ.

Problem Two

2.   An inference is required in matching the response to "a friendship should be sincere" in CJ; cf. Affiliation norm, Stage 3 Aspect 1(c): "if you are a **real** friend." Also, the adjective "loyal" is not scorable since it can reflect meanings ranging from Stage 2 to Stage 4.
3.   A slight inference is required.
5.   A slight inference is required in matching "should be allowed to have that awarded to them" to "the money is their reward."

Scoring Key For Protocol 9

Question Referent: Aspect Citation: Stage or Transitional Level

Problem One
Affiliation
1:    3; 1
2:    6(d); <u>2</u>
3:    5; 1
Life
4:    4(a); <u>1</u>
Law
5:    1(a); <u>1/2</u>
6:    unsc.
Legal Justice
7,9: unsc.
Conscience
8:    unsc.

Problem Two
Family Affiliation
1,4: unsc.
6:    3(b); <u>2</u>
Contract
2,3: 3(a); <u>1</u>
Property
5:    unsc.

Protocol Stage Rating
Modal: 1
SRMS: 150
Global: 2(1)

Annotations

Problem One

3.   An inference is required.

Problem Two

6.   The inconsistency between the evaluation and the justification is not unusual at the lower stages. Such responses may nonetheless be scorable.

Scoring Key For Protocol 10

Problem One
Affiliation
1:    unsc.
2:    6(d); <u>2</u>
3:    unsc.
Life
4:    2(g); <u>4</u>
Law
5:    unsc.
6:    3(b); <u>3</u>
      6(f); <u>2</u>
Legal Justice
7:    3(b); 2/3
9:    1(b); <u>3/4</u>
Conscience
8:    1; <u>3/4</u>

Problem Two
Family Affiliation
1:    3(b); <u>2/3</u>
4:    6(a); <u>2</u>
6:    1(a); 2/3
Contract
2:    1(a); <u>3/4</u>
3:    3(a); <u>2/3</u>
Property
5:    4; <u>2/3</u>

Protocol Stage Rating
Modal: 3
SRMS: 306
Global: 3

Annotations

Problem One

1.   Without "if it makes sense," the response would have been scorable as Stage 1.
2.   Stage 2 Aspect 6(b) is not an appropriate citation because "risk his neck" can be interpreted as "risk his life." The response is nonetheless scored because of the use of the interogative.

8.   An inference is required, but the opening phrase ("cases like Mr. Jefferson [sic]") is helpful.
9.   This is a hard one. An inverse as well as a considerable inference is required in matching the response to the CJ.

Problem Two

1.   An inverse is required.
2.   An inference is required in matching "part of freindship [sic] is not lieing [sic] to each other" to "honesty is important for any relationship" in the CJ. The response is also equally matchable to Stage 3 Aspect 1(a), but by Rule 3 the upper adjacent level (Transition 3/4) is assigned.
3.   An inference is required.
5.   The reference is scorable because of its prescriptivity, although the overall response is very close to the disclosure category.

Scoring Key For Protocol 11

Practice Item: Aspect Citation; Stage or Transitional Level

Problem One
Affiliation
1:   unsc.
2,3: 6(d); 2
Life
4:   6(d); 2
     6(a); 2/3
Law
5:   unsc.
6:   6(f); 2
Legal Justice
7:   4(a); 1
     unsc.
9:   8(a); 2/3
     6(a); 2
Conscience
8:   unsc.

Problem Two
Family Affiliation
1:   unsc.
4:   1(a); 2/3
6:   3(a); 2/3
Contract
2:   4(f); 2/3
3:   6(g); 2
Property
5:   5; 2
     6(a); 2

Protocol Stage Rating
Modal: 2
SRMS: 229
Global: 2(3)

Annotations

Problem One

1.   The interpretation of the response is problematic.
5.   The response is merely an opinion and hence is not scorable.
9.   "In peace" in the response is matched to "makes things safer" in the Transition 2/3 CJ.

Problem Two

2.   A considerable inference is required in matching the response to "they are not important . . . to you" in the CJ.
4.   An inference is required in matching "they had you" in the response to "if it weren't for your parents, you wouldn't (even) be here" in the Transition 2/3 CJ.
5.   An inverse inference is required in matching "wouldn't be able to go no where [sic]" to "can have fun" in the CJ.
6.   The preference element must be inferred.

Scoring Key For Protocol 12

Practice Item: Aspect Citation; Stage or Transitional Level

Problem One

Affiliation
1,3: 1(b); 3
2: 8(a); 2/3
Life
4: 2(c); 2/3
Law
5: 3(b); 1
    4(a); 2
    5(a); 2
6: 6(f); 2
    3(b); 3
Legal Justice
7: unsc.
9: cf. Law 4; 2/3
    1(a); 1/2
    3(b); 3
Conscience
8: 4(a); 3/4

Problem Two

Family Affiliation
1: unsc.
4: 3; 1/2
    4(b); 2/3
    6; 3/4
    2(a); 3
6: 7(a); 3/4
Contract
2: 4(b); 2/3
    4(a); 2/3
    6(b); 2
3: 3; 4
    4(c); 2/3
Property
5: 6(a); 2
    2; 2/3
    2(c); 3

Protocol Stage Rating
Modal: 3
SRMS: 319
Global: 3

Annotations

Problem One

8. The rating of "still knew the consequences" as Transition 3/4 can be bolstered by an additional, irregular citation to Legal Justice Transition 3/4 Aspect 4(a).
9. Note that the citation for Transition 2/3 required a foreign-norm citation (Law).

Problem Two

2. A transverse from "that friend" to "you" is required for the match to "you may need **help.**"
4. "Respect" in the response is matched to the Transition 3/4 CJ. Also, an inference is required in matching "not hold grudge just for 1 mistake" to "the child should forgive or understand" in the Stage 3 CJ.
5. An inference is required in matching "in poverty" to "having hard times."

Scoring Key For Protocol 13

Question Referent: Aspect Citation: Stage or Transitional Level

Problem One

Affiliation
1,2: unsc.
3: 2(a); 3
    6(d); 3/4

Problem Two

Family Affliation
1: 9(a); 3/4
4: unsc.
6: 2(a); 4

Life

4:    unsc.

Law

5:    4(b); 3/4

5,6:   1(a); <u>4</u>

6:    5(a); 3

Legal Justice

7:    2(g); <u>4</u>

9:    2(a); 4

      2(a); 4

      6(b); 3/4

Conscience

8:    1; <u>3/4</u>

Contract

2:    1(a); 3

      2(a); <u>4</u>

3:    unsc.

Property

5:    3(b); <u>3/4</u>

Protocol Stage Rating

Modal: 4

SRMS: 379

Global: 4

Annotations

Problem One

3.   Transition 3/4 is ppropriate because the respondent relates the drug-
      gist's greed to the life value (specifically, to the consequent death of
      the friend). An inference is required, however, in matching the response
      reference to the druggist's "more than ample profit" to the Transition
      3/4 CJ reference to the druggist's "greed."

6.   The match to Stage 3 requires an inference.

8.   "It was the only moral thing to do" is unscorable.

Problem Two

6.   Aspect 2(a) is more appropriate than Aspect 1(a), since the latter aspect
      specifies an obligatory element missing in the response. "Well being" is
      matched with inference to "welfare" in the CJ.

INDEX

DATE DUE

ILL 6234225

BRODART, INC.   Cat. No. 23-221